Multiculturalism
Some Inconvenient Truths

Multiculturalism

Some Inconvenient Truths

Rumy Hasan
Politico's

First published in Great Britain 2010 by
Politico's Publishing, an imprint of
Methuen Publishing Ltd
8 Artillery Row
London
SW1P 1RZ

10 9 8 7 6 5 4 3 2 1

Copyright © Rumy Hasan 2009

Rumy Hasan has asserted his right under the Copyright, Designs and Patents Act 1988 to be identified as the author of this work.

A CIP catalogue record for this book is available from the British Library.

ISBN 978-1-84275-237-1

Printed and bound in Great Britain by CPI Antony Rowe, Chippenham, Wiltshire

This book is sold subject to the condition that it shall not by way of trade or otherwise be lent, resold, hired out, or otherwise circulated without the publishers' prior consent in writing in any form of binding or cover other than that in which it is published and without a similar condition being imposed on the subsequent purchaser.

Contents

Acknowledgements vii
Introduction 1

PART I Multiculturalism and its consequences

Chapter 1
Descent into Multiculturalism and Multifaithism 7
- Four phases of ethnic minorities in Britain
- Key concepts and critique of multiculturalism
- Dangers of ethnocentricity and faith exemptions
- Hindrance to integration
- Race, ethnicity, and 'cultural racism'

Chapter 2
Origins of parallel lives: cultural and religious factors 63
- Official racism and neglect
- Focusing on the Asian population
- Virtual Asian absence from the public domain
- Culture, family, and segregation

Chapter 3
Multiculturalism and 'Psychic detachment' 95
- Segregation and psychic detachment
- Components of psychic detachment
- The central role of culture and religion
- Some consequences

PART II Focus on Key 'Muslim Issues'

Chapter 4
The misplaced doctrine of 'Islamophobia' 121
- Examining the doctrine
- Evidence against
- Islamophobia as an offspring of multiculturalism

Chapter 5
**Reflections on the veiling of Muslim women
in Western Societies** 155
Background
- Why the shift to veiling in the West?
- Veiling and *laïcité*: the debate in France
- Social and health consequences of veiling

PART III Obstacles and Solutions

Chapter 6
Obstacles 193
- Segregated schools and the threat of minority-faith schools
- The difficulty of 'White liberal post-colonial guilt'
- The weakness of secularism

Chapter 7
Solutions 229
- Breaking down segregation, increasing integration and cohesion
- Challenging oppressive cultural and religion mores
- An identity based on commonality not difference

Chapter 8
Concluding remarks 267

Bibliography 275
Index 289

Acknowledgements

I owe warm thanks to several people. Geoffrey Toy read the whole manuscript and made numerous corrections, offered detailed comments and criticisms and, at several junctures, tempered the tone of my writing. Moreover, as a principled anti-Orientalist and someone who still retains some sympathy for the ideas embedded in multiculturalism, his observations and insights have been invaluable. Maykel Verkuyten provided helpful advice in clarifying my ideas in Chapter 3. My original thoughts on this chapter were presented as a conference paper at the ICAS (International Convention of Asia Scholars) conference in Kuala Lumpur in August 2007 – the ensuing lively discussion was also useful in clarification of the issues. Similarly, the core ideas of Chapter 5 were presented as a conference paper at the British Sociological Association, Sociology of Religion Study Group Annual Conference in Oxford in April 2007, which also resulted in a fruitful and robust discussion.

My warm gratitude is also due to Jonathan Wadman, former Commissioning Editor of Politico's at Methuen Publishing, for commissioning the book; and to Sam Carter at Methuen for being so thorough and diligent in copy editing the manuscript. Finally, I owe an enormous thanks to Paola for her unstinting encouragement and support.

Introduction

At the start of the new millennium, a report commissioned by the Runnymede Trust, 'The Future of Multi-Ethnic Britain', felt sufficiently confident to recommend that the government formally declare the United Kingdom to be a 'multicultural society' (The Parekh Report, 2000, p. 313). It seemed that 'multiculturalism' had taken very deep roots and was a fact of British life and society. Accordingly, the recommendation seemed natural, just, and unproblematic. But, as the events of the following five years would show, this was far from reality and the report masked profound tensions in society and unease with what multiculturalism represented and its advocates demanded. A defining moment was the 7 July 2005 suicide bombings in London. This naturally aroused great concern regarding the situation of Muslim communities in Britain and a number of issues were aired and observations made in the aftermath, including the deep alienation and disaffection from mainstream British society of many Muslims, especially young Muslims. Open disquiet came to be voiced of the deep-seated segregation and 'ghettoisation' that has become prevalent in several British – especially English – towns and cities, and appeared to emanate from the policies of multiculturalism.

One influential voice has been that of the Chair of the Commission for Racial Equality (now Equality and Human Rights Commission), Trevor Phillips. In a well-publicised speech on 22 September 2005, two and a half months after 7/7, Phillips argued that 'we are sleepwalking our way to segregation. We are becoming strangers to each other, and we are leaving communities to be marooned outside the mainstream.' Indeed, the phenomenon of segregation and ghettoisation is not just peculiar to Muslims – the vast majority of whom are Asians from a

Pakistani and Bangladeshi background – but also manifests itself in other religious-ethnic minority communities. Phillips' intervention caused, and continues to cause, much re-thinking and debate among the various 'stakeholders'.

This book is a contribution to this rethinking and debate. It aims to critique the theoretical and philosophical basis of multiculturalism, and to highlight some of its effects in Britain; though there is also discussion of related issues in other countries, notably Canada, France (especially in Chapter 5) and the Netherlands. By so doing, it can be seen to be a corrective to the dominant discourse in academia and, until quite recently, in mainstream political circles regarding Western societies with significant numbers of ethnic minority citizens. Importantly, the argument is made that there has in Britain increasingly been a transformation of multiculturalism to a variant where religious identity appears to have become overwhelmingly predominant, which can be termed 'multifaithism'. The book seeks to provide previously lacking analyses and arguments, suggesting that many of the beliefs and cultural/religious practices of religious-ethnic minorities are oppressive – especially concerning women and children – and that, contrary to the proponents of multiculturalism and multifaithism, these are profoundly damaging the lives of many of those now trapped within what, in reality, are 'mono-religious, mono-culture' segregated communities. To a very significant extent, these citizens have become what I term 'psychically detached' from mainstream society – and indeed from other minority communities. I make this assertion in the full knowledge that living amongst 'one's own' can provide succour, familiarity and security. One egregious outcome indicated by the London bombings is that, to put it somewhat euphemistically, legitimate foreign policy grievances (the reality is nothing short of incandescent rage) have been internalised to such an extent so as to forge a pernicious and fanatical religious identity among a section of young British-born Muslims.

Undoing such damaging societal outcomes is not feasible (hence not desirable) under policies emanating from a multicultural/

multifaith discourse. I make an explicit value judgement in regard to this subject matter: the book aims to set out a vision of society that is based on the erosion of the leading of 'parallel lives' and segregation, and the concomitant rejection of oppressive and divisive cultural and religious practices.

The book is organised as follows. Part I, Multiculturalism and its Consequences, is divided into three chapters: Chapter 1 analyses and critiques multiculturalism and its recent transformation into 'multifaithism', focusing particularly on oppressive practices within religious-ethnic minority communities; Chapter 2 examines the origins of 'parallel lives', with particular reference to aspects of culture and religion; and Chapter 3 provides an examination and understanding of the phenomenon of 'psychic detachment' among segregated communities. Part II is entitled Focus on Key 'Muslim Issues'. Given the concerns regarding Muslims since 9/11 and 7/7, special attention is provided in two chapters relating to the 'Muslim community': Chapter 4 subjects to close scrutiny the notion of 'Islamophobia' that has gained currency in public discourse in recent years, whilst Chapter 5 critically discusses a phenomenon that has become so prevalent over the past decade and a half in Western societies: the veiling of Muslim women. Part III, Obstacles and Solutions, has two chapters: Chapter 6 discusses particular obstacles to the goals of integration and social cohesion, and Chapter 7 provides solutions to these, from an egalitarian universalist perspective, in opposition to multiculturalism. Chapter 8 provides concluding remarks.

PART I

MULTICULTURALISM AND ITS CONSEQUENCES

Chapter 1
Descent into Multiculturalism and Multifaithism

Four phases of ethnic minorities in Britain

The place of ethnic minorities in post-war Britain can be seen as traversing four different phases. The first phase – roughly from the beginnings of mass migration in the late 1940s through to the mid–late 1970s – designated non-White settlers from the Commonwealth as 'coloured immigrants'. This epithet was deemed to be racist and demeaning by ethnic minorities and, given the pervasive racism of the period, justifiably so. By the time of the passing of the Race Relations Act in 1976 by the Labour government, there was a genuine attempt to tackle in both real and symbolic manner the pervasive racism and discrimination that afflicted Britain. This gave way to the second phase which occurred (with hindsight somewhat paradoxically) during the heyday of Thatcherism in the 1980s, when ethnic minorities began to be viewed as legitimate citizens by mainstream society, including all the major political parties (though the Conservative right was always reluctant to do so). One crucial factor in bringing about this change was the riots that had occurred in major cities (including Bristol, Brixton in London, Birmingham, Liverpool, and Manchester), in the first half of the decade (1980, 1981, and 1985) which were a generalised rebellion against injustice (Keith, 1993). Whilst the majority of the rioters were young Black men, there were also significant numbers of Asians and Whites, so these were not, as is often portrayed, typical 'race riots'. No longer denigrated as 'coloured immigrants', the epithet 'Black British' became readily accepted to describe migrant settlers from the Caribbean and Africa ('Afro-Caribbeans') and South Asia and East Africa ('Asians'). In this second phase, the drive to full citizenship intensified as it became clear to all, whether they liked it or not, that these citizens were here to stay for good, Accordingly, the struggle against racism and for equality deepened, to include a significant input from ethnic minorities themselves either acting within or without the Labour party.

Soon after came into fruition a third phase which characterised Britain as being a 'multicultural' society – taken to mean that it had citizens from 'different' cultures. A better epithet would have been 'multiracial' (with 'race' being a politcal concept, given its lack of foundation in biology) or, better still, 'multi-ethnic' society. But, with 'race' being discredited, the somewhat euphemistic 'multicultural' gained legitimacy. However, with the advent of this conception came the fissuring of the unity that had existed under the umbrella term 'Black British' – a unity expressed by non-Whiteness (notwithstanding the fact that many Asians resented being labelled as 'Black'), and facilitated by being to a large extent working class. It was these characteristics that led to ethnic minorities overwhelmingly voting for Labour in elections and joining trade unions in proportionally higher numbers (see, for example, Anwar, 1998). However, the 'multicultural' turn and, in its wake, attendant embrace of 'multiculturalism' launched a divisive dynamic. In local communities in particular, this led to pork-barrel politics* whereby councils began to channel funds and resources to various 'ethnic', 'cultural' and, more recently, 'faith' communities in return for votes. One inevitable consequence of this was increasing levels of segregation and concomitant ghettoisation in many inner areas of towns and cities.

This dynamic was given a wake-up call by riots in the summer of 2001 (importantly, all these took place *before* 9/11) in the northern English towns of Bradford, Burnley, and Oldham. These riots were, in crucial respects, markedly different to the riots of the 1980s, especially by virtue of being comprised almost entirely of young, male Muslim Asians. The riots shone a piercing light on an uncomfortable reality that encompassed widespread racism, threats from far

---

* Though this term is more in usage in the USA, its meaning is universal: government funds that confer certain sections of society with resources which, in turn, yield political benefits. As such, it can be a highly effective divide-and-rule tactic.

right groups, social deprivation, and profound levels of segregation. Indeed, a report on Bradford *before* the riots pointed out some stark truths that had been submerged in popular and political discourse:

> So called 'community leaders' are self-styled, in league with the establishment key people and maintain the status quo of control and segregation through fear, ignorance and threats ... There is resentment towards the Asian community by sections of the White community who perceive hostile and mono-cultural religious leaders as *the advocates of segregation*' (*The Bradford Race Review*, 2001, p. 10, emphasis added), (*The Ouseley Report*).

The fourth phase, whose start can roughly be gauged to be post-9/11, is the transformation of multiculturalism into 'multifaithism', where primacy began to be accorded to the religion of ethnic minorities and attendant religious (or 'faith') identity. Accordingly, Britain is not only considered a multicultural country but also a multifaith country. An indication of this was provided by the Islamic pressure group FAIR (Forum against Islamophobia and Racism) that was formed in 2001, whose literature stressed 'promoting a multi-faith and multi-ethnic Britain' (FAIR, 2001); for this group, the epithet 'multicultural' had presumably become obsolete.

One crucial consequence of this transformation has been the fissuring of identities of British Asians. From being 'Black British' and the generic 'Asian', they have become disintegrated into religious categories (in the main, Muslim, Hindu, or Sikh). Furthermore, and increasingly, Muslims identify with the *umma*, Hindus with *Hindutva*, and some Sikhs with *Khalistan*. These religious identities are invariably also accompanied by a national (predominantly Indian, Pakistani, or Bangladeshi) and regional (e.g. Bengali, Gujarati, Kashmiri, Punjabi etc.) identity. The logical progression of this would be further fissuring into religious sects: hence, Muslims would fall into the categories of Shia and Sunni (and smaller sects such as Ahmadis), and of Hindus and Sikhs into different castes.

Among Asians, these self-descriptors have long been a commonplace, a natural legacy of the origins of the first generation of settlers, but gradually they have come out into the public domain. Thus, at the point when the unifying 'Asian' should have been passed down to the second and third generations, it became enormously weakened and replaced by religious and national signifiers.

Pork-barrel politics ratified this transformation, whilst the problems and tensions between different communities were spilling out into the open. So, on the one hand, the government, recognising communal strains, highlighted the importance of 'community cohesion' whilst, on the other, increasingly allocated funds to what it termed 'faith communities'. Indeed, the focus on community cohesion is a recognition of the lack of cohesion between communities, but there has been little acknowledgement that prior multicultural policies may have contributed to this grave problem.

From the mid-1980s, then, the approach taken by governments and local authorities of all the major political parties in regard to increasing segregation can be summarised as being that of benign non-intervention, justified under the rubric of 'multiculturalism'. As the term indicates, broadly speaking, multiculturalism describes the existence of different cultures within a state. However, in the modern Western context, it is taken to mean the prevalence of 'minority' cultures alongside the culture of the indigenous majority. Specifically, these minority cultures are, in the main, the cultures of ethnic and racial minority settlers. The key aspect of this is that they are 'different' – in many crucial respects markedly so – from the dominant culture, and it is the tolerance and acceptance of this difference that lies at the core of multiculturalism's policy prescriptions. There may be some overlaps between the cultures but what makes these distinct and different to others, in particular to the major dominant culture, is that they share a common language, history, set of religious beliefs, moral values, and geographic origins. In sum they belong to a specific *group* (Watson, 2000, p. 1).

Even though we can locate the UK as being designated a

multicultural country by approximately the mid-1980s, in the sense of non-intervention in regard to the situation of ethnic minorities, we can contend that national and local governments had, unknowingly, adopted what can be described as a 'soft' form of multiculturalism (West, 2005, p. 3) or, more accurately, cultural laissez-faire. Under this approach, migrant communities have been allowed to lead their lives pretty much as they would have done in their 'home' countries. By so doing, these communities naturally retained, almost *in toto*, cultural and religious customs and traditions. A corollary to this has been that the mixing with those not from one's 'own' religious-ethnic community has been minimal and possibly declining – to the point where, for perhaps the majority living in segregated neighbourhoods, it is virtually non-existent. This has forcefully been described by Trevor Phillips, Chair of Commission for Racial Equality (now Equality and Human Rights Commission):

> Residentially, some districts are on their way to becoming fully fledged ghettoes – Black holes into which no-one goes without fear and trepidation, and from which no-one ever escapes undamaged. The walls are going up around many of our communities, and the bridges that so many of you in RECs [Race Equality Councils] and the voluntary sector have laboured to build are crumbling (Phillips, 2005).

What is curious and seemingly paradoxical about 'the walls going up' and contemporaneous lurch to religious identity among some (especially Asian) ethnic minorities is that it has taken place at precisely the time that indigenous White society (of all classes) has been decisively 'removing the walls' emanating from religious belief so that, barring the unusual case of Northern Ireland and small pockets in Scotland, faith identity is practically of no consequence. Long gone are the days when in mainland Britain one was referred to as 'Catholic' or 'Protestant'. On the contrary, there has been a profound decline in both 'believing' (in a religion) and 'belonging' (to a church) (Voas and Crockett, 2005)'. So, we can with confidence assert that in every sphere of their lives the majority now has a strongly secular outlook. True, there has been a rise in 'new age' movements and myriad superstitions but these beliefs tend to be private and do not interfere with or dictate life beyond a very narrow private range so that for adherents of such superstitions, the social and public sphere remains overwhelmingly secular. So the intensification of multiculturalism and rise of multifaithism is very much against the grain of the direction in which British society at large has been taking – and indeed this is true of Western Europe as a whole.

The origins of segregation and attendant ghettoisation lie in the post-war migrations of people from the former British colonies to work in mills, factories, foundries, and public services in various parts of Britain, though concentrating mainly in Greater London, the West Midlands, Yorkshire and Humberside, and the north-west. They often came from poor rural communities with a high degree of illiteracy. For reasons of 'choice' (that is, culture, language, religion, ethnicity, regional origin) and 'constraints' (racist councils, landlords, and estate agents) (Lakey, 1997), the settlers congregated in certain parts of towns and cities (Hiro, 1992, parts I and II). This offered some security, succour and protection from the at times harsh racism they were to encounter. The governments of the day (be they Labour or Conservative) failed to make migrants feel welcome and secure; moreover, they failed to make any credible attempts to bridge links with local Whites – and encourage the latter to offer a welcoming hand of friendship (Foot, 1965). This gross negligence and irresponsibility has had negative consequences whose effects still linger, regardless of problems of language and customs.

It is important to note, however, that middle class Asians have never been ghettoised in terms of where they live. Rather, they head for the suburbs and, as a result, see a much greater mixing of their children with locals. Moreover, because of the transferability of their skills, they tend to be much more mobile geographically, further eroding their potential ghettoisation. This is not to say that middle class people are devoid of all 'ghetto traits' or thinking. On the contrary it is often the case that, though they may live in a predominantly White or mixed area, away from work they often lead a separate existence in the sense of minimal interaction with those not part of the wider family or circle of friends from a very similar ethnic group. Thus, Muslim middle class people often tend to fraternise mainly with fellow Muslims, Sikhs with fellow Sikhs, Hindus of a particular caste with those of the same caste, and so on. We can postulate that the more 'traditional' the outlook and practices, the greater the reluctance to mix socially with others.

* * *

Key concepts and critique of multiculturalism
We can distinguish two groups of theorists, commentators and activists who espouse multiculturalism. One comprises White liberals and progressives who oppose western imperialism, colonialism, and dominance over non-White peoples (amongst the most influential of these are Will Kymlicka, Charles Taylor, James Tully and Iris Young). Accordingly, they also tend to be principled anti-racists with a genuine concern for ethnic minorities in the developed West. Naturally, they are animated by, and fearful of, the charge of 'racism' that may be directed against them (for an elaboration of this see Chapter 6). Therefore, meticulous care is taken to avoid subjecting the *modus vivendi* of ethnic minorities to any sustained scrutiny or criticism, for to do so may redound on them with this wounding charge. The moral, philosophical, and political bases of multiculturalism provide the elegant and convenient solution of 'live and let live'. A less generous indictment, however, would be that this provides an elaborate shroud for pusillanimity.

The second group is that hailing from ethnic minorities – who can collectively be described as 'cultural nationalists' (the most prominent in the UK are Bhikhu Parekh and Tariq Modood). They are animated by protecting and preserving the ways of living of ethnic minority settlers and see cultural and religious attributes as a defining feature of self-being and identity. Albeit for different reasons, members of this group also fail to apply strong critiques to ethnic minorities and again, multiculturalism provides a neat solution to this. The less generous indictment in this case is that multiculturalism provides a cover – or 'do not disturb' notice – for myriad reactionary beliefs and practices.

Again what unites the two groups is a commitment to anti-racism and anti-discrimination. Crucially multiculturalism can be seen as a logical outcome of the implementation of anti-racist policies, given that 'cultural minorities' are invariably 'racial minorities' in the Western context (leaving aside the migration of large numbers of White East Europeans into Western Europe in recent years). But, the equating of 'culture' with 'race' or 'ethnicity' is a sleight of hand. The anti-racist struggle was, and remains, a struggle for *equality* in every facet of life whereas multiculturalism is demands for *separate* rights, exemptions, and provisions.

The original and in some respects key theorists and proponents of multiculturalism emanate from Canada, the most notable of whom are Will Kymlicka and Charles Taylor. Taylor's major – and highly influential – contribution to the literature is the concept of 'recognition' and his argument for the need and demand for recognition by and on behalf of minority groups, and the 'supposed links between recognition and identity where this latter term designates something like a person's understanding of who they are, of their fundamental defining characteristics as a human being'. But the vital importance of recognition, for Taylor, resides in its obverse, that is, '*mis*recognition' because:

> Nonrecognition or misrecognition can inflict harm, can be a form of oppression imprisoning someone in a false, distorted, and reduced mode of being ... misrecognition shows not just a lack of due respect. It can inflict a grievous wound, saddling its victims with a

crippling self-hatred. Due recognition is not just a courtesy we owe people. It is a vital human need (Taylor, 1994, p. 25–26).

The supreme importance of recognition of cultures for multiculturalists is highlighted in Joseph Raz's assertion that: 'even oppressive cultures can give people quite a lot'* (cited in C. Tyler, p. 21, 2004). Lash and Featherstone (2001, p. 13) draw out the logical conclusion: 'for Taylor, recognition of authenticity is as important a source of the self as dignity-recognition: *cultural justice [is] as central as universalist justice*' (emphasis added). *Ipso facto*, to ensure that such harm, oppression, and self-hatred do not arise, it is incumbent on the polity that minority communities are given due recognition and that their cultural differences with the majority society are accepted and embraced.

Taylor utilises a concept that has become vital to multicultural philosophy, that of 'difference', which was the subject of Iris Young's influential book *Justice and the Politics of Difference*. The thrust of Young's argument is that 'where social group differences exist and some groups are privileged while others are oppressed, social justice requires explicitly acknowledging and attending to those group differences in order to undermine oppression' (Young, 1990, p. 3). Armed with this doctrine, Taylor now posits an astonishing claim with profound implications and one which he supports (*ibid.*, p. 43):

> the supposedly neutral set of difference-blind principles of the politics of equal dignity is in fact a reflection of one's hegemonic culture. As it turns out then, the minority or suppressed cultures are being forced to take alien form. Consequently, the supposedly fair and difference-blind society is not only inhuman (because suppressing identities) but also, in a subtle and unconscious way, itself highly discriminatory.

---

* The obvious response to which seems to have escaped Raz: indeed they can – a lot *of oppression*. Is this justified under the rubric of 'tradition', 'recognition', and 'way of life'? My argument is that it cannot under the principle of increasing liberation for humanity.

A further assumption is

> the imposition of some cultures on others [and echoing Edward Said's *Orientalism*] with the assumed superiority that powers this imposition. Western liberal societies are thought to be supremely guilty in this regard, partly because of their colonial past, and partly because of their marginalization of segments of their populations that stem from other cultures (*ibid.*, p. 63).

Given this, there follow the demands for cultures being allowed to defend themselves within reasonable bounds and to 'recognize the equal value of different cultures; that we not only let them survive but acknowledge their worth' (*ibid.*, p. 64). Those who oppose multiculturalism are assumed to do so because of 'a mixture of prejudice and ill-will [so] the multiculturalists charge them with the arrogance of assuming their own superiority over formerly subject peoples' (*ibid.*, pp. 67–68). Naturally the implications of this are that attempts to treat all with not only 'equal dignity' but also with 'equality' is a chimera and should be rejected – for to do so would force minority cultures to take an 'alien form'.

Taylor's arguments have provided powerful tools for advocates of multiculturalism and, if true, are certainly powerful indictments of Western liberal societies: any attempt on their part to provide legal and constitutional guarantees of equal treatment cannot be accepted in good faith for they necessarily stem from *mauvaise foi*. But they are far from being true; on the contrary they are bald assertions rooted in a colonial epoch and, crucially, are not backed up with hard evidence. For example, does misrecognition really lead to crippling self-hatred? Are opponents of multiculturalism really fired by prejudice and arrogance? These sound suspiciously like 'guilt-tripping arguments'. Concern about the marginalisation of ethnic minority groups is right and proper but this does not emanate from equal treatment before the law but from racism and attendant discrimination, that is, from *lack* of equal treatment. And it is precisely the universal application of the law that can assist in tackling racism and marginalisation. Indeed, there is much evidence to suggest that strong cultural and religious identities can *cause* marginalisation (see Chapters 3 and 5), not least for the most vulnerable. Take, for example, the case of Asian girls who are prevented from pursuing studies by their parents so that they can be married off at a young age – frequently to a relation from the country of origin. In the 'Biraderi system' – which is common to migrants from Kashmir and a part of their cultural heritage and identity – a marriage agreement by the parents is often struck when the girl is a pre-pubescent child, with little grasp of the language or society (for a discussion of Biraderi, see Bolognani, 2007).

This inevitably leads to a high degree of marginalisation from mainstream society – but then this is the desired outcome of many religious and community leaders who do not wish their girls and women to be contaminated by the emancipated lifestyles of Western society. If, as Taylor asserts, recognition forges identity (*ibid.*, p. 66), then such recognition can also engender marginalisation that ensues from the formation of tight-knit communities based on a strong cultural or religious identity.

Moreover, we are not provided with what precisely 'recognition' entails, and why its non-existence should necessarily cause harm to minority groups (and why just these groups). That said, Taylor has added to the lexicon of multiculturalism so that, in debates pertaining to it, it is difficult to side-step issues of recognition and the survival and equal value worth of all cultures – what is commonly referred to as cultural relativism, which can be thought of as the philosophical and normative basis of multiculturalism.

That Canada should have been an early focus for multiculturalism is understandable given that it is a country with an indigenous people and a colonial settler population from Britain and France. The Canadian polity came to be dominated by English-speaking settlers and their descendents, but there remained a significant Francophone population, concentrated in Quebec, that wished to retain its distinctiveness and, above all, the French language. Equally, indigenous tribes wished to retain their identities and the right to live in a traditional manner; accordingly, they demanded resources and exemptions from the law. The relationship between these three culturally distinct populations, and the search for an amicable resolution to the tensions that naturally arose therefrom, provided the *raison d'être* for thinking about multiculturalism. An important consideration was that this was the lesser evil given that, within Quebec, there was a strong secessionist movement – which has been placated somewhat by the 1983 Meech Lake Accord that granted Quebec certain exemptions from the Canadian Charter of Rights so as to ensure its distinctiveness and 'survival' (Taylor, 1994, p. 52-53), notwithstanding the fact that the majority of non-French Canadians opposed this accord and rejected outright its putative successor, the Charlottestown Accord, the aim of which was to give Quebec 'special status' (Barry, 2001, pp. 310-313).

Into this mix came new migrants, including those such as Muslims and Sikhs, with a very different but strong cultural and religious identity. Those who wished to be 'recognised' for their identity were helped by Canada's espousal of multiculturalism which became codified into law by the passing of the Canadian Multiculturalism Act of 1988. Furthermore, some assert that section 15 (2) of the Canadian Charter of Rights and Freedoms provides for separate laws, programs and activities on the grounds of ameliorating disadvantaged groups: 'Subsection (1) does not preclude any law, program or activity that has as its object the amelioration of conditions of disadvantaged individuals or groups including those that are disadvantaged because of race, national or ethnic origin, colour, religion, sex, age or mental or physical disability' (CCRF, 1982).

Inevitably, traditionalists within these new communities began to assert the politics of difference that had been legitimated by this Act, and to press for separate rights (for example, see Chapter 7 re demands for Sharia Law in Ontario). There appeared a seamless progression from separate rights for what, in effect, were 'national' peoples of indigenous tribes and the French settlers who had claims to significant tracts of the Canadian landmass to the new economic immigrant settlers of the post-Second World War era. Kymicka (2003, pp. 11–26) acknowledges this distinction within 'cultural pluralism' by his bifurcation of a 'multination state' (encompassing nations – but he also ascribes this to be 'peoples' and 'cultures') and a 'polyethnic state' as a result of immigration (rather than being 'national minorities', these are 'ethnic minorities').

A moment's reflection tells us that there is a marked difference between the two minorities, and the two groups (national groups and immigrants) cannot be theorised about in the same way. In the case of the former, one can readily discern the difficulty of asserting a 'difference-blind' politics of equality, for to do so risks demands for national separation and the break-up of the state. Accordingly, the granting of certain exemptions and rights is done on the pragmatic basis of the politics of a lesser evil. However, to offset incessant separatist demands, strict limits to these may be required to prevent the rupturing of the polity; but if these are rejected by the majority of the national minority, secession becomes inevitable. But these inordinate difficulties do not arise with respect to recent migrants and, therefore, exemptions can be disallowed on the grounds of equality and universalism. While it may be 'axiomatic for Quebec governments that the survival and flourishing culture in Quebec is a good' (Taylor, 1994, p. 58), the same is most certainly not the case for recent migrants given the oppressive and obscurantist aspects of their cultures; indeed it is decidedly a harm.

Given this problematic, divisive, dynamic, and the later lurch to multifaithism, it is *prima facie* surprising that multiculturalism attracted so much support, and so little sustained criticism. Certainly, most commentators of liberal and left persuasions have openly advocated it as a positive social development, whilst on the right, until the start of the new century, there was a hesitancy to openly attack it or deny that Britain had become a multicultural society. Let us, therefore, subject multiculturalism to a critique from a universalist egalitarian perspective.

Indeed, we are fortunate that a most powerful, sustained critique of multiculturalism has been undertaken by Brian Barry in his magisterial *Culture and Equality: An Egalitarian Critique of Multiculturalism*. Barry carefully analyses the assumptions and practices of multiculturalism and shows that they are in fundamental breach of liberal doctrines. His foundational stance is that uniformity (or equality) of treatment is the enemy of privilege (Barry, p. 10);[*] and given that multiculturalism necessarily breaks from this, it unavoidably leads to unequal, regressive outcomes for large sections of 'cultural minority' populations. Given the importance of this work, we shall refer to many of its key points whilst not refraining from offering some critical remarks.

Accordingly, the politics of difference and recognition irrevocably lead to the breach of universalistic notions of human rights, justice, and equality. When adopted by the government, multiculturalism becomes an official policy of recognising differences in ethnic minority 'cultural communities' – and of *celebrating*, and of even *encouraging* these by channelling resources. The *raison d'être* of this is taken from an anti-racist discourse, that is, public recognition of ethnic minority cultures equates to the recognition that ethnic minorities are a legitimate and integral part of society. This seems, *prima facie*, a progressive, fair-minded policy with the added advantage that the self-perception of the White majority to think of the nation state in mono-racial and mono-cultural terms is no longer deemed to be correct nor, indeed, acceptable. Multiculturalism, therefore, lays down a new marker, points to a new reality, and provides for a new discourse.[†]

---
[*] But importantly, it is also the enemy of *oppression*.
[†] Kelly (2002, p. 1) has coined the phrase 'circumstances of multiculturalism' to suggest that '[a]ll modern states face the *problems* of multiculturalism even if they are far from endorsing multiculturalism as a policy agenda or official ideology'. But surely if a state does not practise or espouse multiculturalism, it cannot suffer problems emanating from it. What many (not 'all') modern states experience is the interaction between migrants from developing countries and the indigenous population where the former, in crucial respects, have significantly different cultural and religious practices and beliefs. This is simply the fact of people from various cultural backgrounds living within the same polity and geographic proximity – but this

However, evidence suggests the effect of multiculturalism has been at variance – and increasingly so – with this appealing scenario. Indeed, what has been set in train is a case of unintended consequences. That is to say, rather than a new respectful, tolerant, all-encompassing, socially-cohesive society, we see evidence of segregation, ghettoisation, resentment, alienation, communal stress and the leading of what Cantle (2006, p. 4) has termed 'parallel lives'. The attempt to forge a unifying 'British identity' should be seen as a belated, half-baked, and quarter-hearted attempt to counter the deep divisions that have arisen: no more than papering over the cracks. The truth is that it will take a far more vigorous, principled approach that is backed up by appropriate measures to deal with the cracks properly. But there is no sign of this; moreover, pressures to maintain the multicultural policies remain, whilst in some respects such as the expansion of faith schools, and the funding of 'faith communities', the government has deepened multiculturalism by its transformation into multifaithism.

These pressures are elucidated with the help of the 'rule and exemption' approach (Barry, 2001, p. 33) whereby exemptions to laws and regulations are demanded by ethnic minorities on the grounds of religion or culture. There is nothing exceptional in seeking exemptions – indeed exclusionary clauses are widespread in law-making. The motive for such opt-outs is the belief that, following Taylor, equality of treatment is harmful to a minority group. Indeed, many laws are based on this very premise and, accordingly, stipulate exceptions. For example, tax exemptions for those earning below a threshold is based on this consideration: loss of income through taxation has a proportionately greater impact on the low paid. However, in regard to exceptions on cultural and religious grounds, the putative 'harm' that is thought to emanate from the principle of equality before the law is a contrived sleight of hand to shore up minority beliefs and practices. Moreover this brazenly distorts the true meaning of 'equality'. What we have, therefore, is a world turned upside down: whereas

does not necessarily imply that a policy of multiculturalism is operational to bring about its 'circumstance'.

equality is considered disrespectful and harmful; unequal treatment is just, shows respect and, indubitably, is beneficial. Individual rights are trumped by group rights for members of ethnic minorities – this is the price (but portrayed as benefit) of preserving the culture and way of life that have been imported from various developing countries.

In multicultural societies, newly arrived minority groups are confronted with Durkheim's 'social facts', that is, the conventional way of doing things. Often, however, the social facts of the dominant culture are deeply alien to ethnic minorities – to the extent that they are avoided, rejected, and even denounced. Yet, similar behaviour by members of the majority society, with respect to minority cultures, can lead to accusations of 'racism' or 'misunderstandings'; usually as a means to deflect critical surveillance. Now rigid adherence to the social facts by the White majority would lead to much shunning of contacts with 'different' members of the minority groups so that meaningful acquaintances and friendships are not forged. But, in the modern era, this would rightfully be considered bigoted behaviour and such bigotry and parochialism does, of course, exist but is unambiguously deemed to be reactionary and intolerable. Yet the same reasoning, with the use of a multicultural compass, does not apply when the same bigoted behaviour emanates from the ranks of ethnic minority groups. What conclusion can we draw from this? A rather harsh one: that this is again an affirmation of the play of double standards that lies at the core of multiculturalism.

Watson (p. 3) argues that in a multicultural society the state has two choices: either destroy multiculturalism and transform society into being mono-cultural, or celebrate and encourage multiculturalism so that all cultures are endorsed by the state. Given these choices, most liberal-minded people would reject the former for the latter. But this is a false dichotomy for there is a third option which is superior, that is, ethnic minorities adopt significant elements of the dominant culture whilst the indigenous majority society adopts aspects of minority cultures to bring about cultural fusion and transformation. Such a 'creolisation' process has enormous advantages which we can deem to be an advancement (this point is elaborated in Chapter 7). Indeed, to some extent, this has already happened and is happening in Western societies without any state endorsement (see the example of Frankfurt at the end of this chapter).

In Britain, some ethnic minorities have integrated better into the host society through cultural adaptation (notably large sections of Black Caribbeans) whilst others have not (Asians in general, and Muslims in particular). At the same time, significant sections of the host society (of all classes) have adopted new cultural norms emanating from ethnic minorities, notably with respect to cuisine, music, and the arts. The key contention is that a unified culture, broadly defined, with elements of the 'new' for all, must abandon *oppressive* beliefs and practices from wherever they emanate. In debates of multiculturalism, insufficient emphasis has been given to this vital issue. Here a fundamental result ensues: adherents of multiculturalism do not, and will not, argue in a principled, cogent manner against the often extraordinarily oppressive beliefs and practices within ethnic minority groups; in contrast they will excoriate oppressive practices emanating from the majority society. Supporters of multiculturalism fear that to argue against or critique oppressive beliefs would lead to 'misrecognition' of minority cultures and leave them open to the charge of being disrespectful of their very being. Moreover, the logical outcome of this would be the haemorrhaging of multiculturalism. It is, therefore, curious how multiculturalism's defence of many illiberal beliefs and customs (which often originate from societies where freedom of expression is usually intolerable and met with firm censorship and severe legal sanctions), is done via the use of liberal channels. Lest one forget, such channels are not the gift of the gods but are rightfully cherished as the result of hard-won struggles over a very long period. In regard to the attempt to impede criticisms and critiques of reactionary aspects of minority cultures under multiculturalism's emphasis on 'recognition', respect, and causing no offence, what this is tantamount to is the use of freedom of expression in order to suppress it. Barry (*ibid.*, p. 32) takes to task Bhikhu

Parekh when he asks the rhetorical question: '... what would be the prospects of freedom of speech if ideas such as those put forward by Parekh became dominant in currently liberal societies?' As a staunch supporter of multiculturalism, the answer would indeed and unambiguously be its curtailment to a stifling degree.

Indeed, Barry's concerns regarding Parekh's views are entirely legitimate given that the latter is perhaps the most influential theorist and proponent of multiculturalism in Britain. Parekh's influence on this subject is attested by the fact that it was he who was asked to chair The Runnymede Trust's Commission on the Future of Multi-Ethnic Britain which yielded the report *The Future of Multi-Ethnic Britain* (also known as *The Parekh Report)* in 2000. This report came soon after Parekh's book, *Rethinking Multiculturalism*, and is greatly influenced by it.[*] Examining Parekh's understanding of multiculturalism takes us to the heart of multicultural thinking in Britain. In essence, both works are profoundly conservative (with a small 'c') given that they accept and legitimise the status quo of traditional cultures and religions of ethnic minority communities who have settled in Britain and, by implication, in other Western states. Parekh only resorts to criticisms of the most egregious cultural practices (such as female genital mutilation, *sati*, and forced marriage) and argues that Western states must veer away from their legal and public commitment to liberal universalism so as to accommodate these minority cultures and faiths.

Given his strong commitment to ethnic minority cultures, Parekh on occasion resorts to tendentiousness and specious arguments in order to support his claims. For example, in discussing Raz's ideas on autonomy, Parekh asserts (2001, p. 93) that Asian immigrants to Britain have prospered and achieved 'remarkable material success ... precisely because they do not set much store by autonomy [taken to mean individual liberty] and draw on the ample resources of a flourishing and tight knit community with readily available network of social support'. This is an example of the 'social capital' thesis

---

[*] For a powerful critique of both these works, see Brian Barry (2001b).

(see Chapter 3) and is certainly true for *some* Asian immigrants (most notably from East Africa). However, it is not at all the case for very significant numbers of migrants from Bangladesh and Pakistan. Evidence shows that these communities are at the bottom of the socio-economic ladder (as discussed in the following chapter). Given that males from these communities tend to have low levels of qualifications, they also overwhelmingly are employed in unskilled and semi-skilled work. When these are combined with large family sizes, the result is a high level of poverty. This can be contrasted with other ethnic minorities – notably those from an Indian background, which is now close to, or above, the White average. Accordingly, we cannot pinpoint racism as the key factor in the relative disadvantage of Bangladeshis and Pakistanis, for the racial disadvantage is likely to be the same for all South Asians. Nor can we apportion the cause to 'Islamophobia' on the grounds that most Bangladeshis and Pakistanis are Muslims, and that the prevalence of Islamophobia has taken its toll on Muslim communities. The reason for this is that the 'scissors' of relative socio-economic standing of Bangladeshis and Pakistanis in comparison with Indians had opened up well before the supposed rise of Islamophobia (see Chapter 4).

This leads to the conclusion that *internal* factors have depressed socio-economic advancement of Bangladeshis and Pakistanis. Such factors emanate from culture and religion which strongly mould the identity of these ethnicities and, moreover, induce high levels of psychic detachment and attendant harmful effects (see Chapter 3). A crucial cultural trait concerns the status of girls and women and the constraints put on them. One consequence of this is the very low levels of employment of women in these communities (as elaborated upon in the following chapter). This leads to the ineluctable conclusion that culture and religion are powerfully acting as a hindrance of women in these communities to the world of paid work which, in turn, is contributing to their relative poverty and deprivation. Accordingly, we can see here a clear link between cultural norms and value systems, and poverty. To then argue that carte blanche respect and recognition be shown to the cultures of these communities is to deflect from the causes of their poor socio-economic situation; indeed, it is a profound disservice to their well-being.

Moreover, what evidence is there to suggest that, if given genuine opportunities, large numbers of Asians would *not* set great store by autonomy? Indeed, multiculturalism's fixation on recognition, difference and identity provides powerful ammunition to community leaders and family elders and traditionalists who actively seek to deny autonomy to their flock, especially to girls and women. Indeed, one reason why the suicide rate among Asian women and girls is far higher than the average is precisely because they are often denied any semblance of autonomy, find their tight-knit families and communities truly suffocating, and desire to leave for a life more akin to those of their fellow non-Asian citizens in mainstream society. Not for them a strong attachment to the 'Asian values' that are supported by Parekh (*ibid.,* pp. 136–141).

Parekh makes a play on the grounds of equality for granting minority cultures special status (*ibid.,* p. 101): 'if a society happens to be culturally homogenous, all its members enjoy the benefits of a stable cultural community. The problem arises when it is multicultural ... the majority community then exercises its cultural rights but minorities do not'. But what does this mean? Some 'cultural rights' cannot be exercised if they break the law – whether they emanate from the majority or minority culture (or community). Take the following example: throughout the world, and since time immemorial, it has been a 'cultural right' of parents to indulge in corporal punishment of their children under what can be termed the parental prerogative. Indeed, and almost universally, such a cultural right was also granted to school teachers: this was certainly *de rigueur* in British public (that is, private) schools where teachers, acting *in loco parentis*, ensured that discipline was instilled in their charges by periodic bouts of a 'good thrashing' through use of the belt and cane. But widespread revulsion at this barbarism, and pupil and parental opposition, eventually put sufficient pressure on governments to outlaw such a 'cultural right' in schools, allowing society to become more civilised. Similarly, this aspect of the parental prerogative has, in recent years, also been denied in many West European countries (though not yet fully in Britain) which is clear affirmation of the simple fact that cultures, and rights therein, are not fixed and timeless.

Suppose, however, that the right of parents and teachers to discipline children by physical punishment is deemed to be of supreme importance to many ethnic minority communities (because it has long been so in their home 'nations' and 'societal culture'). Proponents of the practice argue that misrecognition and denial of this cultural trait and right can lead to harm of the communities concerned and their sense of self, integrity, and pride. The presumption must be that Parekh and Multiculturalists in general would seek to grant them an exemption from the law. If so, then they are providing justification for oppressive, barbaric practices – one outcome of which would be more cases of the Victoria Climbié type.* If an exemption is not granted, then it is not clear what the normative basis for this is. Crucially, however, such a refusal puts firm limits on demands for 'cultural rights'. Contrast this with the clear, principled, anti-oppressive stance based on universal rights of the child: this would outlaw physical violence against children, whether in Western Europe or anywhere else. Appeals to tradition, culture, or religious doctrine are dismissed outright. The moral of this case is that there is a clear and present danger of the corrosion of civilised morality on the grounds of cultural sensitivity and accommodation.

Writing very much as if he was a Hindu *pandit*, and, likewise, without offering much evidence, Parekh (*ibid.*, pp. 158–160) stresses

---

* This is the notorious case of the eight-year-old girl from the Ivory Coast who was murdered by her carers (her great-aunt and her boyfriend) in February 2000 after suffering months of physical abuse. At the hearing into the case, the social worker (of African-Caribbean descent) said she had assumed Victoria's timidity in the presence of her great aunt and boyfriend stemmed not from fear but from the African-Caribbean culture: 'respect and obedience are very important to the African-Caribbean family script' (BBC News, 2001). There was cultural relativism at play in this reasoning as it implied that in order to instil 'respect and obedience', African-Caribbean families were entitled repeatedly to thrash their children.

the importance of 'loyalty to culture' and makes great claims for the benefits that accrue:

> our culture gives coherence to our lives, gives us resources to make sense of the world, stabilises our personality ... Its values and ideals inspire us, act as our moral compass, and guide us through life ... no culture is wholly worthless [would he apply all these attributes to say Nazi, slave plantation, or apartheid cultures?] ... No culture is perfect, and it is bound to include beliefs and practices that are perverse and sit ill at ease with its values and ideals. To love one's culture is to wish it well, and that involves criticising and removing its blemishes.

But is this feasible? The reality of tight-knit communities, and a key *raison d'être*, is that it is extraordinarily difficult to indulge in honest, constructive criticisms in an attempt to remove 'blemishes'. Tradition and religion, in combination, provide powerful reinforcing ballasts against challenges from within. Moreover, it is often not the blemishes that need removal, but much of the foundation which gives rise to 'perverse beliefs and practices'. Parekh clearly disliked Salman Rushdie's *The Satanic Verses* and supported its censorship in India (*ibid.*, p. 320) – in his terms, Rushdie had shown little loyalty to his culture and religion (setting aside the fact that he had little choice in the matter but, in regard to the religion at least, rejected it by exercising his autonomy and intellectual faculty) and gone way beyond the bounds of acceptable criticism and attempts to expose blemishes.

Moreover, what defines the boundaries to 'loyalty to culture'? Are these different to loyalties to other beliefs, practices, or organisations? Without making this explicit, what Parekh seems to be advocating is some kind of equivalence to patriotism (loyalty to nation) or 'company man' (loyalty to company). These set limits to criticisms of the 'loyal opposition' type, so just as unpatriotic behaviour or 'whistle blowing' on companies are frowned upon by the powers-that-be in the nation or company, so too is the case with the Parekhian guardians of culture. In regard to religion, the test for loyalty tends to be even stricter, whereby none of the fundamentals (the existence of God, the prophets, rituals etc.) can be subject to criticism let alone denied, so that criticism is confined to interpretation, which is usually the preserve of the layer of priests and equivalents. But even this has dangers for Parekh because this 'can easily violate the integrity of the texts and the tradition …' (*ibid.*, p. 88). This reasoning simply ignores or disallows questions such as this by the Dutch-based Iranian scholar, Afshin Ellian: why should westerners be the only ones to dissent from their traditions? (Buruma, 2007, p. 28). So if, in Samuel Johnson's memorable phrase, 'patriotism is the last refuge of the scoundrel', then it is not too uncharitable to think the same regarding loyalty to culture; which is to assert that apologetics and timid criticism are of little use to the cause of cultural advancement and social progress.

The dangers of, and rejoinder to, Parekh's strong defence of culture and abrogation of universal rights were provided long ago by John Stuart Mill. In *On Liberty* (p. 9) he insisted:

> there needs protection also against the tyranny of the prevailing opinion and feeling; against the tendency of society to impose, by other means than civil penalties, its own ideas and practices as rules of conduct on those who dissent from them … This all but universal illusion [that rules appear self-evident and self-justifying] is one of the examples of the magical influence of custom … The effect of custom, in preventing any misgiving respecting the rules of conduct which mankind impose on one another, is all the more complete because the subject is one on which it is not generally considered necessary that reasons should be given …

In regard to Parekh's attacks on Rushdie, this is Mill's firm stance (*ibid.*, p. 27):

> Strange it is that men should admit the argument for free discussion, but object to their being 'pushed to an extreme'; not seeing that un-

less the reasons are good for an extreme case, they are not good for any case. Strange that they should imagine that they are not assuming infallibility, when they acknowledge that there should be free discussion on all subjects which can possibly be *doubtful*, but think that some particular principle or doctrine should be forbidden to be questioned because it so *certain*, that is, because *they are certain* that it is certain.

Parekh's *Rethinking Multiculturalism* and *The Parekh Report* both came out in 2000 (importantly, before 9/11). Soon after 9/11, however, especially in regard to Muslims, debates on multiculturalism increased and attacks on it intensified. In this harsher political terrain for multiculturalism, in a 'comment' piece in the *Guardian* in 2005, 'Multiculturalism is a civilised dialogue', Parekh attempted to provide a succinct defence of multiculturalism – whilst recognising that the sort of blanket support he had hitherto given to ethnic minority cultures would cut little ice even with the readership of a liberal paper. He begins with a frank acknowledgement that 'no culture is "self-authenticating" or above criticism. All have their share of unacceptable practices and these must be exposed and fought'. But these sentiments and injunctions are, in fact, a veering away from cultural relativism that asserts a non-judgemental stance regarding cultures; the *raison d'être* of a relativistic stance. He provides severe criticisms of aspects of Asian cultural practices such as the high incidence of domestic violence, coerced marriages, sexism, and gender inequality. Now all these clearly point to the generally poor treatment of women within Asian societies – and within the family structure which is at the heart of Asian culture and 'Asian values'. But he goes on to say that we need to 'cherish the Asian family structure' – yet it is this very family structure which is often brought about by coerced marriages (this does not apply just to 'forced marriages', but also to 'arranged marriages' as these can be underpinned by a degree of coercion), and which has a high incidence of sexism, domestic violence, and gender inequality. So how can we cherish this?

He proceeds to assert that 'this is why an equal and robust dialogue between different cultures benefits them all'. But surely this involves mutual criticism – and again we then have to breach the normative basis of multiculturalism, that is cultural relativism where cultures are provided with 'do not disturb' signs and therefore are not open to robust dialogue. Parekh then goes on to say that 'multiculturalism is about sometimes friendly and sometimes tense critical engagement between cultures. It is not about shutting oneself up in a communal or cultural ghetto and leading a segregated and self-contained life'. But this has exactly been the reality – brought about in good measure by multicultural policies – in so many towns and cities and which has spawned government desire to increase 'community cohesion' and counter 'parallel lives'. If you allow people to live their lives according to their culture and religion and, moreover, argue that this is perfectly fine, that it is a democratic right, and that such differences in cultures and religions should be afforded public 'recognition' and even 'celebrated' – which, after all, are the foundational principles of multiculturalism – this is not a recipe for critical engagement, tense or otherwise. Experience strongly indicates that people in segregated communities in general, and community and religious elders in particular, simply do not open themselves to criticism from others – so as to learn 'from their insights and criticisms and growing as a result into a richer and tolerant culture'. This all seems to be wishful thinking, and goes against the grain of the reality – which critics of multiculturalism have argued would be the outcome of multicultural policies.

Parekh then argues that 'our musical, artistic, literary, culinary and other areas of life are the richer for being the products of intercultural fusion'. But intercultural *fusion* is the antithesis of multiculturalism. It assumes that cultures are not fixed, immutable, do not have 'essential' characteristics and, moreover, that cultures must be allowed to transform and develop, in the context of people *mixing with one another* with high levels of points of contact. But when you have segregated communities and ghettoised schools, the prospect of intercultural fusion taking root is well nigh impossible. Moreover, he further thinks that this is 'also true of our religious life where each religion is subtly shaping the self-understanding of all others'. Now there is not much evidence for this and nor for any 'inter-religious fusion'. Indeed there remain very high levels of alienation, friction, and even hostility between the main religions, not least between Islam and Hinduism, and Islam and Judaism.

Parekh concludes by arguing that 'our task is to encourage the process of unplanned social and cultural integration by creating conditions in which our different communities can carry on their formal and informal conversation and help evolve a shared but plural way of being British'. This is laudable but naive. Integration cannot genuinely arise alongside robust multiculturalism whereby people adhering to their own cultural and religious norms are separated into their own neighbourhoods and communities. Integration can only flourish when rigid communal identities and attendant 'communities' are dismantled by very high levels of interaction and mixing – including forming relationships. Yet, evidence strongly shows that this is prevented under multiculturalism and, with greater intensity, under its successor 'multifaithism' (of which more below).

Writing in the post-9/11 era, Tariq Modood, a close intellectual ally of Parekh and academic adviser to *The Parekh Report*, acknowledges that multiculturalism has been subjected to severe criticisms and, in those countries that have advocated it, is under retreat. Yet his book *Multiculturalism: a Civic Idea* largely fails to discuss and take account of the criticisms and objections of multiculturalism but instead focuses on debates *within* multiculturalism. Instead, he devotes a whole chapter to Will Kymlicka's theory – but critiques this with the view to extending it, so as to cover post-colonial immigrants into Western Europe. Thus, he argues 'the only additional questions, for Kymlicka, that political multiculturalism has to consider in relation to religious minorities are exemptions, rather than, as in the case of cultural groups, demands for democratic participation, for public resources or institutional presence ... we seem therefore to have a certain blindness here; something we might characterize as a secularist bias' (Modood, 2007, p. 26–27). It is curious that he includes 'democratic participation' here, as it is precisely the threat to this that can stem from multiculturalism. Furthermore, the foundational approach of theorists of multiculturalism is based on the rejection of 'blindness' that egalitarians argue is a *sine qua non* for equality. In essence, this is Modood wishing to assert an even 'deeper' multiculturalism (or, *de facto*, multifaithism) than Kymlicka – one that rejects the neutral role of the state (which, in any case, Kymlicka deems to be impossible). Instead, he wishes the state to adopt a non-neutral, proactive stance so as to materially assist those minority groups that define and assert their identity in avowedly religious terms. Rather than seriously engaging with critics, Modood retreats into the multiculturalist *laager*, but by so doing resorts to arguments that are not only unconvincing but indeed, at this juncture, rather pointless.*

In an edited collection that focuses on the challenge for multiculturalism regarding Muslims in Europe, Modood and his co-editors argue that owing to this challenge, there needs to be rethinking as to what secularism is, and that 'a focus on Muslims exposes and contests the narrow definitions of racism and equality and [once more] the secular bias of the discourse and policies of multiculturalism in Europe' (Triandafyllidou, Modood, and Zapata-Barrero, 2006, p. 3). The overcoming of these supposed problems is done by a rethinking that leads to definitional change, so that secularism – the separation of religion and the state – is abandoned in order to accommodate Muslim demands for their 'just claims to [the holy trinity of multiculturalism] difference, recognition and multicultural citizenship rights' (*ibid.*, p. 4). By which criteria are these demands 'just'? Only those criteria that privilege them over equal rights and treatment; and, as we shall see, it is the widespread recognition and dislike of

---

* At the back of Barry's book is the following (in my opinion, entirely justified) claim by Ian Shapiro: '*Culture and Equality* is without doubt *the* critique that defenders of multiculturalism will have to answer'. Alas, this is what Modood singularly fails to do in this work. Indeed in his *Multicultural Politics* (2005), there is not even a single reference to Barry's work.

this stark reality that lies at the heart of increasing opposition to multiculturalism. One avers that it is this plain but powerful truth that escapes theorists of multiculturalism and, accordingly, demonstrates their own inherent bias.

In a response to Barry's book, Parekh (2002, p. 147) points out that despite his uncompromising attacks on multiculturalism, Barry tends to have similar views to most multiculturalists on concrete issues (on the 'softer' variety of cultural and religious practices, such as those listed below, there is agreement that these should be allowed; on the 'hard' variety, such as female genital mutilation, there is agreement for banning them),* though the grounds given for the toleration tend to be different. In all the cases given, for multiculturalists the reasons are the familiar ones of justice for ethnic and religious minorities, respect for culture and for public manifestations of differences, equal opportunity, and freedom of choice. Examples Parekh provides include allowing the following: i. American Indians to ingest peyote (a proscribed drug) on religious grounds (for multiculturalists, this is a case of justice but for Barry, it is on the grounds of a prudent and enlightened public policy). ii. Opposing the law which requires French schools to proscribe the wearing of a headscarf by Muslim girls (though Parekh does not mention that this includes *all* conspicuous religious symbols, and is wrong to suggest that they allow Christian insignia – see Chapter 5). Barry's argument on this is that as the headscarf does not hamper the proper functioning of the school, it should be permitted. iii. Multiculturalists advocate allowing Sikh boys to wear the turban in schools that otherwise proscribe it as part of their requirement on school uniforms – Barry agrees with this on the grounds of equality of opportunity plus, again, as with the *hijab*, on the grounds of school functionality not being interfered with. A further, related, example is that of Sikh men being allowed to wear turbans on building sites (rather than helmets which are required by

---

* Though it is not clear what precisely the grounds for 'soft' and 'hard' practices are: for example, the scarring of faces that is common in some African societies is illegal in Britain. But is this any 'worse' than the wearing of the turban or *hijab*?

law) – Barry agrees with this on the grounds of equal opportunity given so many Sikhs work on building sites.

Indeed this is a legitimate and rather clever manoeuvre by Parekh, for it does highlight the fact that although Barry provides a sound philosophical and normative basis for egalitarian universalism, in cases such as these, he veers away from it by allowing numerous exemptions to universal laws and regulations; yet it is precisely the thrust of his argument against multiculturalism that such exemptions are detrimental to egalitarian universalism. Unfortunately, by so doing, Barry arguably gives too many hostages to fortune to multiculturalism, because the grounds for exemptions in most cases are insufficient to justify a breach of universalism: *ipso facto*, this weakens his case. I shall discuss the weakness of his and multiculturalist arguments regarding the veil issue in Chapter 5. Here, I wish to comment on the related issue of the wearing of turbans in schools.

Barry (2002, p. 213) points out that the EU's Council Directive states that non-discriminatory laws can be unjust if they have a differential impact on people, unless objectively justified as a 'legitimate aim and the means of achieving that aim are appropriate and necessary'. Now, the British government has accorded great importance to achieving 'social cohesion', that is, minimising inter-communal stress and tension, and increasing integration of ethnic minorities. Evidence suggests that a key factor for lack of social cohesion is divisiveness caused by conflicting religions and religious identities. Therefore, the reduction and minimisation of such divisiveness is a legitimate societal aim; it follows that a prerequisite to achieving this aim is to significantly reduce public manifestations of religion and religious identity. This applies *a fortiori* to schoolchildren who are not old enough to make an informed and free choice about religious allegiance. There is much to commend Bertrand Russell's belief (1987, p. 19) in the 'immensely strong hold of early associations'. Often, where a child is found to be noncompliant with these 'associations', some stern sanctions, including, as we have seen, a good thrashing soon brings him/her back into line. The policy prescription flowing from this legitimate aim and the reality of divisiveness on religious grounds is obvious and compelling: that is, to proscribe *all* manifestations of religion in school. Otherwise, religion and religious identity are accorded a privileged status over other beliefs and identities, and this is necessarily done on the basis of discrimination (of which more below).

Barry, however, agreed with the House of Lords ruling (on the *Mandla* v. *Dowell Lee* case, 1983) that was made under the Race Relations Act 1976. This involved a private school in Birmingham refusing admission to a turban-wearing Sikh boy on the grounds that this breached the school's rules which 'prescribed a particular uniform, including a cap, and required boys to have their hair cut short'. The House of Lords ruled that the imposition of the school uniform policy was tantamount to the denial of equality of opportunity of education. In Lord Fraser's words, the school failed 'to provide a sufficient justification for what was *prima facie* a discriminatory rule'. The way the Lords squared the circle for the purpose of the Race Relations Act was to designate Sikhs as an ethnic group (other Asians are not accorded this status) on the grounds that they were a 'separate and distinct community' (Barry, 2001, pp. 61–62; 2002, p. 213).

But this is not correct – in fact it is confused and contradictory. The reason being that it is quite impossible to distinguish Asian Sikh and non-Sikh women, and Asian Sikh men who do not wear a turban and non-Sikh men. Moreover, there are many other groups which can also be designated as 'separate and distinct communities'. What the ruling clearly implies is that, by virtue of wearing a turban, Sikhs are accorded the status of a separate ethnic group. In reality, this is tantamount to the unequal, privileged treatment/status of the Sikh faith and, unsurprisingly, it set a precedent whereby adherents of other faiths demanded the same privileged status.

The counter-argument to the House of Lords and Barry's position is compelling. The ruling completely overlooked the *harmful* effects of turban wearing: most obviously, it is highly divisive given that it sets Sikh boys very visibly apart. Indeed Barry (2002, p. 228) refers to

Aguilar's observation about cultural 'recognition' constituting a form of 'symbolic separatism' and it is this which is precisely the outcome which, in the school context, undermines the 'legitimate aim' (as provided in the EU's Council Directive) of cohesion among school pupils. The obvious question is this: why should school children be subjected to this unnecessary and potentially counterproductive form of separatism? Furthermore, it is precisely because the wearing of the turban (as with the *hijab* or veil for Muslim girls and women, or the yarmulke for Jewish boys) is not based on genuine choice[*] but rather on coercion from the parents, family, and wider 'community' arising from accident of birth, that it is imperative that boys from a Sikh background should be offered a milieu where their press-ganged 'Sikh identity' is not displayed and which, in turn, also helps prevent religious tribalism in schools. There is also the not insignificant *effort* that is required on a daily basis for the wearing of this religious accoutrement throughout a Sikh male's life. It is also the case that wearing a turban can prevent in the partaking of certain sports and leisure activities, for example, the playing of football at professional level. Given that football is the UK's and indeed the world's most popular sport, and can offer a highly lucrative and rewarding career to the most talented and dedicated, the complete denial of this path to fame and fortune to young males on the grounds of their parental religion and identity is unjust and can, therefore, indeed be considered harmful.

Barry argues (2002, p. 206) that multiculturalism derives from communitarian and New Left politics. But these are strange bedfellows given that the former has a strong conservative element whilst the latter is avowedly progressive, even revolutionary. But the fact

---

[*] That is say, not a choice arising from whimsical reveries or desires of children. Allegiance to sophisticated beliefs – be they religious, political, ethical etc. – requires careful evaluation and thought which children largely do not possess. So, just as it is strange to view primary school children having reasoned political views, so too it is the case in regard to religion. There is also the following indisputable *fact* regarding the absence of genuine choice: children almost *never* adopt a religion (and religious attire) that is not of their parents'. It is this striking fact that leads one to think that parental coercion is the most decisive factor.

that these two very different political streams merge in regard to multiculturalism highlights the strange turn that so many erstwhile progressives have taken. That said, there may, in fact, be a better progenitor in regard to New Left multiculturalists, that is, 'Third Worldism' (see, for example, Harris, 1986, ch.1). Multiculturalists have close affinity to the ideological underpinning of 'cultural nationalism', which was a central feature of Third Worldism in the post-colonial era of the 1950s and 1960s. At its core were two tenets: first, Whites must offer solidarity with, and refrain from criticism of, the new independent countries; second, politics emanating from the 'third world' were axiomatically progressive given that their basis was the struggle by the oppressed colonial subjects for liberation and independence. In the early years, there was certainly much truth in this, but it is no exaggeration to assert that the history of post-colonial leaders and rulers has been, on the whole, abysmal. Nowhere has there been a firm commitment to emancipatory politics and enshrining of rights and freedoms; on the contrary, the reality has been (above all in Africa) one of rampant corruption, trampling of rights, repression and, by hook or crook, the clinging on to power by those who had earlier fought for liberation from the colonial yoke (Amnesty International's reports over the years, for example, provide ample testimony for this assertion). Thus, adhering to Third Worldism is no guarantee of reaching decisions that further the cause of human liberation and development.

Also influenced by Third Worldist ideas are those who actually hail from the third world in whose adherence to multiculturalism we can also discern a more personal form of cultural-religious nationalism. This is clear from the following example of Parekh's (2002, p. 143): 'although political obligations generally override ethnic and religious obligations, there can be occasions when this is not the case. If the state were to require me to betray my parents and friends, spy on or malign *my ethnic community*, or convert to another religion, I would find its demands unjust or unacceptable and unworthy of my respect' (emphasis added).* Similarly, Tariq Modood (2005, pp. 4–5) describes his '... identity – composite and shifting but ultimately settling on Muslim – should be accepted with pride ... my emphasis on ethnic pride and an ethnic diversity in which Muslim identity has become prominent ...'

As such, their theories accord well with the insistence that cultures and beliefs of ethnic minorities in former colonial heartlands should be afforded, writ large, recognition, great sympathy and understanding. Furthermore, these should be offered protection by the granting of legal exemptions and generally be 'celebrated'. As a corollary, there is little by way of critiquing cultures and beliefs of ethnic minorities from an egalitarian, anti-oppressive perspective. The intellectual armoury of this can again be traced back to Said's *Orientalism*.†

Some advocates of multiculturalism recognise the dangers of abandoning universalism in favour of accommodating cultural rights of ethnic minorities, not least because this can leave women and children at the mercy of dominant, invariably male, group leaders. One such is Ayelet Shachar (2001) who forcefully attempts to reconcile the two seemingly irreconcilable positions by attempting to reduce injustice *between* groups, together with the enhancement of justice *within* them. This seems a propitious course of action but, as we shall see, suffers from fundamental weaknesses.

Shachar stresses the oft-problematic nature of minority group cultures by observing that practices and traditions pertaining to the family therein often impose disproportionate costs on women

---

* Depending on context, the overall sentiment is laudable. Perhaps Parekh took inspiration from E. M. Forster who, *In Two Cheers for Democracy* (1972 [1951], p. 66), famously and controversially wrote: '... if I had to choose between betraying my country and betraying my friend, I hope I should have the guts to betray my country'.

† This is not to detract from the importance of Said's work – a powerful corrective to the long history of Western colonialist and racist discourse in regard to the Middle East (the 'Orient'). But it is important to note that Said became uncomfortable with some of the unfounded and extravagant uses of his book – including by Islamists – as he made clear in the 'Afterword' to the 1995 edition, which is reprinted in the 2003 edition.

and proceeds to make the following admission and indictment of multiculturalism:

> still less consideration has been given to the ... often injurious impact that state accommodation policies can exert on individuals within minority groups – an impact which can be so severe as to nullify some individuals' basic citizenship rights ... multiculturalism begins to present a problem whenever state accommodation policies intended to mitigate the power differential between groups end up reinforcing power hierarchies within them (*ibid.*, pp. 11, 17).

This is patently true and the honesty of it is most welcome but, again, does this not say something of vital importance about the culture of some minority groups? Indeed it does: that they are often founded on intense patriarchy with strict gender roles, often with high levels of gender segregation. The question, resolutely avoided by multiculturalists, therefore, naturally arises: are these cultural practices worth preserving and hence being accommodated by the granting of rights, exemptions, and privileges? It is my contention that an egalitarian, anti-oppressive stance must firmly answer *no*: the tackling of oppression of any kind should be a central goal of enlightened governments and non-state actors.

But there is no *a priori* reason for state accommodation (that is, multicultural policies) mitigating the power differentials between groups. We can take 'mitigating of powerful differentials' to mean the raising of key socio-economic indicators of members of hitherto disadvantaged ethnic minority groups to the national average. This can, however, better be achieved by recourse to two alternate sets of policies. The first, and most important, is to ensure maximum equality of opportunity and outcome, especially by the implementation of laws that prevent discrimination on grounds of race or ethnicity. Second, if need be, enact positive discrimination laws in favour of a group/groups that are, or have hitherto been, systematically discriminated against – as in the case, most famously, in the setting up of affirmative action programmes and quotas for Blacks in the US in a variety of areas (see, for example, Darity and Myers, 1998). Crucially, moreover, the enacting of multicultural policies cannot *per se* be said to reduce power differentials between groups. On the contrary, such measures are likely to have zero or minimal effect – for giving ethnic minority groups cultural autonomy is not *necessarily* going to increase their absolute or relative power. The channelling of significant resources to such groups is obviously the necessary prerequisite, but there is always the danger that this merely facilitates increasing the power of 'community leaders' rather than individual members (whose position may not alter at all), thereby entrenching group power hierarchies. Moreover, as commented upon earlier, a further danger is the manifestation of pork-barrel politics and heightened divisions between communities that can ensue through use of such policies.

In fact, increasing group rights may lead to the *diminution* of power of some sections *within* a group – as Shachar rightly notes, it is women who tend to be trapped in an oppressive position within minority groups. Consequently, if the socio-economic and political status of women is kept suppressed, this must inevitably mean that the power of the group *as a whole* is weakened. Or, in Shachar's terms, the corollary of 'the reinforcing of power hierarchies' may result in the *worsening* of power differentials for the group as a whole.

Shachar proceeds to present a dilemma that is supposed to be the norm in minority communities: either participate in the minority culture (and risk losing some rights that are granted to the rest of society) *or* abandon the culture (*ibid.*, p. 86). But this is a false dilemma for it ignores the capacity of the state to *mitigate* those aspects of a culture that are in breach of laws and universalist norms of justice operating in the wider society. In her discussion of 'consensual accommodation' (where individuals can choose, in certain matters, either group or state legislation – so that a 'consensus' has been reached between groups and the state), Shachar argues that group members themselves are in the best position to evaluate their attachments to their group. However, she acknowledges that 'it is easy to imagine how a person might choose to remain under traditional authorities out of submission to familial, cultural, and group-based pressures, or because insufficient knowledge or resources limited his or her ability to imagine a life outside the *nomoi* group" (*ibid.*, p. 106, 108).

But this rather downplays the often systematic and unrelenting indoctrination and coercion that ensures a powerful attachment to the group culture – so much so that 'detachment' from the group becomes well-nigh impossible even to conceive, let alone effect. So even if resources are available – and in the developed world, there is the existence of extensive social service provisions as well as refuges for women – the incidence of 'exit' from a group remains minimal (for an enlightening discussion of 'exit costs', see Barry, 2001, pp. 150–151). Shachar thinks that the role of the state is to ensure that the individual is not subjected to duress and not forced into an unwanted religious or customary marriage. But this turns on how one defines 'duress' – indeed, in regard to many cultures, it may be possible to make a cogent case for arguing that their very basis rests on duress. Hidden away in a footnote, Shachar recognises that 'choice-based' approaches upon which her own thesis rests for sharing jurisdictional authority between groups and the state pay *'too little attention to the constraints imposed on the individual by the institutional context in which her choices are made'* (*ibid.*, fn. 45, p. 108, emphasis added). This is indeed a powerful truth the impact of which is to severely weaken the case for consensual accommodation. Moreover, a key constraint for individual members – especially children and women – is precisely the duress that they are subjected to in all aspects of life within their community. Thus, Shachar calls for 'certain limits' by the state on how far a community can impose controls on its members. But this begs the question of what kinds of limits, and who should decide what these limits should be. Importantly, the imposition of such limits can severely encroach upon multiculturalism and the autonomy of groups;

---

* By which she means primarily religiously defined groups of people that share a comprehensive world view and extends to creating laws for such groups (Shachar, 2001, fn 5, p. 2).

and this is precisely what universal egalitarian norms of justice should do.

Dangers of ethnocentricity and faith exemptions
What proponents of multiculturalism do not fully appreciate, do not take cognisance of, or simply ignore, is that the strong adherence to a minority culture and identity may, in some instances, *exacerbate* racism and discrimination, and this represents a very grave danger. Suppose, for example, that a White Briton marries someone/has a partner from an ethnic minority background. What is the likely impact of this on the attitudes of his/her family and friends regarding ethnic minorities in general, and of the ethnicity of the partner in particular? One can reasonably conjecture that, over time, assuming that the relationship is reasonably successful with at least some interaction between the couple and members of family and friends, that attitudes will either become positive, or remain positive, in regard at least to the ethnicity of the partner, and perhaps to ethnic minorities in general also. Hence, a generalised corollary to the development of such positive attitudes can be the challenging of bigotry and racism residing within the majority White society. Indeed, we can postulate that it is precisely this type of interaction – of ever increasing numbers of people from the majority society having relationships and relatives from a different ethnic background – that has been a contributory factor in the decline of racist attitudes among the White British population over the generations.

Now look at this 'marrying out' phenomenon from a multicultural perspective, perhaps thinking of the example of 'traditional' Asian families and communities. Unless the 'outsider' converts to the faith and complies fully with the cultural practices of the community, this represents the strong possibility of dilution of the faith and customs on the part of the person marrying out. Moreover, there arises a concomitant 'danger' that outside beliefs and practices will permeate the extended family and community – assuming that contacts are maintained – emanating from the 'demonstration effect' of the mixed couple. Accordingly, this is considered an undesirable outcome – especially if the person marrying out actively proceeds to challenge the core beliefs and mores of the family and community; and nothing worries community and faith leaders more than an intellectual and social challenge to their faith and customs from the outside.

Consequently, these twin dangers are sufficient to warrant great care in regard to the socialisation of the young so as to ensure their full compliance with the central tenets of the faith, culture, and traditions – a process in which all manner of coercive practices (including threats and cajoling) are systematically and mercilessly used, the aim of which is the prevention of marrying out and threat of 'exit'. Religion is crucial to this socialisation process – and places of worship especially are of central importance to the community. To leave the faith and to stop frequenting the mosque, temple, gurdwara etc. is to distance oneself from the community. Non-attendance is detected quickly and pressure applied to attempt to ensure that the recalcitrant individual returns to the flock. If the dissident refuses then there is the likelihood of being shunned by the community (and concomitant loss of social capital) with the attendant accruing of significant material losses (that is, loss of 'economic capital').

From this perspective, it is clear that 'outsiders' are generally not welcome into the ranks of the family and community, and are likely to be considered potentially hazardous, unwelcome intruders. Naturally, such stringent ethnocentric behaviour is likely to have a profoundly alienating affect on the White partner and his/her family and friends; this alienation, in turn, may reach a point that engenders hostility to the family, community, and even to the ethnicity of the partner – perhaps to the point of prejudice and racism. It is this sort of scenario, given succour under multiculturalism, which can poison community relations. The blunt refusal of an ethnic community to mix, that is associate, with people from the majority community and integrate into wider society has become a pervasive phenomenon of ghettoised neighbourhoods and its profoundly negative effects, such as in this hypothetical example, have not sufficiently exercised the minds of proponents of multiculturalism.

As ethnic minorities have become established in Western countries, often in highly segregated neighbourhoods, many have, with ever greater conviction, tried to reconfigure the terrain upon which they inhabit according to traditional customs, cultural, and religious norms, which are often at sharp variance with prevailing norms in the rest of society. Certainly, for perhaps the majority of settlers from South Asia in segregated areas, this has been done with a remarkable thoroughness. Separation and segregation facilitates the socialisation of – or embedding in – community members according to traditional cultural and religious mores. In turn, this has increasingly given rise to demands for what must be deemed as special pleading or privileges, including separate provisions and exemptions from certain laws on the grounds of religion or culture. These are *privileges* because they are denied to individuals or groups who identify themselves on other criteria.

This is a cause for further alienation of the majority society from ethnic minority groups that are vociferous and insistent in their demands for special status and, as such, from multicultural policies in general. This can be illustrated with basic examples rooted in multicultural reality. Suppose, for example, a school has a uniform policy but allows exemptions to certain groups on religious grounds (such as Jewish boys being allowed to wear the yarmulke, Sikh boys to wear turbans, and Muslim girls to wear the *hijab*). At the same school, some parents of children closely following the local football team as part of a long-standing family and community tradition wish their children to be allowed to wear the club's football shirt to school, and so also be granted exemption from the standard school uniform. If the school insists on maintaining its policy on uniforms (let us not be detracted here about the merits and demerits of school uniforms, or indeed of uniforms in general), it can only refuse the exemption with respect to football shirts on the grounds that an identity based on allegiance to a football club is less than an identity based on religion.

Precisely the same thinking will apply, for example, to motorcyclists seeking exemption from wearing a helmet in hot weather conditions; an exemption that is granted in law to Sikh men. Indeed, on rational grounds, an exemption from helmets on the grounds of high temperature is rather more persuasive than one based on religious superstition but is denied in law. Similarly, if Muslim girls are permitted to wear the *hijab* at school, then why not permit other boys and girls to wear hoods, caps, or balaclavas?

Now let us take an example from the 'home' society concerning a group that has long been a highly unusual minority – the gypsies. Among British gypsies lack of literacy – to the point of illiteracy – is considered a mark of distinction and of ethnic identity. Consequently, gypsy children encounter 'cultural dissonance' (that is, the mismatch of gypsy culture with that of mainstream culture) when they enter schools: the high value placed on literacy, books, and acquisition of knowledge through reading clashes fiercely with their upbringing (Levinson, 2007). The presumption under cultural relativism must be that gypsy culture's pride in illiteracy is of equal cultural status as that of a culture that places high value, backed up by resources, on literacy. Presumably also, therefore, the United Nations Development Programme's Human Development Index's inclusion of literacy as a key component of 'human development' is misplaced and, from a consistent multiculturalist view, should be removed. But if advocates of multiculturalism and cultural relativism reject this reasoning, then we are again in the realm of differential standards.

To further stress this crucial point, we can offer this example. Suppose that a worker leaves an organisation with strong union representation that offers effective protection against egregious acts by the employers in order to join a non-unionised workplace. We can adduce sharply contrasting 'corporate cultures' in the two organisations. The obvious question presents itself: should a tougher, perhaps uncompromising, stance by the latter employer be excused under the pretext of 'respect for a different corporate culture'? Most are likely to reply in the negative on the grounds that this reasoning and justification is illegitimate; this would certainly be the case with those rooted in the left-wing politics of the labour movement. Thus, again, under the banner of cultural relativism, corporate culture is treated with an entirely different yardstick to that of the culture of religious-ethnic minorities.*

What this decidedly asks of us is to cede a privileged status to 'recognition of cultural and religious differences'. It therefore follows that higher ethical standards are accorded to certain cultures and religions than to other (non religious, non ethnic minority) cultural manifestations from which flow the policy prescription of granting rights to some groups but not others.† But it is precisely this differential standard that is likely to generate an alienating and divisive dynamic that can – and does – generate increased hostility by the sections of the majority society to multiculturalism. It is indubitably the case that significant sections of the majority may not readily understand,

---

* Note that 'corporate culture' need not be reified for it is also based on ethics and values of human beings, albeit in a specific namely, organisational, setting

† It is not just ethnic minorities who seek exemptions to the law on religious and cultural grounds. Till recently, the Church of England had been granted a powerful exemption from the right to freedom of expression on the grounds of blasphemy. In early 2007, the Catholic Church put pressure on the British government in regard to allowing Catholic adoption agencies exemption from the law which provides for the right of gay couples to adopt – and indeed had sympathy and support from the Prime Minister at the time, the Catholic convert Tony Blair. Though the exemption was denied, this brought into sharp relief the true nature of what exemptions from the law on grounds of religion (often asserted as the 'right of religious expression') can mean: the right to wilfully discriminate. Another example is that of the long campaign to outlaw fox hunting. A constant refrain used by supporters of fox hunting was that it was a long standing tradition and vital part of rural culture. That much was true, though, in reality, it had been the preserve of a wealthy elite. But opinion polls had consistently shown large majorities in opposition to the practice, and there was a majority from even those residing in the countryside. Yet, cultural relativist arguments were never accepted as valid by the population at large and eventually also by the Labour government that introduced the banning legislation. The key ethical and universalist consideration was patently clear, that is, the appeal to culture or tradition could not justify animal cruelty. Nor was this a novel turn for the same principle had earlier applied to dog and cock fighting that had also been outlawed, though the latter 'traditions' had been the preserve of working-class men.

or approve, of the normative basis for this blatant discrimination that appears so obvious and compelling to multiculturalists and is rationalised under the rubric of cultural relativism.

Multiculturalists may well argue that such alienation and resentment is churlish and displays an absence of sympathy for the profound cultural and religious needs of ethnic minorities striving for acceptance and recognition of their ways of life. But this discounts the fact that the majority view may be highly egalitarian; one that insists that the polity should consistently accord *equal* treatment to all and, as such, be also strongly in favour of anti-discriminatory legislation with strong powers of enforcement. It further discounts the corollary to this which is that separate 'group rights' may lead many in the majority society to the view that they cannot view all their fellow citizens in a shared and inclusive manner. A divisive dynamic can ensue which can entrench the feelings of ethnic and religious minorities as not truly 'belonging' to, and being part of, society and, by so doing, perpetuates and even accentuates the 'strangers in our midst' mentality. Moreover, exemptions granted to one group can trigger a demonstration effect so that other minority groups begin to seek similar legal exemptions and provisions. The danger is clear: differences between individuals and communities become codified in law and enormously entrenched.

There is a further danger: multiculturalism and concomitant segregation, in combination with the rise in religious identity, is aiding the development of extreme right-wing forces that emanate from two sources. The first is the case of avowedly racist, far right organisations preying on the acute levels of alienation brought about by divisive policies and divided communities. Towns and cities divided along ethnic lines present potentially fruitful pickings for such organisations who wish to incite base feelings of resentment, bigotry, and hatred. This has precisely been the strategy of the BNP and its targeting of Muslim communities in particular – importantly long before 9/11. The party has made political inroads in deprived White estates in several towns and cities. They have been assisted in this by the strong segregation of communities, with little interaction between them – that is, by the existence of 'parallel lives'. Problems have been accentuated by pork-barrel council politics (the BNP has vigorously pushed the line that 'Asian' or 'Muslim' estates receive more resources than 'White' estates) in combination with multicultural policies and the strong religious identity of Muslims, whose cultural and religious norms sharply collide with those of mainstream society. Given that there is very little inter-racial mixing and integration, the room for enlightened forces to challenge such naked divide-and-rule politics is naturally curtailed. All these factors have intensified the resentment and alienation felt by many sections of the White majority, a section of society that has become overwhelmingly secular and, in all likelihood, not too enamoured by obscurantism and religious superstitions (this is discussed further in Chapter 6).

The second is the rise of chauvinist 'faith organisations' – most notably, an array of Muslim organisations, but also Hindu and Sikh organisations. Religious identity is indubitably fuelling sectarian hatred, and it is traditional right-wing forces within religious minorities which are benefiting from this and, in turn, accentuating divisions – for it is in their interests to do so. Consequently, there has arisen a panoply of groups and individuals who resist any dilution of their religious identity and, thereby, hinder community cohesion and inter-cultural, inter-faith, dialogue. Put simply, the problems of multiculturalism are intensified when groups of citizens are deemed to be members of 'faith communities', which we have argued is the transformation of multiculturalism into multifaithism. The lesson is clear: dividing people up according to religious beliefs can be enormously divisive – the history of Northern Ireland attests this and provides a warning that should be heeded. As stated earlier, what we have is a case of the law of unintended consequences where the result is the converse of the intent. In fact, what multifaithism does is to accept the reality of segregated communities, and cement them into 'faith groups', rather than countering the divisive dynamic that has contributed to segregation.

Just because myriad cultural and religious attributes and practices have existed for a long time and are derived from religious edicts and rituals does not mean that a laissez-faire, let alone a respectful, approach should be taken in regard to them. The principle must always be based on the understanding and cognisance of any oppression of members within a particular culture. An equivalent to the Hippocratic Oath needs to be at the centre of government policies, that is, religious and cultural practices should do no harm. Defining what constitutes 'harm' in this context is likely to be problematic but, clearly, there can be little disagreement in regard to the most egregious practices such as *sati*, female genital mutilation and self-flagellation,* where physical harm is central to these practices.

But harm can come in other ways also, as already noted in regard to the example of turban wearing. Suppose the culture of a 'community' is so much at variance with that of the rest of society as to *prevent* its members from interacting with others in anything more than a superficial manner. Should this be considered a problem which is socially harmful? If one adopts the normative stance that the close mixing of peoples is good, desirable, and helps 'community relations', then, from this perspective, given that the inevitable outcome of this community's culture is self-enforced segregation, it can be viewed as an undoubted social harm. All those with a progressive outlook would indubitably oppose the enforced separation of peoples as occurred in the southern states of the US post-slavery, in apartheid South Africa or, currently, in occupied Palestinian territories. If these are considered damaging and detestable then, we can legitimately ask, why not also – even with milder revulsion – the segregation that occurs from religious-cultural practices and beliefs? In other words, why should

---

* This is the practice of flogging oneself (on the back) with a 'zanjeer' whip with curved blades during the Shia ceremony of 'Ashura'. For the first time (in 2008), the Crown Prosecution Service prosecuted a man for encouraging two boys (both under 16) to beat themselves up. The jury duly convicted him on the grounds of child cruelty. The judge told the defendant: '[y]ou must realise that the law recognises that children and young persons may wish to take part in some activities which it considers they should not. It is sometimes expressed as protecting themselves from themselves' (BBC News, 2008).

segregationist practices within many communities be considered acceptable or tolerable? On the contrary, one must assert that they are indeed harmful.

Hindrance to integration
What do we mean by integration of ethnic minorities? By integration is understood that ethnic minorities, new to the country of settlement, overwhelmingly reliant on work, will interact in a significant manner with those of the indigenous society. It can be defined as systematic and widespread 'points of contact' by ethnic minorities beyond their 'own' groups, above all with people from the majority society and culture (this is discussed further in Chapter 3). Such points of contact – which can be shallow or deep – occur across the spectrum of their lives: officialdom, the world of work, education for children, social, leisure, civic and political activities. Crucially, however, integration requires the freedom of members of minority groups to choose their activities, place of residence, cultural and religious mores, friends, and partners.

The key aspect is meaningful, sustained dialogue and social intercourse – at the lowest level this is formal either in relation to officialdom or in regard to market-based contracting. At the highest levels of integration, there arises the fusing together of lives through the forging of strong friendships and relationships (marriage or equivalent).

Where there is legalised, enforced separation of peoples, integration is wilfully prevented. When these impediments do not exist, integration can proceed, even if there is some initial resentment, suspicion, hostility, and resistance. In regard to migrants from the developing world (in particular, former colonies) to developed, Western countries, it is important to acknowledge that there has been no legal, enforced separation. However, a further generalisation is that, to all intents and purposes, no purposive effort was made by governments to facilitate integration; at most there was the provision of some language tuition and rudimentary assistance in regard to dealing with officialdom. Indeed, rather than government measures, it has been the advent of time, mutual familiarity, and gradual interaction that has brought about whatever integration has taken place. Time can be a great healer: with its passing, there has indubitably arisen, in many of the heartlands of Britain and other West European countries, the healing of divisions and enmities, including overall declining levels of racism, and the forging of real interaction between ethnic minority settlers and the majority White society.

The central argument against integration – in its extreme form referred to as 'assimilation' – is that it leads to the dissolution of the distinctive cultural identity of minority groups. This implicitly assumes that cultures are fixed (or change at a glacial pace) and is predicated on the belief that this fixity is an unalloyed social good and that, somehow, preservation of cultural forms has the same virtue as preservation of species. Yet such reasoning is profoundly retrogressive, and counterproductive in the sense that, rather than helping ethnic minorities, over the long term it is damaging to their interests. Why this should be so is that adhering to a mono-cultural identity inevitably leads to the converse of integration, into the trap of segregation and ghettoisation with all the attendant problems this generates. In stark contrast, integration is invariably desirable: the mixing and meaningful interaction of people from different backgrounds indubitably lessens the probability of segregation. Crucially, the forging of friendships, solidarity and unity across racial, ethnic, or religious divides are a natural outcome; it is a supreme prize for society at large.

At this point, it needs to be emphasised that though I firmly oppose the imprimatur given by multicultural policies to ethnic minority cultures and beliefs (and consequent segregation), I am not at all suggesting that governments should instead 'create' some kind of standard culture for all its citizens. Clearly this is intolerable: to do so would necessitate the exercise of coercive political power and hence would breach Rawls' (2005 [1993], p. 36) requirement of 'reasonable pluralism' for a democratic society. Accordingly, the role of the government should be to encourage and facilitate the mixing of peoples from all backgrounds in a non-oppressive manner – in education, places of work, and in civic and leisure activities. Representations of such interaction should be a prominent feature of the mass media so that it is viewed as the norm.

Issues of multiculturalism and the problems of (especially the Islamic) faith and integration have arisen in a particularly acute form in the Netherlands in recent years. The Mayor of Amsterdam, Job Cohen, applying a formulation in accordance with multicultural and multifaith principles, has argued that 'the easiest way to integrate these new immigrants [Muslims] might be through their faith. For that is just about the only anchor they have when they enter Dutch society in the twenty-first century' (cited in Buruma, 2007, p. 245). The Somali-born former Dutch MP Ayaan Hirsi Ali took him to task for this:

> he seemed to be making an appeal to the Dutch people to adopt an unreflective, unexamined tolerance of Islamic communities and their activities. With this 'appeal', however, he blatantly ignored the desperate situation of Muslim women in his own city. And he seemed to believe – mistakenly – that this 'benevolent' sentiment and attitude would help the integration of Muslims into Dutch society. It will not. It does exactly the opposite: it makes a virtual institution of Muslim self-segregation and isolation' (Hirsi Ali, 2007, p. 15).

This is a cogent response for it focuses attention on *self-segregation* and the plight of Muslim women which, under these conditions, is likely to amplify their isolation and, in turn, intensify 'power differentials'. The prospects then of 'integration through faith' is nothing more than wishful thinking; a chimera born out of a convoluted, relativistic logic.

The foundational argument is that religion is a major factor – indeed perhaps the single most important factor – in *preventing* integration and this is equally true for the first generation of settlers as it is for subsequent generations born and/or brought up in the West. To describe their faith as the only 'anchor' Muslims have in Dutch (or Western) society, as Job Cohen does, is to show ignorance of the reasons for this. Why does this reasoning not apply to other migrants to the Netherlands from non-Muslim backgrounds? Evidence shows that they manage to integrate far better than Muslims without relying on the sole anchor of their faith (Buruma, 2007). It is so precisely because 'their' faith is either of much less, or perhaps of no, concern to them or, even if it is important, does not require them to 'submit' every aspect of their lives to its doctrines. In sum, it does not act as a *barrier to integration*. This is in no way to suggest that difficulties in regard to integration are not encountered by other ethnic minorities for clearly they are, and racism and discrimination is an ever-present danger. What it does suggest, however, is that successful integration requires two necessary, mutually reinforcing, conditions to be fulfilled: first, the 'host' polity and society must provide equitable and just treatment to newcomers; and second, on the part of the settlers, a willingness and effort to play a full part in their new society and not to isolate themselves away by self-segregation, immersed in customs and practices as if still in the 'home' country, that are in sharp conflict with egalitarian universalism.

For the first generation of settlers, experience shows that fulfilling the above condition is often difficult: aside from language difficulties, they naturally bring with them all manner of cultural accoutrements and value systems which the indigenous population sometimes finds alienating. In some cases, however, integration can be achieved with relative ease – particularly from settlers of educated, professional backgrounds and, more naturally, from those who speak the same language and with a similar culture. We can postulate the stricter the mores on the part of migrants, the more resistance there will be to integrate meaningfully and, accordingly, the more isolated they will become; fomenting a high incidence of self-segregation and ghettoised neighbourhoods. This is precisely the concern regarding, above all, Muslims in the West – though the stringent demands of other faiths and cultures also drive insularity and self-segregation.

In contradistinction, the closer proximity of West Indians to White British society (including language, culture, religion – the vast majority are Christians) facilitated integration despite their being subjected to the most appalling racism, especially in the early decades of post-war settlement. The racism and rejection included being shunned by many Christian churches, yet Black Caribbeans were, and largely remain, highly devoted to their faith (Hiro, 1992). Another, albeit rather different, example is that of Polish migrants who also settled in the post-war period: clearly, however, being White ruled out the racism that Blacks were subjected to. Nonetheless, they had a strong 'anchor' of Catholicism, plus a different language. But, with the aid of a significant indigenous Catholic population, and cultural mores that were not too far removed from those of the majority society, they seamlessly integrated into British society (Sword, 1996).*

With respect to Asians, there was no section of the indigenous White population which practised any of their major faiths. So, increasingly, the religious anchor plus attendant cultural mores that were significantly different from the majority's kept very significant numbers marooned from the shore of mainstream society in their own islets.

Race, ethnicity, and 'cultural racism'

Since the 1970s, the concept of biological racism has been challenged and exploded so that its scientific credibility is now zero. In its stead has arisen the epithet 'ethnicity' which is rooted not in biology but in society. It has, therefore, a social meaning (Giddens, 2001, p. 250). Yet this distinction is problematic in that it suggests that discrimination against peoples is based on social grounds rather than on bio-

---

* This is highlighted by Sword's remark that 'I have deliberately used the expression "Poles in Britain" rather than "the Polish community in Britain" since ... the latter expression implied a degree of involvement and affiliation with formal community life that may not be justified of all individuals who might be cast as "Polish" or "a Pole"' (Sword, 1996, p. 74). Though the point is very clear, it is curious, however, that the sub-title of his book is 'The Polish community in Britain'.

logical traits. The reason for this is that inherited characteristics are crucial to the notion of ethnicity, above all that of skin colour; the epithet 'visible minority' is helpful precisely because non-White skin colour defines 'visibility'. Hence 'Black' refers to people of African origin with Black skin; 'Asian', within the UK, refers to people whose origins reside in South Asia and who overwhelmingly have a brown complexion. In contrast, however, in the US the generic 'Asian' refers, in the main, to those hailing from East Asia (China, Japan, Korea, Vietnam etc.) as these groups far outnumber those emanating from South Asia – though the 'hyphenated American' is the norm for a more precise ethnic background (Chinese-American, Japanese-American etc.); whereas in the UK, until the recent fissuring into faith identities as identified earlier, the hyphenated 'British-Asian' has been the sole ethnic categorisation.

To further clarify the point, suppose a person of Black Caribbean parentage were removed at birth from his/her biological parents and brought up by White adoptive parents and acculturated in the latter's lifestyle and social milieu. By what ethnicity should this person be designated? Without hesitation, it would be 'Black' because, biologically, that is what the person is. We should not forget that 'White' is an ethnic category too – in the West, it is the ethnic majority. In contrast, migrants with White skin colour to Britain from Ireland, the Mediterranean, or Eastern Europe, are generally not considered sections of ethnic minorities, as they are not 'visible'. Indeed it may be legitimate to consider them as forming part of the White ethnic majority, even if their culture and religion is quite distinct.

However, an exemption to this link between ethnicity and 'race' (skin colour) is that of Jews. Nominally a faith designation, the category 'Jew' became racialised or 'ethnicised' in Europe as a result of extreme anti-Semitism. Yet, Jews in the UK are overwhelmingly White, and this is why they are *ordinarily* not considered an ethnic minority. But, for very specific historical reasons which do not apply to other White minorities (including the Irish, a minority that had long subjected widespread discrimination), they are accorded the status of an 'ethnic group' and so covered under the provisions of the Race Relations Act 1976.*

If 'race' does not have scientific validity, the concept 'racism' certainly is a social, economic, and political reality (Rose, Kamin, and Lewontin, 1984). When ethnic minorities are subjected to systematic discrimination on grounds of skin colour, they suffer from racism and not 'ethnicism'. Indeed it was the racism suffered by Afro-Caribbeans and Asians post-Second World War that justified both sets of people as being united under the umbrella 'Black': whether Asians liked it or not, for racist Whites they were Black – period. Naturally, White minorities were not designated as Black and nor did they suffer the same level of discrimination and vilification.

Both at a formal (or 'institutional') level and at an informal ('personal') level, therefore, the key animating factor in racial prejudice remains that of skin colour; this provides the signal 'difference' between various groups of people – as we have seen, it is non-Whiteness that predominantly lends itself to the potential for racist thoughts and actions. But, as legislation and public opinion have turned against racism, the ability to openly express racist views has concomitantly declined. This has undoubtedly been a major advance notwithstanding the fact that some right-wing critics derogate this as 'politically correct'. Yet, the discrediting of first biological race and, later, increasing intolerance of racism may have helped in their disappearance from public discourse; nevertheless, racism remains a persistent and pervasive phenomenon.

A crucial reason for this persistence, it is argued, is that paralleling skin colour has arisen the notion of 'cultural' characteristics as the basis of racism – what became known as the 'new racism' or, more pointedly, the oxymoronic 'cultural racism'. In Britain, a decisive impetus for this was a remark by Margaret Thatcher in 1978 about

---

* As we saw earlier, following the 1983 House of Lords ruling, Sikhs are also accorded the status of an ethnic group. Other groups have not been granted this but the Employment Equality (Religion or Belief) Regulations 2003 Act, and the Equality Act 2006, outlaw discrimination on the grounds of religion.

the possibility of Britain being 'swamped by people with a different culture' (Barker, 1981, p. 15). Though she did not refer to people of different colour or physical traits, her remark certainly had racial connotations and had hit the right note with her racist supporters; they certainly understood that those doing the 'swamping' also happened to be non-White. This becomes clear if we consider the settlers from the West Indies – especially Barbadians. They have close cultural affinities to the British (closer certainly than White people from the Mediterranean or Eastern Europe) yet continued mass migration from the Caribbean islands would doubtless have drawn the racist ire of Thatcher and her supporters. It is of course also true that cultural factors were an important consideration for Thatcher but, plainly, not the decisive one (certainly her personal culture clashed sharply with that of, for example, striking miners in the mid-1980s), for this undeniably remained skin colour, the visible factor.

However, the belief that culture was driving the 'new' racism led to a certain defensiveness on the part of anti-racists in regard to cultural differences between non-White migrants and the indigenous community – a defensiveness that resulted in silence in regard to the various reactionary and oppressive cultural and religious practices among migrants. This chimed in well with the multiculturalist imperative: a studious silence in regard to asserting value judgments with respect to cultural and religious beliefs and customs, excepting the most egregious. For example, Modood (2005, pp. 6–8; 27ff) considers that 'antiracism and racial equality have been too narrowly defined' (being solely focused on colour racism) given that South Asians also suffer from what he asserts as 'cultural racism', that is, 'a certain culture is attributed to them, is vilified, and is even the ground for discrimination'. Accordingly, Asians are subjected to a 'double racism'. But, given the thrust of this chapter, and indeed of the book as a whole, we reject this faulty, tendentious analysis – which is tantamount to an apologia for myriad oppressive cultural and religious beliefs and practices. We need now to move beyond what has become the suffocating bind of 'cultural racism' – which is not the same as racism – and firmly assert that challenging reactionary cultural practices is not racist but a progressive and necessary act.

Tiryakian (2004, p. 9) has made the interesting claim that multiculturalism shares features in common with earlier broad movements of modernity, such as the labour movements and the nationalist movements of the nineteenth and twentieth centuries, and can be considered an element of 'new social movements'. This is a tempting analogy but describing the assertion of separate cultural and religious rights and identity by 'cultural minorities' in metropolitan heartlands as a 'movement' is rather over-pressing the point. Moreover, whereas labour and national (in the case of oppressed nationalities) movements come under the umbrella of 'progressive', this cannot be said of multiculturalism. One of the fundamental charges against multiculturalism is that it is women and children who tend to suffer the most from policies under its auspices (see, for example, Okin, 1999). Moreover, Tiryakian's reasoning can lead to the sleight of hand of including multiculturalism within the anti-racism movement in the western context – a tactic that has been successfully employed by myriad Muslim groups in the post 9/11 era (see Chapter 4). The anti-racism movement was/is a struggle for *equality* for non-White people, in all aspects of life, whereas multiculturalism demands *separate* rights and provisions, and legal exemptions that, as we have stressed, can (and indeed, often do) result in the diminution of equality for members within a minority grouping.

The development of a people's or society's culture depends, of course, on a multitude of factors: political, economic and social factors, technological development, levels of immigration and the interaction of different peoples generally. To this we can add a less considered factor, that is, *resistance* to mainstream ideas, culture, and traditions. We might think of those, usually younger, sections of the population, who are at the forefront of this resistance, as cultural 'iconoclasts' who can instigate cultural advances that are elemental and persistent – but which are often later absorbed in mainstream society. As a generalisation, such iconoclasts tend to be imbued with a progressive bent. Yet, when it comes to ethnic minorities, under multiculturalism, it is not an exaggeration to suggest that truly iconoclastic behaviour is rarely contemplated; the focus is on propping up those (invariably the most vociferous men and women) who campaign to preserve their 'traditional beliefs and practices', free from scrutiny or censure, including the oppressive elements. Given that the unflinching rule is that there should be no dilution of culture, resistance and iconoclastic behaviour are severely suppressed within segregated 'cultural' or 'faith' communities.

Contrast how different is the thinking when multiculturalism is applied to cultural iconoclasm emanating within the White majority in the West. The following example from Germany – a country not renowned for advocating multiculturalism – illustrates this well. In his discussion of Frankfurt becoming a 'multicultural metropolis' post-1989, Radtke (2004, p. 89) notes how the cadres for this came from the Green Party and its electorate which included 'rootless new leftists' and their 'tolerance of unconventional lifestyles and milieus, performing a culinary-consumatory [*sic*] attitude towards culture(s)'. What is suggested here is indeed true of sections of the White majority in Western countries who are happy to adopt (or consume) 'ethnic' cultural traits and internalise them as their own: in the main, these are cuisine, music, fashion, literature, cinema and the performing arts. By so doing, they become bearers of a multicultural lifestyle. But what they do not, in their overwhelming majority, do is to internalise the mass of the cultural forms beneath this tip of the iceberg – brought about by the overbearing influence of religion and attendant taboos: the most important of which are espousal of a strong religious identity, the highly restrictive family and community structures, arranged and forced marriages, the fawning deference to community and religious 'elders and 'leaders'. In regard to the bulk of this cultural iceberg, the *soi disant* multiculturalists tend to adopt a resolute silence. Whilst free to adopt a 'buffet' approach to cultural manifestations of ethnic minorities, they pay lip service to the fact that members from these communities are denied this approach – which includes, moreover, often being denied the right to adopt cultural norms from the host society.

So, true, the espousal of some cultural norms of migrant settlers by large sections of the host society – especially the young – is an unalloyed positive. Moreover, it contributes to an anti-racist and non-nationalistic (even internationalist) outlook which adds to the public good. But, contrary to the impression often given, this is emphatically *not* multicultural*ism*; but rather a manifestation of cultural eclecticism.

Drawing this chapter to a close, we can assert with confidence that multiculturalism essentially views cultures as static which, in regard to the modern developed world is a profoundly *ahistorical* approach. It is also ultimately *conservative* because it fears change, including *progressive* change, and is resistant to shocks to the cultural identity of ethnic minorities. Furthermore, given its implicit assumption that a person from an ethnic, religious, or national minority is subsumed within a cultural or religious group, multiculturalism is also a *totalising discourse*. Now, it is true that some cultures and religions do have a totalitarian quality, but this is hardly a reason to accept them on their own terms. Rather, this should be considered problematic and, where doctrines breach egalitarian principles of human rights, be firmly challenged. A caveat of vital import is that the abandonment of universalism is a slippery slope to division, segregation, needless antagonisms, tensions, and fractures. We shall explore these issues of supreme importance in later chapters.

Following the collapse of the Soviet empire and the rise of a 'new Europe', Brubaker (1996, ch. 6) used the poignant phrase 'unmixing of peoples' to describe the effect of separatist nationalism in the region. Indeed, to some extent, 'unmixing of peoples' is also felicitous in describing precisely what has occurred under multiculturalism/multifaithism and augmented by the 'hindrance to mixing of peoples' that arises from its policy prescriptions. Paradoxically, however, many of the new 'unmixed' nation states of Eastern Europe actively sought, and then proceeded with great alacrity, to 'mix' with the peoples of the European Union, and had few qualms about acceding to the mass of EU legislation and regulations. We do not, as yet, see similar signs of 'mixing' on the part of many ethnic minority and faith communities that have unmixed with fellow citizens; and nor will we do so if multicultural/multifaith policies retain their hold.

Chapter 2

Origins of parallel lives: cultural and religious factors

Official racism and neglect[*]

In this chapter we examine the rise of segregated communities and the way some religious-ethnic minorities in Britain lead parallel lives. In the main, the discussion is focused on Asian minorities as multiculturalism has primarily taken account of, and accorded privileges to, their cultural and religious beliefs and practices. Accordingly, relatively little attention is given to West Indian communities on the grounds that their cultural practices, broadly defined, are considerably less restrictive and hence more in accordance with mainstream British society – though that is not to ignore that there are some major issues relating to young Blacks in particular.

During the Second World War many from the colonies fought for Britain. By so doing we can, with some legitimacy, suggest that they accepted a broader 'imperial British identity'. It was the genius of the British Empire that this should have been so and, indubitably, a crucial ingredient in its success. In recognition of this, one imagines that the government would have actively attempted to instil such an imperial identity in migrants from the colonies, at least in the early period of immigration. But this was most definitely not the case. Happy to have the millions they subjugated fight and die for them (against fascism and for the empire), there were no attempts to forge any kind of unifying identity. True, in later post-colonial years, there emerged the notion of a 'Commonwealth identity', but this was devoid of any substance – for, by that stage, the populations of the Commonwealth were firmly denied entry to the 'motherland'. As such, the many tours by members of the Royal Family to former

---

[*] This chapter draws on Hasan (2003).

Commonwealth colonies under the pretext of visiting members of a 'wider family' were manifest humbug.

That is not to say there was a complete absence of an imperial identity on the part of at least some migrants – indeed this was likely within the ranks of those who had served in the British Army and other military bodies, and also possibly within some bureaucratic circles and educational institutes. True, for some migrants there was an undoubted emotional attachment to Britain. But, soon after their arrival, they were overwhelmingly disabused of such an attachment being reciprocated by members of officialdom and the general public. On the contrary, theirs was a rude awakening of suspicion, indifference or even some hostility. The host society tended not to recognise any common identity or commonality. Thus, whatever vestiges of an imperial identity there may have been during the Second World War, it did not spill over into the post-war era and the rise of mass migration. On the contrary, it was the fact of racial difference of the new migrants that animated British thinking.

Kenan Malik (1996) has helpfully revealed how the concerns of governments regarding immigration post-Second World War were indeed rooted in racial thinking (there was no discernible difference between Labour and Conservative governments). Thus, as early as 1949, The Royal Commission on the British Population cautioned that, 'immigration on a large scale to a fully established society like ours would only be welcomed without reserve if the immigrants were of good stock and not prevented by their religion and race from intermarrying with the host population and becoming merged with it'. By 1955, as a Cabinet minute reveals, such caution was translated into the fear that 'if immigration from the colonies and, for that matter, from India and Pakistan were allowed to continue unchecked, there was a real danger that over the years there would be a significant change in the racial character of the English people'. The Colonial Office epitomised this thinking by its reasoning that 'a large coloured community as a noticeable feature of our social life would weaken … the concept of England or Britain to which the people of British stock throughout the Commonwealth are attached'(cited in Malik, 1996, p. 20). Malik is right to conclude from this that 'for the British elite, its sense of self and identity [were] mediated through the concept of race. Britishness was a racial concept and large-scale migration from the colonies (and former colonies) threatened to disrupt the racialised sense of national identity' (*loc. cit.*).

Implicit in this view is that the authorities decried the inter-marrying between non-White immigrants (including those who were 'not prevented from doing so for reasons of religion and race') and indigenous Whites. Yet, almost from the beginning, there was mixing and inter-marrying between West Indian men and White women, notwithstanding the opprobrium that was often heaped upon the latter within their own communities, in the context of a society where overt racism was still rampant. It appeared that the core characteristics of attraction, romance, and falling in love just could not be legislated away or swept aside by social engineering, or nipped in the bud by racist and demeaning taunts. Prevention of inter-marrying would have required legislation of the type that had been implemented in apartheid South Africa, or a history akin to that of the southern states of America, which Britain had never had. This was unthinkable: after all, this was a society that took pride in defeating fascism and proudly upholding democracy where, nominally at least, all, no matter their skin complexion, were equal before the law. No matter their dislike of it, the authorities appreciated fully that the freedom to choose a partner is a fundamental human liberty and civil right.

It was this inter-racial mixing – in very small numbers at first – which would have a profound effect in years to come on West Indian communities in particular. In stark contrast, rejection of mixed-marriages – that is, marrying-out of both racial and religious boundaries – has always been the norm for Asian migrants. This stems not from notions of 'racial purity' or even of 'self' and 'identity' but rather from preservation of the faith, culture, family and community; as well as the inculcation of values attached to these pillars to future generations. In so doing, control of members of a family or community is more easily afforded.

Rather than being viewed as a positive development, we might view the subsequent *outcome* of multiculturalism as being analogous to the divide-and-rule policies of empire within the 'mother' country itself. For an elite steeped in the arrogance and superiority of empire, with concomitant contempt for colonial subjects, a sudden change in thinking in regard to some of these 'natives' settling into the mother country was unlikely. Indeed, such condescension may precisely explain not only the avowedly non-interventionist, even neglectful, stance adopted by post-war Labour and Conservative governments but also, implicitly at least, the divide-and-rule policy. As such, even if unintentional, this can, with some justification, be viewed as a *de facto* racist stance in regard to non-White migrants.

Compounding this was the uncertainty about possible alienation and hostility to non-White migrants by the indigenous White community – yet such potential dangers would become a self-fulfilling prophecy (though this must not be exaggerated) given the failure to systematically implement policies which could tackle such alienation and make migrants feel welcome into Britain with the aim of fully integrating them into society. The assumption in the early years was that migrants would return to their countries of origins in the former colonies – that is, that the overarching motive of those coming was short-term economic gain with little desire to stay permanently and plan for the future in the new country. Consequently, no encouragement was given for long-term settlement and integration into society; this somewhat haphazard policy was similar to that of the 'guest-workers' policy of Germany or Holland (see, for example, Radtke 2004; Buruma, 2007).

This can be sharply contrasted with migrants from the UK to Australia or New Zealand, where there was a clear assumption that this would be a permanent move to start a new life and, in due course, become citizens in the fullest sense of the word (that is to say, not just passport holders with very little interaction with the host society). The signal given out was, therefore, overwhelmingly positive: we want you to come to our country to settle, work, and to be fully part of the society and country and become its citizens. Future prospects for you and the family would be bright. Of course, given the shortage of labour and these countries' desire – for decades ossified into a racist immigration policy in Australia – for English-speaking, White migrants, from the 'homeland' (but, as second best, from other European countries), an unequivocal welcoming stance was a *sine qua non* for attracting the right type of people to such far-away lands.

It was undoubtedly true that, for many non-White 'Commonwealth' migrants, the motivation was indeed to escape poverty and poor job prospects with the hope of working and saving money in order to attain a better standard of living. For significant numbers, we can conjecture that the plan was eventually to return to their home countries, which is what was also hoped for by the various governments. Reality, however, took an opposite course: the vast majority of migrants were reluctant to return and so stayed and settled. This happened despite generally their not being *welcomed* in the manner of migrants to Australasia; on the contrary, for far too many, hostility and resentment from the indigenous population was often the norm. True, as the years rolled on there was some, albeit minor, recognition of the needs of non-English speaking Asians such as the provision of TV programmes.[*] But there was never any systematic attempt to educate locals as to the background of the new migrants and to encourage them to offer a hand of friendship, solidarity, and empathy. We can conjecture that the decisive, though unplanned, intention on the part of the government and various agencies, including local government was *separation* of ethnic minority settlers. Later, this reality was to be, by default, acknowledged under the rubric of multiculturalism. Because Britain had people from different and distinct cultural, religious, and ethnic backgrounds, it had become a 'multicultural society' (the third 'phase' noted in the last chapter).

---

[*] The first was the BBC programme 'Make yourself at home' for Indian and Pakistani immigrants, launched in 1965.

Nonetheless, separation was by no means what the settlers themselves desired. The clearest example of this was of West Indian men, aided by closer cultural norms to the host country including the same language. They generally had few qualms about forming long-term relationships with local White women, many of whom, to their great credit, resisted abuse and excoriation from racists in their midst and gladly reciprocated the sentiment. What enabled such liaisons to develop with relative ease was that, notwithstanding the empire and its view of colonised non-Whites as second class, British society did not have the pernicious legacy of slavery of the US, with its hysterical fear and loathing of Blacks whereby relationships between Black men and White women became well nigh impossible in southern states and hugely difficult in even in the more progressive northern cities.

But what is now forgotten is that there were similar outward-looking Asian men (albeit in much smaller numbers) who also formed relationships with local White women.[*] They represented the thinking that settling in the UK was not simply a money-making and saving exercise, with the hope of returning at the soonest possible moment; or, indeed, what would become prevalent, the re-creation of 'mini-Pakistans' or 'mini-Indias' in the adopted country. It is the vision of settling in fully, that is to say, in the integrated manner that was genuinely desired by many of the early Asian settlers that has vanished under the dead weight of multiculturalism and segregation. The fault is not solely that of the various governments and local councils but also of 'community' or 'religious' leaders who were profoundly traditional and inward-looking. This unfortunate transition was eased by the arrival of many with minimal literacy levels from rural areas. Their mode of thinking and cultural mores and reflexes stemmed from the pre-modern village life; it was transported 5,000 miles to flourish with renewed vigour in a country and society where such a mode of living and thinking had long since

---

[*] For example, a BBC TV documentary, 'Minorities in Britain' showed Asian coffee bars in Bradford where Asian men met local White women in a liberal atmosphere during the 1960s (BBC, 2005).

disappeared. The following section examines the cultural legacies of this pre-modern history.

Focusing on the Asian population
Though it is a truism to say that 'Asian culture' is not homogenous (and indeed it is marked by very significant variations); nonetheless, these are variations on a very similar theme. This enables generalisations to be made owing to the high degree of commonalities, such as the importance of religion and attendant ritual accoutrements, the role of the family and social mores in general, communalism, manner of dress etc. They also encompass mysticism and obscurantism (which leads to the shunning of reasoned and critical thinking); there is intense fixation on caste and class, the oppression of women sometimes to the point of misogyny, and the downplaying of individuality.

What is at the heart of the matter is the contradiction between the freedom of cultural and religious *expression* and the freedom of cultural and religious *oppression* that often emanate from the former. In contradistinction to multiculturalism, the contention I wish to make is that, in many fundamental respects, these cultural and religious mores are antithetical to the aims of egalitarianism and emancipation. Moreover, they often lead to bigotry and divisiveness, which are enormously weakening to the progress of these communities in the developed world. Therefore, whilst freedom of *expression* should be maximised, equally, the freedom of *oppression* must be minimised.

The Asian extended family that is cherished by many multiculturalists does indeed offer protection, succour, and unstinting support to its members (but see the important findings of Hicks and Bhugra discussed below) – though it can be hostile to those not within the family unit. However, its origins are located in agrarian societies without any modern welfare state; in large measure, marriage and family are economic contracts and welfare units so that it is all-too-often suffocating, intellectually sterile, corrupting – especially when spawning nepotism – and crushing of individuality and dissent. An important by-product of its transferral to developed societies has been that it often induces the young to lead what can best be described as schizophrenic lives, often of great anguish and pain. A particularly shocking statistic reflecting this fact is that the highest suicide rate in Britain is that of Asian girls and women (see below for details).

The total ethnic minority (that is, non-White) population of Great Britain was 4.6 million in 2001 (8.1 percent of the total). Of this, Asians comprise just over half and Blacks a quarter. Table 1 provides population estimates of the different ethnic minority groups for April 2001 based on census data.

Table 1: Population by Ethnic Group, Great Britain, April 2001

Ethnic Category	Population (thousands)	Population (%)	Ethnic minority split (%)
White British	50366	88.2	
White Irish	691	1.2	
Other White	1423	2.5	
Mixed	677	1.2	14.6
Indian	1052	1.8	22.7
Pakistani	747	1.3	16.2
Bangladeshi	283	0.5	6.1
Other Asian	247	0.4	5.3
Black Caribbean	566	1.0	12.2
Black African	485	0.8	10.5
Other Black	97	0.2	2.1
Chinese	242	0.4	5.2
Any other ethnic group	229	0.4	5.0
All ethnic groups	57103	100	100

Source: Focus on Ethnicity and Religion 2006, table 2.1, p. 21, ONS

Among Asians, there is now quite a marked difference between the different groups: Indians and East African Asians (who are of Indian origin) are better placed, according to all socio-economic indicators, than Pakistanis and Bangladeshis. The following statistics are for 2002 and 2003. In school education, 70 per cent of Indian girls and 58 per cent of Indian boys achieved five or more GCSEs at grades A*–C in comparison with 45 per cent and 32 per cent for Pakistani and 50 per cent and 40 per cent for Bangladeshi girls and boys respectively (2002 figures). The lowest levels of GCSE attainment, however, are for Black Caribbean: 38 per cent for girls and 23 per cent for boys. In terms of higher education, far more Indians are likely to have degrees than Pakistanis and Bangladeshis (in fact, among women, Pakistanis and Bangladeshis are the least likely to have degrees – just 7 per cent) (ONS, 2005, p. 8).

Pakistanis and Bangladeshis are also the most likely to be unqualified: for men, 28 and 40 per cent respectively; as against 18 per for Indian men; and also suffer much higher rates of unemployment: the respective percentage figures for Indian, Pakistanis, and Bangladeshi men in 2002/3, were 7, 14, and 18 (*ibid.*, pp. 8, 9). In terms of economic inactivity (that is, not available for work and/or not actively seeking work – estimates are for 2007), the percentage rates for Indian men and women are 18 and 32 respectively (the equivalent rates for White British are slightly lower at 16 and 25); in contrast, the rates for Pakistanis and Bangladeshis are much higher (27 and 68) (NOMIS, 2008). The much higher levels of economic inactivity of Pakistani and Bangladeshi women are directly as a result of cultural pressures, rather than labour market characteristics, stemming from marrying and starting families at a young age, and then looking after the family and home. This clearly has an adverse economic impact on these ethnic groups.

When taken together, the much higher rates of male unemployment, the extremely high rates of economic inactivity of women, combined with the fact that Pakistani and Bangladeshi men are overwhelmingly in unskilled, semi-skilled, and skilled manual work (astonishingly, in 2002/3, one third of Bangladeshi men worked as cooks or waiters, and one in six Pakistani men were cab drivers or chauffeurs, ONS, 2005, p. 10), explain the high levels of poverty and overcrowding among the Pakistani and Bangladeshi population.

Thus, whereas the situation of Indians (and East African Asians) has moved towards the White average; the same cannot be said of Pakistanis and Bangladeshis. They, alongside in some respects Black Caribbeans, constitute the most deprived groups in Britain. Given this fact, our argument is that cultural factors that act as impediments to social and economic advancement and which, as we have seen, are sanctioned under multiculturalism, are contributing directly to poverty and deprivation. As such, they cannot be 'cherished' but rather need to be tackled.

As has been noted, whereas there is now significant mixing of Black Caribbeans of all classes with the dominant White community that indubitably acts as a constraint on the development and persistence of segregation, such mixing is much less in regard to Asians in inner city towns ands cities. So the argument that the high degree of segregation of many Asians is mainly attributable to racism lacks validity (see Bradford Race Review 2001; Cantle, 2006).

Living in a segregated neighbourhood leads to what may be described as a 'ghetto mentality', where the outside world (which may be less than a mile away) is often considered hostile terrain full of 'demons and dragons'. This leads to insularity and reinforces a further reliance on the network of family and friends within the ghetto. Such insularity and fear of the outside can be a breeding ground for an array of reactionary attitudes and practices, and cements backward, obscurantist traditions and beliefs. Thus, pressure to conform strictly to religious and cultural traditions becomes highly oppressive. Ghettoisation not only leads to breaking up links with the dominant White society, but also with other ethnic minorities. In fact, the bigotry and sectarian attitudes that bedevil Asian communities *towards each other* are invariably a direct importation of these from the Indian sub-continent (with its long history of British divide-and-rule politics, the legacy of which still lingers), and are passed down the generations.

One consequence of intra-Asian tensions is the creation of 'pure, mono-cultural/religious ethnic' ghettos with powerful ethnic, regional, and religious mind-sets, and marked by hostility to, and resentment of, 'outsiders'. This attitude is ironically reminiscent of the same shown by large sections of the host population in the early decades of migration.* So, it is the case that there is often great distrust and animosity between different Asian groups – something that is not fully appreciated in mainstream society and liberal opinion. The pure ethnic ghetto traps these attitudes within its borders, gives succour to them and, in so doing, reinforces itself. Inevitably, therefore, progressive (that is to say secular and inclusive) politics are marginalised – and, over the years, there appears to have been an intensification of sectarian attitudes which, under the imprimatur of multiculturalism, have been quietly tolerated.

It is the oppression of women that raises the greatest call not simply to ignore the egregious cultural practices within Asian communities. Leila Ahmed (1992, p. 7) makes the point (equally valid for most other religions) that: 'in establishment Islamic thought, women, like minorities, are defined as different from and, in regard to legal rights, lesser than men'. And it is the 'establishment thought', propagated by uniformly male religious leaders, that tends to dominate religious practice in all major religions. Consequently many of the oppressive practices are enforced and justified on religious grounds.

Boys and young men do not escape either from cultural and religious coercion, for they are also forced to pray, to wear 'traditional' forms of dress (such as the ubiquitous shulwaar-kameez – the

---

* For example, in Bradford, Sikhs and Hindus have long been gravitating towards Pudsey, leaving the Asian inner city areas predominantly to Muslims (Bradford Race Review, 2001, p. 9). Moreover, a degree of inter-ethnic sectarianism appears to have taken hold in voting habits. In the Bradford West election in 1997, for example, 61 per cent of Pakistanis voted for Mohammad Riaz, the Conservative candidate, compared with only 35 per cent for Marsha Singh, the winning Labour Candidate. By contrast, 74 per cent of Indians voted for Singh and 23 per cent for Riaz (Anwar, 1998, p. 20).

baggy trousers and long shirt),* if Muslim to fast during the month of Ramzaan (or Ramadhan) and grow 'religious' beards, and if Sikh to wear a turban etc. If there is segregation from the outside world, then within the community there is a strong element of gender apartheid. From a young age boys and girls are separated. In teenage years, having boyfriends and girlfriends is disallowed, and in adulthood there is often a separation of the sexes in public life and even within family gatherings. Such strong levels of gender segregation must inevitably have an impact on the psyche and mentality of both men and women: in men, to the extent that a very deep sexism becomes ingrained, taken for granted, and perpetuated; in women, a toleration and internalisation of such male attitudes.

A particularly repressive cultural practice that has gained prominence in recent years is that of forced marriage. Following sustained campaigning and pressure by women's groups, the government introduced legislation against this practice and set up a Forced Marriage Unit (FMU), under the aegis of the Foreign and Commonwealth Office, to provide assistance to various interested parties. The FMU's website gives an example of what is involved in forced marriage: confiscation by the family of passport and phone, 'locked in the home and beaten before being forced to marry a man you've never met. And then you're raped on your wedding night' (FMU, 2008).

Also prominently displayed on the website is the following statement by the Home Office Minister, Baroness Scotland: 'Forced marriage affects children, teenagers and adults from all races and religions, including Christians, Hindus, Jews, Muslims and Sikhs. And it is not solely an issue facing Asian communities. We deal with cases in the Middle East, Western Balkans and Africa.'

Though strictly correct, this is nonetheless grossly misleading. Unpublished data provided to the author by the FMU for 2007 show

---

* Sahgal gives the example of fundamentalist groups in Punjab and Kashmir who, as part of their strategy to forge group identity, forced women to wear 'traditional' clothes. Thus, in Kashmir, women started to wear the veil where traditionally they had not done so; in Punjab, women were prevented from wearing dresses and jeans and forced to wear shulwaar-kameez (Sahgal, 1992, p. 167).

that nearly 90 per cent of 'overseas assistance' cases relate either to Pakistan (68%) or Bangladesh (22%). Although the data is not broken down in terms of religion, we do know that the ethnic Pakistani and Bangladeshi population is overwhelmingly Muslim, so we can safely conclude that, contrary to the impression given by Baroness Scotland, forced marriages appear to predominantly affect Muslim girls and women with family connections in Bangladesh and Pakistan.

A report by the women's refuge and campaigning organisation, Southall Black Sisters (2001, p. 4), provides a more detailed breakdown of the suffering that candidates for forced marriages are subjected to: 'physical and sexual violence; threatening behaviour; imprisonment; abduction; mental and social pressure, including emotional blackmail; restrictions on lifestyle such as limitations on movement, association, dress, education and career choices; oppressive financial controls; and other demeaning, humiliating and controlling actions'.

A woman who breaks free from a forced marriage can expect to be hunted down by 'bounty hunters', private detectives, or organised gangs of networks of men, be intimidated by them and forced to return home, where she will inevitably face further punishment. And she may end up paying the ultimate price for her disobedience: death. This was the tragic fate of Tasleem Begum from Bradford who, after leaving her husband from a forced marriage, was killed by her brother-in-law (who, no doubt in the name of multiculturalism, had his sentence commuted from murder to manslaughter on the grounds of 'provocation' – presumably stemming from the 'shame' and 'dishonour' she had brought his family). Scandalously, religious leaders, though not condoning this, asserted that 'according to the Koran, killing this woman was correct' (SBS, 2001, pp. 8, 7). Suffice to say that the signal this gives out to women contemplating deviating from the path chosen for them is enormously powerful. Moreover, it is a clear illustration of the often prohibitively high 'exit costs' (reaching life-threatening proportions) from a religious-ethnic community.

Asian children and young adults are denied access to an array of activities that are readily available to others. Think of the restrictions placed on a young Asian girl or woman (whilst accepting that there is a degree of over-generalisation here): discouraged from playing with boys after a young age and, when she gets older, forbidden to have boyfriends. Pubs or clubs are no-go areas, she is dissuaded from attending leisure centres and swimming pools; discouraged from going to 'Western' concerts, or on holidays with friends to some seaside resort at home or overseas. She would be told to wear the traditional attire of say shulwaar and kameez, and be forbidden to wear skirts or shorts, even in sweltering heat. If she were from a Muslim background, she maybe told to wear a *hijab* outside her home, including in school. In sum, she would be denied various liberties that Western women have for generations fought for and won, and now take for granted. Thus, an Asian girl from a segregated community, fortunate enough to have say White or Black girlfriends, can legitimately ask why she cannot do all manner of activities her friends can and which, in wider society, are considered so utterly normal. It is for this reason that Asian girls (to a lesser extent this is also true for boys) often lead, as we have suggested, schizophrenic lives, brought about by living in families and communities whose mode of thinking and living is so starkly different to what is typical of non-Asian peers.

It is this crushing of individuality, and the pressure to conform to pre-ordained norms, that so often leads to a torn existence. It is why problems related to mental health and self-harm abound, and why the rate of suicide for Asian girls and women is much higher than the average. Research by Dinesh Bhugra of the Institute of Psychiatry in London has found that the rate of attempted suicide of Asian women in London is 1.6 times that of White and Black women and 2.7 times that of South Asian men. But this average masks some extraordinary differences when we look at age-specific rates. Thus by far the highest rate is that for young Asian women aged between 16 and 24: this is 2.6 times that of White women, 2.5 times that of Black women, and an astonishing 7.5 times that of Asian men of the same age cohort. The rate, however, declines rapidly as the age of the cohort increases – strongly suggesting that it is young Asian women who are most vulnerable to suicide (data from Bhugra, 2007). Hicks and Bhugra (2003, p. 455) argue that 'sociocultural factors may play a significant role in the suicidality [sic] of South Asian women'. Their research (sample size of 180 Asian women) on perceived causes of suicide attempts included marital problems, violence by the husband, family conflict or pressure, being trapped in an unhappy family situation, in-law problems, depression (though this is, in fact, an effect), and fear of shame, rejection or loss of reputation in society. All these had the combined response of 'strongly agree' and 'agree' of over 80 per cent (*ibid.,* table 1, p. 457).

Earlier research by Newham Inner City Multifund and Newham Asian Women's Project (1998, p. 57) was in accordance with the findings of Hicks and Bhugra, but also provided other areas of concern to young Asian women, which may lead to their self-harm:

> issues around honour and shame; stresses around fragmentation and leading dual lives; the experience of sexual abuse; marital difficulties and domestic violence; high academic expectations; the pressure of unwanted arranged marriages (or a lack of choice in this situation); socio-economic disadvantage; racism; lack of flexibility around Asian cultural traditions, and a lack of communication with parents.

This is in consonance with one of the types of suicide in Durkheim's influential typology, that of 'fatalistic suicide', which stems from 'excessive regulation, that of persons with futures pitilessly blocked and passions violently choked by oppressive discipline' (Durkheim, 1996 [1897] p. 276, fn. 25).

What is interesting in the Newham study, and perhaps surprising, is that the categories 'racist abuse' and 'financial and housing problems' were considered 'exacerbating factors' (*ibid.,* p. 51); in other words, the bulk of factors which directly trouble young Asian women emanate from *within* the family and community, and not from a hostile external environment. Here we have direct evidence of how cultural entrapment is causing great anguish and harm to girls and young women from an Asian background. Those who espouse multiculturalism and advocate cherishing 'Asian culture and family values' should take particular heed.

But there is also what may be described as a perverse response by some Asian women to the rights, freedoms, and independence gained by women not just in the West, but the world over: where these are viewed in a derogatory manner, unbecoming for a 'modest' Asian girl or woman. Given that such a view is customarily instilled from a very young age, girls are weaned away from critical thinking well before they have matured (the same – though not with the same intensity – could be said for boys) and so often end up accepting and justifying the restrictions placed upon them. Commands and threats can instil such an enormous fear in Asian youngsters that they find it well nigh impossible to cast aside oppressive cultural mores in adulthood. Unless one agrees with Joseph Raz (noted in the previous chapter) that even 'oppressive cultures can give a lot', this is quite indefensible.

Nonetheless, so many Asian women not only accept their lot, but confirm Raz's view by gaining an inverted sense of righteousness and pride from their restrictions. In so doing, they *internalise their oppression*, whereby they come to fully agree to conforming to their group's beliefs and customs, no matter how oppressive.[*] Though it was Freud who first hypothesised the importance of internalisation to a child's personality development, feminists in the 1970s utilised this concept in analysis of women's oppression (see, for example, the remarks on Millet below). Women apologists for their subservience have similarities with the 'Uncle Toms' of slavery for whom ideas of liberation were thought dangerous and to be opposed. Such 'Uncle Tommery' is explicable if social conditioning is so powerful as to prevent the questioning of even the most repressive forms of the status quo. Particularly in the context of 'culture clashes' and hostility

---

[*] This can be contrasted with *compliance* whereby there is *apparent* but not real acceptance and conformity, and so fundamental disagreements and dissent are masked. Coercion can, however, be the motor for both internalisation and compliance.

from the majority society, it can become twisted into a virtue, and brazenly defended. The following example graphically highlights the extent to which internalisation of oppression can reach: it is that of Mauritania's ninety thousand slaves for whom 'the possibility of rebellion, like the possibility of a world made up entirely of free men and women, is inconceivable among people who have lost their collective memory of freedom' (Burkett, cited in Okin, 1997, p. 142, fn. 1). Similarly, many Asian women in close-knit families and communities find it inconceivable to challenge their oppression and so internalise it. They do so either by taking pride in such an identity or by not thinking of the restrictions on their lives in such terms; or indeed by simply adopting a resigned acceptance in accordance with Panglossian principles.

Back in the heyday of feminism in the early 1970s, Kate Millett (1971, pp. 26, 31) famously pointed out the vital importance of conditioning and socialisation from early childhood to explain the assent given by both sexes to gender inequalities. In a controversial work, this was nonetheless an important insight – which we argue applies *a fortiori* to the present reality of Asian girls and women in the West. Yet, there is a dearth of systematic analyses in such a vein in regard to this group of females. Indeed, it is not too uncharitable to express Western feminist thinking as thus: yes, there must be a principled opposition to women's oppression in all its forms – *except* in regard to Asian (especially Muslim) girls and women in 'their' communities. The *raison d'être* for this curious silence resides, of course, in cultural relativism – but also, as we shall argue in Chapter 6, in 'White liberal post-colonial guilt'.

As stressed in Chapter 1, culture in the modern world, is not static or 'essential' – on the contrary, it constantly adapts, changes, and evolves. Indeed, we can argue that the mixing of peoples greatly energises cultural advancement and social progress, helping to break, on the one hand, the 'Little England' mentality of the indigenous population and, on the other, similar ethnic or religious fixations of the settlers – thereby shifting mental and political dispositions in the direction of opposition to bigotry and 'group closure'. Indubitably, significant advances have been made in the past 60 years, whereby the culture of Britain has been transformed through interaction with settler communities through music, cuisine, dress, manner of speaking, what might be termed 'generosity of spirit and hospitality', and the challenging of existing ideas vis-à-vis non-White people.* This runs counter to the fear held by some in minority groups that 'their cultures' would simply assimilate away under the tidal wave of the dominant culture; analogous to the fear of Aldous Huxley's dystopian 'Brave New World'. However, it is certainly the case that the 'cultural impact' of Black-Caribbeans has been noteworthy: far more than might be expected from a group constituting not only such a small proportion of the population, but which also resides near the bottom of the economic ladder.

To stress again, what is important here is interaction and mixing of peoples at all levels – not a slavish adherence to what one believes to be unchanging values and traditions. And throughout the country there *has* been a mixing of peoples – with the most profound one being the ever-increasing numbers of inter-racial marriages and partnerships (see below for a discussion of this). But in regard to Asians such mixing and interaction is much less and in some cases (especially of segregated Muslim communities) is negligible, such that we can consider many citizens to be virtually imprisoned in a geographical and cultural/religious milieu from which it has become exceedingly difficult to break out.

Moreover, once segregated neighbourhoods become ossified into

---

* In many ways Britain is, in this regard, at the forefront in Europe. Look, for example, at the contents of supermarkets now compared with, say, forty years ago. True, this is so because the proliferation of different products from across the globe has become profitable; supermarkets do not sell these out of the goodness of their hearts. But, it is also an indication of the willingness of the White population to buy types of foods that their parents or grandparents would not have dreamed of doing, regardless of reasons of availability or cost. In the culinary sense, there has been a real breaking out of the 'Little England' straitjacket. In the same vein, British tourists often consider Indian and Chinese restaurants in Mediterranean resorts as providing 'home food'. This is certainly a healthy sign in more ways than one.

ghettos, a territorial attitude towards 'outsiders' takes hold, akin to that of the manner of hostile Whites to non-White migrants in the early post-war years of immigration. Stark examples of this were provided in a documentary, shown in 2004 by Channel 4 Television, by the well-known commentator on Black issues Darcus Howe. Howe's premise was that whereas White racism has now been accorded pariah status, inter-ethnic conflict is a 'plague of our time'. This is a frontal challenge to mainstream thinking, including that of multiculturalism. On his visit to the West Midlands, Howe found tensions between young Blacks and Asians including 'tribal warfare' and 'no-go areas' in Walsall where Black boys were terrorised by Pakistani youths (with their refrain that 'we have to look after our own people'); similarly, in the Alum Rock district of Birmingham (a segregated Pakistani Muslim area), 'outsiders' were shown to feel threatened. His other examples included disparaging – *de facto* racist – remarks made by 'successful' Asians against Blacks, which clearly revealed both ethnic and class hostility to a fellow settler community; and in London, he revealed crude hostility on the part of Black Caribbeans towards the recently arrived Somali community.

Howe was clearly shaken by this coruscating experience and expressed deep sadness at the loss of solidarity between Blacks and Asians that had earlier been so robust (when the political epithet 'Black', as we have seen, was a unifying symbol for the two groups of people). It certainly seemed as if their history of decades-long unity and joint struggles had been forgotten. Decades of self-segregation and narrowing of identity had ruptured the earlier sense of unity – a unity which had been based, lest it be forgotten, on secular foundations, notwithstanding the pervasive influence of religion. Indeed, the documentary's portrayal of the rise of tensions among ethnic minorities is powerful testimony to the failures of multiculturalism. In October 2005 riots in the Handsworth-Lozells area of Birmingham between Black Caribbeans and Muslim Asians seemed to confirm Howe's thesis. An article on these riots in the *Observer* newspaper (Townsend, 2005) was entitled: 'The new colour of British racism:

Behind the riots lies vicious hostility between the Asian and African-Caribbean communities in Birmingham'; which accords well with 'inter-ethnic conflict is a plague of our time'.

What the documentary did not show, however, were intra-Asian tensions that have also developed significantly in recent years and have pivoted around religious identity, notably between Muslims and Hindus/Sikhs.* One manifestation of this has been, among sections of the Hindu and Sikh communities, the refrain of not wishing to be designated as 'Asian', so as not to be associated with Muslims. Acknowledging the lack of firm corroborative evidence we can, nonetheless, hazard the conjecture that this is not the dominant thinking among non-Muslim Asians – yet it does highlight in an acute manner the fissuring of the unity that had previously existed.

Interestingly, and revealingly, a similar pattern of identity disintegration has not arisen among Black Caribbeans – either along religious lines (though most are Christians and attend a variety of churches) or on the basis of origins of island. Thus, even though most hail predominantly from Jamaica, this is not translated into an island identity. However, it appears that the unifying 'West Indian' identity is, nonetheless, inexorably falling into disuse and, even among Caribbean countries, seems now only to apply to the cricket team. Overwhelmingly, those with origins in the Caribbean are now simply 'Black British'. In regard to Africans, they too are referred to as Black and, as with Caribbeans, there is no significant sign yet of this fissuring into an array of religious identities. However, given the divisive dynamic among Asians along religious lines, one cannot rule out – in the absence of a countervailing unifying force and challenge to multiculturalism – a similar scenario occurring with respect

---

* Although tensions between Hindus and Sikhs also exist. Writing about Southall, Sukhwant Dhaliwal observes: 'Alongside the railway station there is freshly daubed graffiti. The first few lines read "Rak Karega Khalsa" ("Khalsa rules" – a reference to the birth of Sikhism and the Sikh separatist movement for Khalistan). This has recently replaced appeals to join a debate on the failings of Christianity and the blessings of Islam. The reply reads "Sikhs get out of Bharat [India]. Hindustan Zindabad" and is painted in orange. These are potent visual symbols of an alarming growth of religious divisions amongst Asians in the area' (Dhaliwal, 2003, p. 189).

to Africans. So there may arise a powerful impetus for identity along countries of origin e.g. Nigerian, Ghanaian, Somali, Sudanese (who can further be divided into Arabs or Africans, Christian or Muslim) etc.

Virtual Asian absence from the public domain
There is evidence to show that whereas Black Caribbeans now have exposure on the British media (particularly in television) that is in proportion to – or indeed above – their population, the opposite applies in regard to Asians. In research conducted by the Commission for Racial Equality on the most watched TV programmes shown between November and December 2000 on the five terrestrial channels, British Asians were practically 'invisible', appearing just 0.9% of the total relevant time, in comparison with a population of 3.7% of the total; the respective figure for Black Britons was much healthier: 3.7% on TV compared to their population of 2.1% (CRE, 2001). Unfortunately, a more recent survey of ethnic minority exposure on TV has not been conducted, but one can conjecture that matters in this regard have not appreciably changed.

The relatively high proportion of Black Britons on the media is further boosted by the existence of a plethora of Black sports stars, pop stars, and other media celebrities, so that in a very tangible manner Black people quite rightly have become part of the 'national scenery'. It is to be welcomed that the UK's favourite news presenter was (until his recent retirement) reckoned to be a Black man – Trevor Macdonald – who has been entering millions of living rooms on a regular basis for over a quarter of a century.* The importance of such roles is obvious: stereotypes are broken down and racist attitudes diminished and eroded. The situation, unfortunately, is not nearly as positive in regard to Asians. There are no national Asian pop stars, very few British Asian sports stars (and, in what must be considered something of a minor scandal, none whatsoever in the favourite and

---
* Maybe someone like the Asian George Alagiah, who has in recent years become one of BBC News' main presenters, might do the same in years to come.

most important sport, football.*) This is likely to add to the alienation of Asians from mainstream society and inevitability leads to their shifting away from the major TV channels to the array of Asian satellite and cable TV stations and radio programmes (catering to the all the main linguistic groups) that have mushroomed sine the mid-1990s.

In regard to participation in professional sports, there is a virtual absence of Asians in all the major sports. The one exception is cricket in which a number of Asians are playing at county level and some have gone on to play for England. Enthusiasm for cricket exists because of the considerable passion for it by the older generations hailing from the sub-continent. So, this may have a self-perpetuating effect: participation and the watching of cricket is encouraged by parents alongside a rather better record by the cricketing bodies to take on Asians as playing staff (excepting, until recently, Yorkshire County Cricket Club). Perhaps there may be a breakthrough in football in years to come, as it is a sport that appears to have genuinely become popular with the younger generation of Asians; but at present there is little sign of it.

Similar factors can explain the lack of an Asian presence in popular music. This contrasts starkly with waves of different kinds of music that have come into the mainstream from an array of non-British sources and which, in turn, have had a profound influence on the domestic music industry. The dominant source, of course, is Black American music that can be considered the root of all Western popular music. However, there is also music from other parts of the world, notably from the Caribbean (especially Jamaica). Also popular, albeit to a lesser extent, is Latino music and African drumming and sounds are influential. Yet, perhaps the majority of young Asians (as with cinema) have resorted to a separate music that is peculiar only to Asians whose roots lie in sounds from the Indian sun-continent,

---

* This, however, cannot be attributed to racism. There are very many Black players in all the leagues and also players from all around the world, including from countries such as China and Japan that do not have a particularly strong tradition in this sport.

in particular of soundtracks from Bollywood films. Asian music has never penetrated into the mainstream (the reasons why this is so should certainly make for interesting research). This marginalisation is particularly saddening as popular music, unlike sport, has a unifying quality that cuts across boundaries and is largely devoid of any pernicious nationalism.

It would, therefore, be wrong to think that popular, English-language music is a form of cultural imperialism; this would be to misunderstand its genuine mass global appeal. Take for example the songs of the Beatles – plainly, these are enormously and enduringly popular across the globe. Their popularity has a 'from below' quality, which is to say ordinary people voluntarily take great pleasure from them, and not because they have been foisted upon the uninterested public by the authorities. Indeed, in closed societies such as those of the former Eastern bloc, Western music was enormously restricted precisely because it was considered a component of Western imperialism – but as soon as these societies opened up, the pent-up demand burst forth, as the younger population in particular sought to 'catch up' with their counterparts in the West and elsewhere. Moreover, when Eastern European countries began to enter the annual Eurovision Song Contest during the 1990s their songs, like those from most West European countries)*, were almost exclusively sung in English, usually based on the tried-and-tested format of Western pop songs. And similar phenomena have been replicated in other parts of the world, so these cannot reasonably be attributed to cultural imperialism.

This leads to the conclusion that the strong adherence to Asian music on the part of young Asians – though undoubtedly stemming from cultural influences within the family and wider community – nonetheless can also be considered an expression of alienation, and of a retreat into cultural, linguistic and racial loyalties and identities,

---

* Interestingly, even France, with its long history of protecting the French language and culture (including music), had for the first time an English-language song at the 2008 Eurovision Song Contest.

We can make the admittedly severe judgement that, in sum, this is tantamount to a retreat into a cultural ghetto.

Culture, Family, and Segregation
So, the life of an Asian child born and brought up in a segregated community might be as follows: very little exposure to the English language up till the age of five; little exposure to White people and other minorities in schools that predominantly comprise Asian pupils – hence, friends will also tend to be entirely Asian; little exposure to the major TV channels if the family subscribes to Asian satellite or cable TV stations and, similarly, little exposure to non-Asian radio stations. Trips to the cinema might be concentrated entirely on watching Bollywood films, as the larger towns and cities now have cinemas regularly showing these (if not, then there is an endless supply of such films available on DVDs); and listening predominantly to Bollywood music. Culturally, therefore, many Asian children may end up leading lives that have very few points of contacts with those of White or Black children living, possibly, only a few hundred yards away. Later in life, they will invariably end up in an arranged marriage to a relative or acquaintance from the same religious-ethnic group. The cycle will then start again for the next generation.

Proponents of multiculturalism will doubtless respond that there is nothing to be concerned about in all this. The acculturation of new generations into the cultures and faith of their parents and communities is, in fact, a healthy sign – especially in a globalising epoch where cultures appear to be coalescing around a dominant culture; and popular music attests this (as indeed does the 'McDonaldisation' of culture). From this perspective, therefore, multiculturalism preserves the cultural heritage of ethnic and religious minorities.

Even if this were true, the difficulty is that it nonetheless accentuates the dynamic of segregation, and concomitant problems thereof. Moreover, as already noted, contact and interaction between cultures leads to their change and development so that it is often only through determinedly self-imposed isolation and coercion that cultures and customs retain their 'essential form'. Whilst empathising with the pressures on minority communities to pursue practices that have been passed down the generations, my firm contention is that *all* oppressive cultural practices (whether stemming from the majority White or minority ethnic groups) should be resisted, and that in Britain it is Asian cultural practices that are the most oppressive.* In a rare and piercing critique, written before 9/11, Claire Beckett and Marie Macey (2001, p. 309–310) provide a powerful argument that is in accordance with this author's:

> No such pledge [as that to combat institutionalised racism] has been made in respect of homophobia or sexism, despite their extent and effects being comparable to those of racism, up to and including physical violence and murder ... One of the reasons for this is the dominance of multiculturalism in Britain which has negatively influenced the domains of gender and sexuality as well as ethnicity ... multiculturalism not only exacerbates and legitimises the oppression of already oppressed minority groups, but poses threats to liberal democracy and individual human rights. This is not a popular position to adopt at a time when the dominance of multiculturalism is such that critical voices are silenced, oppressive cultural practices invisibalised and contradictions between the ideals of multiculturalism and those of liberal democracy masked.

---

* It is curious why Asian cultural practices merit such zealous safeguarding. Tellingly, however, the impact of Asian culture beyond its own ranks is negligible. The major exception, of course, is the cuisine – though this has rather been vulgarised into the derogatory term 'curry' (not least because of the willingness of Asian restaurateurs to go along with this) – a travesty for a cuisine that encompasses over a fifth of the world's population, and all the variety this implies. The other exception is possibly literature. Bollywood films have some following in West Africa and the Middle East but, as in the Indian sub-continent, their aim is to provide escapism for the poor, largely illiterate, masses. Their utter fatuousness goes far beyond anything Hollywood can muster and so prevents them from permeating more developed societies (being confined overwhelmingly to the Asian population). True, there is also a tradition of 'Art House' films such as those by Satyajit Ray but sadly their popularity is minuscule in comparison with Bollywood's.

All this contrasts sharply with the situation of Black Caribbeans – who may in fact be seeing a reduction in their ghettoisation. Brixton, for example, was for many years a West Indian ghetto but, over the past two decades, has become much more multi-ethnic (there are a variety of factors causing this, including a degree of economic regeneration following the riot of 1981). But a key factor must be the propensity of Black Caribbeans to mix with others and have meaningful points of contacts with, above all, indigenous Whites. This is made easier, as noted earlier, by language and cultural similarities but there appears not to be the same intensity of exclusion of others, or groups closure, that is so prevalent in Asians.

Perhaps the clearest indicator of desegregation and integration is that of forming a relationship with someone from a different ethnicity – usually from the majority group. Evidence suggests that inter-ethnic relationships do indeed occur in all ethnic minority groups, but there is great variation. Table 2.2 provides data for inter-ethnic marriages based on the 2001 Census data for England and Wales. However, these figures are likely to underestimate the true picture as they exclude co-habiting couples. In over 90 per cent of cases, the marriage is to a White partner.

Table 2.2: Percentage of married people in inter-ethnic marriages by ethnic group and sex, April 2001 (England and Wales)

	Mixed	Indian	Pakistani	Bangladeshi	Other Asian
Male	76	7	5	4	20
Female	78	5	3	2	16

	Black Caribbean	Black African	Other Black	Chinese	Other Ethnic
Male	29	20	48	14	34
Female	20	12	35	28	56

Source: ONS (2005), *Focus on Ethnicity and Identity*, p. 4.

By far the highest rate of inter-ethnic marriage is for that of the 'Mixed' group at just over three-quarters for both genders. The next highest rate is for 'Other Ethnic' group (this is actually not a unified group at all, given that it encompasses people from the Philippines, Malaysia, Japan, Vietnam, and various Middle Eastern countries) with over half the females and about a third of males marrying out. Then follow 'Other Black' (in the main, largely young Blacks born in Britain) at nearly half for males and over a third for females. By far the lowest rate is that for the major Asian groups – all in single digit percentages, with Indians showing a slightly higher rate than Pakistanis and Bangladeshis (by contrast the rate for 'Other Asians' was almost one-fifth) (ONS, 2005, p. 4). It should be noted that these figures include those who would already have been married prior to their arrival in the UK and almost certainly to someone of the same ethnicity. An earlier study showed that the attitude of young people of all groups is much more liberal and, therefore, this is expected to show an increase in the marrying out rate for ethnic groups, including UK-born Asians (Modood and Berthoud, 1997, pp. 315–316). Nonetheless, the rate for Asians is still likely to be far less than for other ethnic minorities.

It necessarily follows that a crucial consequence of high levels of inter-ethnic mixing on the part of young British-born Blacks must be, as suggested earlier, the decline in the levels of segregation; in particular of Black Caribbeans. We stress again the positive aspects of the mixing of peoples: it accelerates cross-fertilisation of cultures and the creation of new cultural norms, reduces fear of those of a different ethnicity and, therefore, reduces bigoted and racist attitudes and behaviour. This then gives rise to an important political consequence: mixed communities will be much less amenable to racist stereotyping and scapegoating in comparison with segregated ones. We have seen that the tactics of far right groups such as the BNP have, of late, focused on specifically targeting Muslim Asian inner city neighbourhoods that border on White estates. Yet, these deprived White estates (which, it must be noted, also fail to gain from the mixing with non-Whites) have much more in common with the at least equally deprived Asian counterparts. Rather than uniting, they can fall prey to divisive politics. Thus high levels of segregation and racial ghettoisation provide fertile ground for such divisions, and the concomitant breeding of suspicion, hostility, and scapegoating: the standard fare of racist politics.

At the heart of Asian culture is the family: it this institution that explains much of the trajectory in life that its constituent members take, and the reason why the rate of mixing with others is so much lower. Ultimately, it is an economic, welfare and recreational unit with origins in pre-industrial, agrarian societies. When couples marry, this is in the form of a contract – 'love marriages' are strongly discouraged, as is marriage across class, religious, ethnic, or racial boundaries; there is often a great stigma and loss of honour attached to marriage to 'outsiders'. The following remark by a Sikh father graphically illustrates the point (the sentiment of which can equally be applied to all Asian groups): 'if my daughter wanted to marry someone who was not a Jat Sikh, she would be chained up. No one has married outside the Jat Sikh caste in my family' (Modood, Beishon, and Virdee, 1994, p. 73).

In fact, the arranged marriage contract is more between two families rather than two individuals. Prior to the finalisation of a contract, an 'invitation to treat' is provided by the parents of a marriage contender (note that no such 'invitation' is allowed for in forced marriages). This can be done indirectly in family gatherings or more directly as in the showing of the 'commodity' (man or woman) to the prospective partner and his or her parents and family. An array of suitability criteria is considered: the right religion, class, and (where appropriate) caste similarity are the *sine qua non*. Other key criteria are family background (marriage to cousins is often desired, with potential for high trustworthiness, as the two partners are literally from the same family – but this can result in various medical problems inherent in such close unions (see, for example, Bittles *et al.*, 1991), the man's job and career prospects, for the woman her age and looks, and for some women, the level of dowry provided by her family (though in Britain this has waned – see SBS, 1994).

The newly married couple is never quite independent and becomes part of the extended family network – similar in many ways to the situation in Britain prior to the First World War. This provides security, support, provision of basic needs where necessary, and a degree of certainty. All in all, therefore, the family acts as a haven in an uncertain and often hostile environment. But it does this at great, often intangible, costs. First, the network and wider 'community', though sealed from outsiders, is rather like a goldfish bowl for those inside it. Consequently, the network systematically acts against individuals obtaining independence – particularly the young, but also the old – so that *self*-reliance, *self*-support, *self*-initiative are all diminished. Indeed, individuality and autonomous behaviour are systematically discouraged so as to prevent any deviation from the very straight and narrow. There is, therefore, great restriction on the development of interests in areas not deemed acceptable or familiar so that horizons become constrained and *social* conservatism becomes deeply ingrained. Nepotism inevitably becomes rife and, with this, the iconoclastic and inquisitive impulses are curtailed.

The preservation of the family's 'good name' within the community centres around two key principles that help explain so much of the motives of individual members. The first is 'honour' (or *izzat* – meaning standing in the community) and the second is 'shame' or *sharam*. In a sense, the family is akin to a large Japanese company of old: members must be loyal, must not damage its reputation (incur shame), strive to improve its well-being and standing (honour), must be submissive to its senior management (the elders),*

---

* There is an array of terms to describe relationships within a family. Much of this is hierarchical (in some ways analogous to terms used by commoners vis-à-vis royalty or the aristocracy) – so much so that elders within a family are given deferential terms and deferential behaviour, and automatic respect (whether it is deserved or not is never for debate) is to be expected and required. For a flavour of these terms, it is worth browsing through any book written by an Asian novelist dealing with family affairs (such as Salman Rushdie's *Shame* or Arundhati Roy's *The God of Small Things*).

and membership involves a lifetime contract. Again, there are advantages to this, particularly if the outside environment is hostile and unwelcoming. But abuses within the family are largely hidden from the outside, and it is women, in particular, who suffer most from the Scylla and Charibdis of honour and shame. Breaching these principles leads to great hardship, particularly for women in close-knit communities. For those unfortunate enough to be in such a situation, they soon find how few, if any, allies are available. Sanctions against them can be severe: there is now a large body of evidence which shows that these could include murder as we saw in regard to forced marriages (see, for example, SBS, 1994, 2001).

Alongside the family, religion plays a vital role. Evidence from the Home Office Citizenship Survey suggests that religious identity is stronger among Muslims, Hindus, and Sikhs (who are overwhelmingly Asians) compared with Christians (who are overwhelmingly White). Hence, 67, 61, and 51 per cent respectively of Muslims, Sikhs, and Hindus considered that their religion said something important about them, compared with just 21 per cent of Christians (ONS, 2006, p. 4).

In families where there is a strong sense of religious identity, strict and coercive enforcement of religious indoctrination begins at a very young age; choice on the matter is rarely on offer. The effects of this can be pernicious as independent and critical thinking is excluded; indeed, there is no need for it as all the answers are provided in a religion's texts and rituals. Moreover, to criticise the religion is deemed blasphemous and invariably leads to being rebuked and ostracised. Hence, perhaps for the majority of British Asians, life must be led in accordance with the dictates of the religion: pray, go to temple, mosque, or gurdwara, conform with whatever eating and drinking requirements and taboos are set out, dress appropriately, marry in accordance with the religion, and so on.

In reality, religion acts as a very powerful *control apparatus,* and religious leaders enjoy respect, power, and influence within 'their' community. Whereas for centuries religion has been used to justify the politics and behaviour of both rulers and the oppressed, in the modern era it is above all in 'Islamic' countries that the political use of religion has become so prevalent. Partly this must be related to the failure of secular political movements to offer credible alternatives; the rise of Islamic parties can be viewed as a backlash to this failure. In a similar manner, the rise of Islam in Britain, and, albeit to a lesser extent, also of Hinduism and Sikhism stems from the inadequacy of the polity, and of an education system that has failed to be secular in a principled manner (see Chapter 6). Furthermore, for reasons of tradition and custom, parents are driven to impose their religion onto their children as part of their duty and requirement: not to do so can lead them into the realm of shame and dishonour within the religious community. Such a scenario is vividly provided in the following illustrative example by Amartya Sen:

> The vocal defense of multiculturalism that we frequently hear these days is very often nothing more than a plea for plural mono-culturalism. If a young girl in a conservative immigrant family wants to go out on a date with an English boy, that would certainly be a multicultural initiative. In contrast, the attempt by her guardians to stop her from doing this (a common enough occurrence) is hardly a multicultural move, since it keeps the cultures sequestered. And yet it is the parents' prohibition, which contributes to plural monoculturalism, that seems to get most of the vocal and loud defense from alleged multiculturalists, on the ground of the importance of honouring traditional cultures, as if the cultural freedom of the young woman were of no relevance whatever, and as if the distinct cultures must somehow remain in secluded boxes (Sen, 2006, p. 157).

This is a cogent rebuttal of multiculturalist thinking and practice and an indictment of Parekh's emphasis on 'loyalty to culture' which we commented on in the previous chapter. Such loyalty nestles agreeably with the same for religion, family, ethnic group, community, and class (the middle class fiercely resists marriage 'downwards' in the class ladder – in a manner that would have made sense entirely to the characters in Jane Austen's novels). There is thus the construction of a powerful edifice within Asian religious-ethnic communities that is extremely resistant to outside influence. The more traditional elements, usually the male elders and religious figures, act zealously in preserving this edifice and rail against the 'corrupting influence of the West'. The hypocrisy of this is self-evident.*

If 7/7 was a wake-up call regarding multiculturalism in general and the situation of Muslims in segregated communities in particular, then events in the northern English towns of Bradford, Burnley, and Oldham in the summer of 2001, a few weeks before 9/11, can be described as a disturbance in multiculturalism's sleep. It is important to note that, in contrast to the major urban riots of 1981 or 1985, the 2001 rioters were exclusively alienated Muslim Asian youths from ghettoised neighbourhoods. In the next chapter, we shall consider the factors that have led to such alienation in more detail.

---

* In an incisive scene from the film *My Son the Fanatic*, based on a script by Hanif Kureishi, the visiting imam from Pakistan asks the taxi driver for legal advice on immigration matters – he wants to settle in the UK and wishes to bring his family over to join him. The taxi driver pointedly asks him: 'Why do you want to stay in this immoral country?' A very good question because it exposes the hypocrisy of those who, whilst railing against the decadent West, are eager to enter it.

Chapter 3
Multiculturalism and 'Psychic Detachment'

Segregation and psychic detachment

Until now the approach taken by governments of both parties and local authorities of all political persuasions in regard to increasing segregation can be summarised as being that of benign non-intervention. This policy, as we have seen, has typically been justified under the rubric of multiculturalism. Under this laissez-faire approach, migrant communities have been allowed to lead their lives pretty much as they would have done in their 'home' countries. By so doing, these communities have naturally retained, almost *in toto*, cultural and religious customs and traditions. A corollary to this has been that mixing with those not from one's 'own' community has been minimal and, evidence suggests, may be declining (Phillips, 2005) – to the point where, for perhaps the majority living in pure religious-ethnic neighbourhoods, it is virtually non-existent. This in turn leads to these communities becoming what can be termed 'psychically detached' from mainstream British society – even though they are *geographically* located in Britain. This phenomenon, in the migrant context, is novel – though variants have existed before or are extant. We explore its attributes and consequences in this chapter.

What does it mean to say that someone, or a group of persons, is/are 'psychically detached' from the society in which they live? A strong definition is one where there are very few 'points of contact' between the individual and group and the rest of society. The phenomenon of 'contact' between people has attracted much research in social psychology under the umbrella term 'contact hypothesis', focusing on the attempt at obtaining an 'optimal contact strategy' (for a good overview of the research, see Dixon, Durrheim, and

Tredoux, 2005).* The optimal contact strategy 'aims to identify and elucidate the conditions under which contact works most effectively to reduce prejudice and, by implication, to increase the possibility of social harmony. For several decades, this approach has served as social psychologists' primary framework for understanding the dynamics of contact and segregation' (*ibid.*, p. 699). We do not, in this chapter, wish to go over the debates in this literature but, rather, to stress the vital importance of points of contact between different peoples in the context of a societal incentive regime that enables this to be done in a meaningful manner, in the endeavour to achieve a more socially cohesive society. In Chapters 6 and 7 we explicitly adopt the value judgement that a *sine qua non* for this is a thoroughgoing secularisation of society.

We can use a somewhat exceptional example to demonstrate the relationship between points of contact and psychic detachment: that of 'company compounds' in Saudi Arabia. Foreign, above-all non-Muslim, workers residing in these separate enclaves can be thought of as being removed to a highly significant extent from practically every aspect of Saudi society. As a theocracy, it is deeply alienating to non-Muslims, secularists, and perhaps even to non-Wahabbi Muslims. Even the most rudimentary norms of democracy are an anathema: the House of Saud reigns supreme, fiercely resistant to challenge and change. Integration into this totalitarian and in many respects tyrannical society – with its state-sanctioned repression and plethora of restrictions – can only occur on the basis of self-denial of an array of basic rights. This would (or ought to) be quite intolerable for those coming from democratic, predominantly secular societies – and indeed is also likely to be the same for those from authoritarian, non-theocratic societies. This form of integration, if it can be described as such, is nothing less than the equivalent of a free person choosing to integrate into a high security prison. It naturally follows that there is no desire whatsoever, among the overwhelming majority of migrant

---
* This paper not only critiques the optimal contact strategy literature, but also provides new and more productive avenues for research. It must be stressed that this important literature has been ignored by theorists and advocates of multiculturalism.

workers, to integrate into Saudi society by adopting its culture, faith, and mores. It further follows that there is no intention to make Saudi Arabia a permanent home. Even if years are spent living in the state, this is not with the view of what is ordinarily meant by permanent settlement – the true home remains, at all times, the country of origin or of passport and the intention is always to return given that, apart from working and making money, there is little reason to remain.

In this highly peculiar situation it is pristine clear that company compound workers are marooned from Saudi society, with very few points of contacts. This represents not only physical but also psychic detachment from the host society. Geographically located in Saudi Arabia, these foreign workers have a mode of thinking, belonging, living and *being* that is rooted elsewhere: that is, their alienation from the host society is such that they may as well be living in another land. Their mind is never rooted in the alien world beyond the compound, is never comfortable with it, so it becomes, in effect, *detached* from it and, in so doing, rejects it. They are, therefore, 'guest workers' in the true sense of the word: after their working stint, they will return home where they will attempt to re-integrate, invariably successfully, with the societies from which they came.

As noted, this unique, even 'artificial', phenomenon does not apply to migrants to the West in general and has not applied to Asian migrants to the UK in particular, a very small percentage of whom have returned to settle in their countries of origin, or have desired to do so. Arguably, the large number of British settlers in other European countries such as France and Spain furnishes evidence of the phenomenon of psychic detachment. Anecdotal evidence suggests that the majority make little effort to learn the local language or adopt the host culture; hence there appears to be little desire for genuine integration on their part and they usually become, to some extent, psychically detached. However, the differences between British settlers in Europe and Asian settlers in Britain are immense and the hitherto lack of enthusiasm for integrating, on the part of the former, should not to be considered anything like as great a societal problem. Thus, there are no significant cultural or religious taboos, on their part, with regard to partaking in the life of other European countries – indeed they readily frequent all manner of social and leisure facilities. Exceptions may occur such as the refusal by the majority of British people (and one can conjecture by many others also) to attend bullfighting events in Spain. Undeniably, however, the key obstacle to lack of interaction remains language difficulties. This is compounded by the fact that English is the global *lingua franca* and so, certainly in tourist resorts, very large numbers of (especially younger) indigenous people now speak English so that some meaningful interaction can still occur without fluency in the local language.

But the most profound difference is the motive for settlement. In the case of Asian migrants (as is the case with the vast majority of migrants generally) the motive was (is) to find work; in stark contrast, the motive for the overwhelming majority of British settlers in Europe is to buy homes, often a second home, usually in countries and regions where the climate is more agreeable. Therefore, the former do so from a position of financial weakness whilst the latter do so from a position of financial strength. It naturally follows that the difference in attitude and confidence is immense – the two groups are largely located at the opposite ends of the socio-economic spectrum. But it remains to be seen whether the British settlers intend to make their adopted countries their permanent home (as was the case with Asians in the UK). Thus far, however, anecdotal evidence suggests that children of settlers tend to go to English-language 'International' schools – with a view to attending university in Britain. Even so, we can assert that the psychic detachment of Asians in Britain is of a different scale and import altogether in comparison with that of the recent wave of British settlers in other European countries. Moreover, in what now appears an iron law, states and their citizens tend to adopt a far more welcoming stance to those who bring investment and spending power than those who offer only their labour power.

As already noted, the overwhelming desire of Asian migrants to Britain has been to make the new country of settlement the permanent home.* Yet, for a significant percentage, permanent settlement is not necessarily predicated on genuine interaction with the host society. This may partially arise because of hostility encountered from the indigenous population and institutions so that there is a retreat to the familiarity and safety of fellow migrants from the home country or region. Indeed, this was a crucial element in the initial formation of separate migrant areas – the 'constraint' factors whose underlying *raison d'être* was racism. But, as the years passed, citizenship was generally granted to those who were eligible and sought it, familiarity with the host society was obtained, including language and customs, and there were overall declining levels of racism and hostility. Meanwhile, the separate areas increasingly became segregated ghettos, driven by 'choice' factors whereby migrants *chose* only to live in areas with their co-ethnic or co-religious brethren. This is seemingly paradoxical as the reality has been that, over time and with increasing familiarity, the indigenous White population has become more willing to establish meaningful points of contact with migrant settlers including, importantly, accepting them as legitimate residents with equal rights (an acceptance all the more readily extended to their children). This also provides a key explanation for the overall declining levels of racism (though it still exists and often with great intensity), and rising level of mixing. Indeed there is much cause to assume that indigenous Whites, in the main, are willing, when opportunity presents, to establish meaningful contacts with migrant settlers and their children (but not necessarily to the same extent as with those from their own indigenous White background), such has been the profound change in social attitudes over the decades. This runs counter to the process within the segregated ghettos where there appears to have been a decline in points of contact with 'outsiders' – either because of unwillingness or lack of necessity to do so.

From this, we can assert that Asian psychic detachment is frequently a 'voluntary', intentional, act on the part of the ghettoised

---

* Whether this will be the case of large numbers of migrants from Eastern Europe in recent years remains to be seen. One can conjecture that proportionally rather fewer will settle permanently in the UK.

communities and cannot any longer be considered as primarily a by-product of the rejection by the majority society. This can, for example, be contrasted with the position of mentally ill people where, notwithstanding the precise causes of mental illness, psychic detachment (albeit of a different nature) is invariably involuntary and unintentional.[*] The very fact of making separate demands, for example, on grounds of religion, constitutes a detachment from the society in which they have settled. 'When in Rome, do as the Romans do' appears an intolerable imposition for many religious-ethnic minority citizens. Again, this alienation is of an altogether different degree than that of the example of British settlers in other European countries highlighted above.

Components of psychic detachment
Psychic detachment is rather distinct from 'social exclusion', which arises in the absence of integration of sections of the population (not necessarily religious-ethnic minorities) into the *labour market* (see for example, Levitas, 1996; Blanc, 1998). It also differs from 'social distance' in that this is predominantly a *class* phenomenon whereby social interaction, within any given society, is a function of an individual's socio-economic position.[†] Obviously, the higher the class position, the greater the resources and potential to partake in the array of activities society proffers; in most societies, there exists a very high multiple separating those at the very top of the class spectrum from those at the very bottom. Hence the *economic* distance between the upper class and the lowest class is a manifestation of differences of income and wealth, hence of economic inequality. The economic distance, in turn, generates *social* distance, which Bogardus (1933, p.

---

[*] Indeed we might hypothesise that 'religious-cultural psychic detachment' may contribute towards a form of 'schizophrenic psychic detachment' – this would certainly be a fruitful avenue of research for psychologists and psychiatrists.

[†] Bogardus (1932, p. 167, fn 2) distinguishes between three forms of social distance: personal or between persons, group or between groups, and personal-group, or between a person and his group. Note that this definition contrasts with the very different one of social distance being a form of personal space, that is, physical proximity between people in social interaction.

270) defines as 'the different degrees of sympathetic understanding that exist between persons'.

But that is not to say that those at the bottom of the socio-economic ladder (for example the unemployed person) would not desire to lead lives that are similar to those at the top: if the means were available, they may well be highly desirous of emulating the latter's *modus vivendi*. It follows that the unemployed are not necessarily *psychically* detached from the upper classes, on the assumption that should the appropriate level of resources become available, there will accordingly be a narrowing of economic distance and, concomitantly, a convergence of social distance and the flourishing of meaningful points of contact between the two. Thus, social distance is a direct reflection of class difference, and associated highly correlative variations. It follows, therefore, that economic distance and social distance are closely correlated with occupation category. Indeed, the influential Cambridge Social Interaction and Stratification scale (CAMSIS) focuses on *occupation group* as its basic unit of analysis because this is considered 'the single most significant and convenient indicator of someone's location in the overall structure of advantage and disadvantage, as well as a major source of identity' (CAMSIS website).

In contrast, psychic detachment in our definition arises with respect to *all* classes and occupations (including, importantly, an individual or group's *own* class or occupation) that are not of the same religion/ethnicity. This goes against the grain of stratification theory – that people of the same class are likely to have more points of contacts with those of the same/similar class (hence social distance is low) than with a different class (where social distance is higher). This is demonstrated by the following illustrative example: suppose a Muslim factory worker in Western Europe works in a factory with significant numbers of non-Muslims – clearly s/he will necessarily engage in work-related activities with non-Muslim colleagues (unless confined to a work section entirely comprised of Muslim workers). Suppose also that s/he returns home to a segregated Muslim community so that the points of contact with non-Muslims reduce to practically zero. Here, on a Likert scale of 1 to 5 (where 1 is zero and 5 maximum), predicted social distance will be 1 (or very low, given that the class position of the Muslim worker and non-Muslim colleagues is identical), 'workplace' social detachment (on this, see below) rather higher at say between 2 and 3 (s/he, for example will prefer to only sit with Muslim colleagues during breaks); but psychic detachment will still be very high – between 4 and 5, meaning that the worker in question is almost completely detached from the wider society, including from work colleagues, with very few points of contact with those not from his/her community. Therefore, *intentionality* in avoiding points of contact with those not of the same religious-ethnic background is crucial. In essence, therefore, 'detachment' is the obverse of 'integration' so that, in this example, the person concerned is very poorly integrated.

The key foundation for psychic detachment is segregation into invariably deprived minority communities from a religious-ethnic background, as already elaborated upon, for reasons of 'choice' or 'constraints'. Segregation facilitates the formation of a heightened religious identity. Key to this is the influence of religious and cultural values, beliefs, and attendant practices from community and religious 'elders' and 'leaders' (for example, the role of imams in mosques, priests in Hindu temples and Sikh Gurdwaras is crucial in Muslim, Hindu, and Sikh communities respectively). As their value systems are often strongly at variance with, and even shun, those of the largely secular mainstream society (and invariably also those of other religious-ethnic minorities), this gives rise to 'normative', that is ideological, detachment.

Segregation, compounded by normative detachment, engenders 'social detachment'. For children, as a direct consequence of segregated schooling, this arises because of very few points of contact with children from the majority society, and indeed also with those from other minority backgrounds. We can hypothesise that schooling in a religious 'faith' school intensifies religious identity and accentuates normative and social detachment.

Growing up in a segregated community and attending segregated schools contributes to socio-economic detachment (that is, working only within one's 'own' community, which could be described as a 'ghetto economy', particularly if qualifications obtained are minimal). Compounding social detachment is the enormous pressure not to marry out of the faith and community. Indeed a cogent case can be made for this being a key determinant of genuine integration (Coleman, 1994). Accordingly, identification with the host society reduces to very low levels or there is, as Verkuyten and Yildiz (2007) have described it, 'disidentification'. It is the combination of normative detachment, social detachment, and disidentification that determines psychic detachment. The greater are the levels of these three contributory factors, the stronger is the likelihood of psychic detachment.

The central role of culture and religion
In Western Europe, religion and supernatural beliefs have long been subjected to sustained scrutiny. It necessarily follows that the worldview and practices of devout believers will inevitably collide with those of the rest of (the now largely secular) society, the points of contact will accordingly be less with those without or with minimal religious belief. Therefore, if heightened religious intensity reduces points of contact with non-believers, it is likely to accentuate psychic detachment.

As we observed in Chapter 1, in sharp contrast to indigenous White society, religion now strongly moulds the identity and community of Asian communities so that there is a high level of self-perception in religious terms. Moreover, I wish to make the case that the formation of a strong religious identity and attendant psychic detachment is directly linked to the formation of segregated communities; in turn, this impacts upon the welfare and prosperity of citizens within these communities. A key outcome is the strong reliance on 'social capital' (that is, 'networks together with shared norms, values and understandings that facilitate co-operation within or among groups' [Cote and Healey, 2001]), and 'cultural capital' (that is, 'forms of cultural knowledge, competences or dispositions' [Bourdieu, 1993, editor's introduction, p. 7]). Within tight-knit religious-ethnic communities, these become the vital conduits for 'economic capital', survival, and reproduction. Importantly, this reliance can give rise to a reinforcing dynamic, whereby religion drives identity, which then engenders a strong sense of religious-ethnic community. Within this community is created cultural, economic and social capital. This, in sequence, reinforces religious identity and accentuates psychic detachment which, in turn, increases the self-perception of religious identity, and so on.

Religions, in essence, are belief systems which impose an array of demands on followers and, unlike most political ideologies, require various acts of worship and ritual usually at precise times, days, and dates – metronomic observance is an absolute imperative. Moreover, the degree of flexibility tends to be very narrow as the core doctrines and rituals are not open to reason, so that religious belief has a 'blind', no-questions-asked, quality. We can postulate that the greater the intensity of observance, the greater will be the shunning of reason and evidence-based viewpoints and arguments. In a society where religious superstitions have been subjected to sustained scrutiny, significantly marginalised in the affairs of state and civil society and, hence, largely rendered impotent, the world-view and practices of devout believers, as noted above, will inevitably collide with those of the rest of society, and the points of contact will accordingly be less with those not (or minimally) fuelled by religious belief. Given that heightened religious intensity invariably reduces points of contact with non-believers, it reinforces social detachment.

The nature of a religion and its development is also important. The greater the restrictions a religion places on adherents, the less flexibility or, to adapt a statistical parlance, the less the 'degrees of freedom' it grants in behaviour and thought; hence the greater the psychic detachment it engenders. What is not in doubt is that each faith can be interpreted in various ways so that the more liberal the interpretation, the greater the degrees of freedom afforded to devout followers; conversely, the more literal the interpretation, the less the degrees of freedom. What is also clear is that each faith has a history and trajectory of development so that in their present state generalisations can be made, with a reasonable degree of validity, in regard to the encumbrances they place. Accordingly, we assume that certain religions afford greater degrees of freedom than others and, within each religion certain interpretations afford greater freedom than others.

We make the assumption that religious beliefs or superstitions are restrictive to a far greater magnitude than what can be described as 'everyday' (strictly-speaking, non-religious) superstitions or beliefs in the paranormal. The latter are non-religious but equally irrational beliefs. They are enormous in number and exist in all cultures – examples include superstitions about the climate, numbers, certain animals (such as black cats), astrology and beliefs in therapies and treatments that have no scientific basis. What both sets of superstitions share is the non-necessity of evidence or reasoned argument for belief: blind faith is a necessary and sufficient condition, although in the case of non-scientific therapies, many believe they have a positive effect based on results – though very rarely is demonstrable evidence provided.* But a vital difference that makes everyday superstitions and paranormal therapies relatively anodyne is that they tend to be personal, are almost entirely voluntary, and can easily be adapted or dropped. True, the same might, in theory, apply to the major faiths but, in reality, this is definitively not the case for the overwhelming majority of religious believers. Any familiarity with the typical, systematic process of indoctrination in religion from a very young age rules this 'innocent freedom of choice' argument untenable. As we have stressed, 'exit costs' from a religious-ethnic minority community can be very high, which is to say that it is enormously difficult to

---

* Richard Dawkins' TV series 'Enemies of Reason' (Channel 4, August 2007) forcefully dealt with the seemingly exponential rise in 'alternative' non-scientific, paranormal, beliefs and therapies. Dawkins argued that 50 per cent of the population believed in the paranormal and 25 per cent in astrology.

exit the community and attempts to do so are often fraught with dangers. It follows that everyday superstitions do not, to any appreciable extent, impinge upon a person's interactions with the wider society – in marked contrast with religious superstitions – hence can be treated as a separate category to religion per se.

Roy Wallis (1984) has used a three-fold typology to describe what he terms 'new religious movements', meaning religions that have developed in the West in the post-Second World War period, especially during the 1960s. The three types of new religions are 'world rejecting', 'world affirming', and 'world accommodating'. As the terms indicate, they attempt to relate new religions directly to the wider society in the modern world. World rejecting religions view:

> the prevailing social order as having departed substantially from God's prescriptions and plans. Mankind has lost touch with God and spiritual things, and, in the pursuit of purely material interests, has succeeded in creating a polluted environment ... They deny the conventional distinction between a secular and religious realm, the secular must be restored to its 'original' religious character ... in the communal life ... they can keep themselves separated, uncontaminated by the worldly order, able to cultivate their collective spiritual state unmolested. The movement is a 'total institution' regulating all its adherents' activities (Wallis, 1984, pp. 10–13).

In contrast, world affirming religions view the:

> prevailing order less contemptuously, seeing it as possessing many highly desirable characteristics ... Movements approximating the world-affirming type claim to possess the means to enable people to unlock their physical, mental and spiritual potential without the need to withdraw from the world ... No arduous prior period of preparation is necessary, no ascetic system of taboos enjoined (*ibid.*, pp. 21–22).

The world accommodating religion:

> is not construed as a primarily social matter; rather it provides solace or stimulation to personal, interior life. Although it may reinvigorate the individual for life in the world, it has relatively few implications for how that life should be lived, except that it should be lived in a more religiously inspired fashion. Any consequences for society will be largely unintended rather than designed ... The benefits it offers are not of the thorough-going instrumental variety to be found in world affirming movements (*ibid.*, pp. 35–36).

It seems enlightening to apply this typology to *all* religions. We can contend that, for both Marx and Freud, religion in the generic form is fundamentally world accommodating. This is evident from Marx's famous remark: 'it is the sigh of the oppressed creature, the heart of a heartless world, and the soul of soulless conditions. It is the *opium* of the people' (Marx, 1977 [1843/4], p. 244).

Freud provided a similar view in *The Future of an Illusion*:

> ... the helplessness felt by human beings remains, as do their paternal yearnings and the gods. The latter retain their triple function of warding off the terrors of nature, reconciling humans to the cruelty of fate, notably as revealed in death, and compensating them for the sufferings and privations imposed upon them by living together in a culture group (Freud, 2008 [1927], p. 19).[*]

What this suggests is that religion is a means by which the helpless and oppressed *accommodate* to the world around them, and *cope* with their suffering, with the promise of a fulfilling hereafter. Though this is a persuasive formulation at a *macro* level, at a *micro* level, in their relationships with the outside world, Wallis' delineation is helpful in establishing the propensity of each religion to have meaningful contacts on an everyday basis with those outside the faith; that it

---

[*] Freud concluded that religion is the 'universal obsessional neurosis' (*ibid.*, p. 55).

recognises the *differences* in religions and this, in turn, for our purposes provides an understanding of the likely degree of psychic detachment that emanates from each.

It is difficult to designate any of the major religions as world affirming (note that the meaning is different to 'life affirming' – certainly all believers can argue that their faith is life affirming). Though there is an element of arbitrariness in any generalisation we can, nonetheless, aver that, in the UK context, world rejecting religions (which have a 'totalitarian' quality) are Hinduism,* Islam, Orthodox Judaism and Sikhism. In the context of the modern, increasingly secular world, this is not an unduly harsh judgement given that in Britain opinion polls indicate there is now an overwhelming majority (82 per cent) that believes that religion does more harm than good (Glover and Topping, 2006). It is surely the case that for the large majority of the population, a very strong adherence to a religion and attendant religious identity (as is the case with Asians in general) is, in a significant sense, tantamount to world rejecting, which we can also think of as being 'society rejecting'. This provides some evidence for our belief that religion is a key contributor to psychic detachment and, as such, hinders integration and accentuates social divisiveness. However, adherents of every religion can each accommodate to the outside world by 'toning down' the outward aspects of their faith, largely confining it to an inner belief system and spiritual salvation; though by so doing, this invariably necessitates the breach of some doctrines and fulfilment of rituals.

But we have seen that there is now a significant difference across various socio-economic indicators between Asians from an Indian background (who are mainly Hindus or Sikhs) and from a Bangladeshi and Pakistani background (overwhelmingly Muslim). Does this suggest that Hinduism and Sikhism are *less* world rejecting than Islam? Or perhaps, unlike Islam, these religions have adapted in significant ways so enabling their adherents to better engage with modernity? Or is it simply that Hindus and Sikhs are rather

---
* Warrier (2007, p. 137) describes 'Hinduism's traditions of yoga and world renunciation'.

less zealous in conforming to the beliefs and rituals of their faiths? There are no hard data on this and, without major surveys of these issues, it is not possible to arrive at sound conclusions (though see the suggestive comments in the following paragraph). But, *prima facie*, there is no reason to think that the beliefs and rituals of Hinduism and Sikhs have become less restrictive than those of Islam. Certainly, we can be assured that in the pure religious-ethnic neighbourhoods, all are extremely exacting in their religious duties – so that it is well nigh impossible to separate oneself away from religious identity, and confine the faith solely to the private sphere. Indeed, it is knowledge of this reality that particularly gives confidence to representatives of such closed communities to demand separate legal provisions for their religions.

We also know that all three religions are male-dominated with women being accorded inferior status. But the much higher levels of economic activity of women from an Indian background, in comparison with their Bangladeshi and Pakistani counterparts, suggest that there may be a greater challenge to male domination within Hindu and Sikh communities. So, a strong religious identity exists in all three faith communities, but appears to be strongest among Muslims and it is this which helps explain their registering the lowest rate of 'marrying out' and of the highest incidence of forced marriages.

A revealing and strangely moving example of the way in which religious taboos can enormously restrict and even prohibit interaction is provided by the Indian mathematics genius Ramanujan. The story of his tenure at Cambridge University during the First World War, although long removed in time, nonetheless resonates today. In his highly sympathetic biography, Robert Kanigal writes of the cultural and religious clash Ramanujan encountered. A South Indian Brahmin,

> Ramanujan was a vegetarian unusually strict in his orthodoxy – if not for South Indians generally then at least for those in England. In crossing the seas he had defied Brahminical strictures. He had

forsaken his tuft. He mostly wore shoes and Western clothes. But as he had promised his mother, he clung fiercely to the proscriptions most central to Brahminic life, on food.

Brahminic food prohibitions dictated that 'from whom you take your food *matters*'. The consequence of this prohibition meant that Ramanujan never ate in his college (Trinity) dining hall: 'there, at High Table during the long winter evenings of 1916, the candles flickered, the conversation hummed. But of all that, Ramanujan never shared' (Kanigal, pp. 240–241).

This is a portrait of a person of formidable intellect trapped in a religious and cultural straitjacket that prevented meaningful social interaction with those not of his faith. It might have been explained away by the peculiar historical circumstances (the high-brow gentility of a Cambridge college was indubitably exceptional, even in the days of empire and attendant patronage towards a visiting colonial subject) and deemed of little consequence. In any case, Ramanujan's hermit-like existence did not prevent him from developing his path-breaking mathematical theories. But wind the clock forward to the era of mass settlement of migrants in Britain's towns and cities. It is this kind of rejectionist behaviour on the grounds of religion and culture that is entrenching psychic detachment and, in turn, generating alienation among the indigenous population who live in close proximity to segregated minority neighbourhoods. Such alienation can beget resentment and hostility so that such communities come to be viewed as the 'other' and not as fellow citizens. Note, however, that this can occur in the context of declining levels of overall racism so that these two phenomena (that is, resentment and hostility on the one hand, and less racism on the other) can exist in parallel.

For devout followers of a religion, their culture, traditions, mores, and folkways are strongly moulded by that religion, to the extent that every aspect of life is guided by religious injunctions. But often we can distinguish cultural from religions customs, whilst being cognisant of the strong conditioning element of the latter on the former. Hence there is a significant overlap. What is key here, as with religion, is the extent to which an ethnic minority culture allows points of contact with the wider society, that is, the extent to which it engenders normative and social detachment, and disidentification. We can once more think in terms of world affirming, world rejecting or world accommodating cultures.

For Asians in Britain, we can postulate two key overarching cultural factors that can be thought as being world (or society) rejecting: gender segregation and (for Muslims in particular) the complete rejection of alcohol. Although alcohol is also prohibited in Sikhism, the compliance with this stricture is not so complete. In contrast, the prohibition on tobacco is much more strictly observed (akin to the taboo on alcohol in Islam). Given the sharp fall in smoking in all sectors of society over the past 50 years, compounded by its being made illegal in public places in recent years, the social impact of a religious prohibition on smoking is negligible. Indeed, it is smokers who have become something of social outcasts.

Gender segregation is of crucial significance for women and girls. From a young age, in all Asian cultures, there is systematic separation of boys and girls that triggers demands for girls-only classes and schools and women-only leisure activities within their 'own community'. Compounding this is the stress on 'modest' forms of attire so that skirts, shorts, t-shirts and swimwear are generally prohibited. For Muslim girls, the imposition of the *hijab* or more intrusive forms of veiling adds to their separation. Accordingly, Asian girls can begin to feel socially detached from other girls – the sense that they are different, not fully able to partake in modes of dress, activities, and behaviour that are considered utterly normal in mainstream society. This can become accentuated in adulthood given that marriage soon follows the completion of schooling, with attendant duties of taking care of the home and husband. This is quickly followed by motherhood so that many women do not experience the world of work (as we have seen, in the case of women from Bangladeshi and Pakistani backgrounds, this is the majority) and many who do work do so in the narrow confines of their community. Such an insular, 'world rejecting' life cycle strongly militates against developing meaningful points of contact with outside society which, in combination with other strong cultural and religious norms, inexorably leads to very high levels of psychic detachment.

The injunction on alcohol mainly affects Muslims. Given the importance of alcohol in so many countries and societies – playing a central role in social gatherings – the avowed refusal to be near the vicinity of places which serve alcohol is a considerable contributor to psychic detachment. Here cultural elements come into play. Islam forbids the drinking of alcohol, but the doctrine does not forbid being physically present in an establishment that supplies alcohol – so for strict believers, imbibing non-alcoholic drinks in such abodes should be permissible. Yet, for perhaps the vast majority of practising Muslims, visiting alcohol-serving premises is a taboo. Consequently, practically the entire raft of places of socialisation become out-of-bounds – including pubs, non-Muslim restaurants, clubs, trade union and working men's associations etc. Truly, there is a self-denial of whole aspects of society that are available for ordinary people. The refusal to frequent such places results in the inevitable diminution of points of contacts with non-Muslims, with attendant insularity and separation.

Further, let us consider Muslim attitudes to dogs. In mainstream Islam the dog is considered, in a manner similar to the pig, an 'unclean' animal that should be avoided – hence Muslims are forbidden to come into close contact with dogs and is why they do not have them as pets (See El Fadl, 2005). Now we know that guide dogs provide a wonderful means for blind persons to constructively engage with the outside world in the literal sense. They are a resource that should be nurtured and treasured. But Islamic doctrine presumably would forbid this and, by so doing, confine devout blind Muslims to the confines of the home thereby increasing their social detachment. We would certainly expect blind Muslims to be more accepting of guide dogs but that does not detract from the fact that the desire to be in ownership of one is a clear breach of doctrine and custom.

Strong affinity with a culture and religion can, therefore, intensify the constituent elements of psychic detachment. Levels of normative detachment may reach such an extent that there is an ever-increasing *hostility* to the host society's culture, values, and mores. A familiar explanation for this, on the part of many Asians, is that they do not wish to partake of a culture that involves getting drunk with fellow lager-louts on Friday and Saturday nights, and they would rather not indulge in abusive chanting at football matches or participate in other social activities in a similar vein. By such denunciations, practically the whole of British – indeed Western – society and culture is generalised and condensed into some of its most vulgar manifestations, and rejected (though there is good reason to think that these distasteful phenomena are of rather less prevalence in other western European countries).

So, far from there being a generational progression towards greater integration and concomitant deeper embedding into all aspects of British society – what might be termed 'deep settlement' – there has arisen within the segregated areas increasing detachment not only from the host society and but also from other minority communities. What we have in the pure religious-ethnic ghettos is precisely the opposite: that is 'shallow settlement'. This is a signal of not truly belonging, of having little desire to seriously embed in the structures of the society in which permanent settlement has taken root. It also involves maintaining the belief that true belonging and identity lies with the 'home country'. It is a manifestation of a rigid, inflexible identity and helps explain, for example, the Muslim community's obsession with notions of *halal* (what is permitted by the faith, most famously pertaining to the manner in which animals are slaughtered for their meat) and *haram* (anything that is forbidden). From this binary, Manichaean perspective a good deal of Western society is simply 'haram'; consequently only within one's own community can 'halal practices' be established so as to encompass all aspects of life: school, work, social activities, food, drink, and religious practices (a poignant example of this detachment is the reference by Schofield-Clark (2007) to the Muslim pop band 'Native Deen' as offering 'halal entertainment' to Muslims).

Some consequences

A rising religious-ethnic minority population in an area of a town invariably dampens demand from indigenous Whites for houses in the area so that house prices rise more slowly than the average, stagnate, or even fall – thereby further constricting demand from Whites. Increasing concentrations of a religious-ethnic minority, in combination with falling house prices, in turn, tend to fuel demand for houses in the area from members of that religious-ethnic minority. The mutually reinforcing factors of increasing ethnic minority concentration and falling house prices not only act as a powerful disincentive for Whites to buy into such an area but also trigger the well-known phenomenon of 'White flight', that is, an acceleration of Whites leaving the area. Ineluctably, therefore, the area proceeds to become a ghettoised religious-ethnic minority neighbourhood. Precisely when the threshold for falling house prices and White flight is reached is uncertain but a reasonable conjecture would be at the point at which the proportion of ethnic minorities is significantly greater than in the country as a whole or greater than the percentage within the town or city concerned (no British city, for example, has a majority of ethnic minorities).

White flight boosts the creation of segregated communities which naturally results in a severe loss of points of contact with the majority society. The physical separation from others provides a firm foundation for an intensification of the process of psychic detachment. Either concurrently or sequentially, the flight of those from a different religious-ethnicity may also occur so that the area becomes a pure religious-ethnic (or mono-cultural) neighbourhood. The implications of this are profound, the most serious of which is the creation of segregated schools in which virtually all pupils emanate from a single religious-ethnic minority (further discussed in Chapter

6). This has become increasingly common and is a sign of drastic failures of national and local government policies vis-à-vis migrants. It means that, by the age of five, children within such schools struggle with the English language. Though not insurmountable, this constitutes a severe handicap in a highly competitive education system. This contrasts sharply with the experience of ethnic minority middle class children in non-segregated schools who invariably speak fluent English, and with the accent of their locality. Thus, educational attainment of children from pure religious-ethnic communities tends to be low which, inevitably, has a deleterious affect on future job prospects. Consequently, in an era of manufacturing decline, these children frequently end up working, as already noted, in the 'ghetto economy' – in shops, restaurants, and local trades, with minimal contact with the majority White community. This naturally leads to insularity and reinforces a further reliance on the network of family and friends within the ghetto. That is, it engenders social and socio-economic detachment. In turn, such an upbringing necessarily accentuates psychic detachment. Crucially, this is not solely from the majority White community, but also, as previously stressed, from other minority communities, contributing to the neglected phenomenon of inter-religious-ethnic stress and tension.

Perhaps provocatively, a case can be made that some of the deeply segregated religious-ethnic communities are becoming akin to the American Amish society in their desire for separation.* Unlike the Amish, however, their separation is not institutional with the granting of an array of legal exemptions. Moreover, they live in close geographic proximity to other communities – and in urban rather than rural areas. But, like the Amish, they do not have a true sense of belonging to the wider society surrounding them and there are enormous coercive pressures on the younger generation, in both groups, to remain in their 'own' areas rather than integrate with 'outsiders'.

---

* A case can perhaps also be made of similarities with Christian fundamentalist/evangelical groups in the southern states of the US who, in many ways, are strongly hostile to, hence psychically detached from, many aspects of mainstream White, 'liberal', society.

Though our focus has been on highly segregated neighbourhoods, we need to acknowledge that there is a *continuum* of psychic detachment – from the complete traditionalists (a not insubstantial proportion) adhering strongly to the religious and cultural mores of their 'home countries' to the modernists (a small proportion, usually younger) who partake fully in the society of their birth, upbringing, and choice; hence of necessity, the latter have carefully given consideration to 'their' traditions, customs, and religions – and largely rejected them for progressive reasons. Without empirical evidence, we can conjecture that the latter are a small fraction of the former. In graphic form (where the horizontal scale is from zero to maximum psychic detachment) this would, therefore, not be a normal distribution curve but one which is skewed to the right.

If we had been thinking of these issues during the 1980s, we might have thought that there would be a generational divide whereby the younger generation of all classes would be rather more integrated than their parents. But not so in the 2000s: high levels of segregation have indubitably militated against the progress to increased integration of the former. It is reasonable to think – which evidence is likely to support – that strict adherence to certain religious and cultural mores lessens the points of contacts with wider society. A crucial outcome of this is the impact on the majority White community, especially on those residential areas and estates that lie in close proximity to religious-ethnic neighbourhoods.

To reiterate the argument already presented: this will have an enormously alienating effect on the part of Whites who, devoid of meaningful contact and interaction, will increasingly shun such 'in-group' communities. The psychic detachment of the latter, therefore, directly contributes to the alienation and resentment felt by Whites. The 'other' of yesteryear, of thousands of miles away, is transposed into the 'other' of near neighbours in the same town or city. This marks an unambiguous change in the mentality of indigenous Whites: whereas, in the initial phase of migration, alienation and resentment by Whites were on the grounds of racism and hostility to newcomers as potential competitors, four or five decades later the same sentiments are aroused because of the shunning, detachment, and insularity (or group closure) by some sections of religious-ethnic minorities – above all, Muslim Asians – in respect of those not of the same ethnicity or religion. Ultimately, we can argue that this has been a decisive outcome of laissez-faire multiculturalism.

We need at this point to provide a caveat, that is, the danger of conflating anti-racism policies (and opposition to these from avowed racists) and hostility to multiculturalism. Such an argument has been made by Roger Hewitt (2005), and provides his contention for the existence of a 'white backlash'. But the two phenomena are quite different. Though there is likely to be a strong correlation between racists and opposition to multiculturalism, one can be an anti-racist yet oppose multiculturalism: this is precisely the stance of the present author. Rather, most people oppose racism and probably by now, multiculturalism, on grounds of equality. That is to say, they advocate equal rights and opportunities regardless of race on the one hand and, on the other, equal treatment without the conferral of privileges on the grounds of religion and culture. There is no demonstrable evidence of a backlash with respect to anti-racism but there is good reason to think that there exists increasing alienation and resentment in regard to the conferral of cultural/religious privileges.

Given the high levels of segregation, ghettoisation, and concomitant psychic detachment, a case can be made that Asians are now the most religious-ethnocentric people in Britain. Under the rubric of cultural relativism, there has been a near absence of systematic contestation of religious beliefs and practices; we must remember that any such contestation would represent a breach of freedom of cultural and religious expression. This absence has, especially for Asians, inexorably and seamlessly aided the transposing of multiculturalism into multifaithism.

It is indubitably the case that socialisation into a culture and religion is vital to the coalescing and bonding of members of a close-knit community which is often a great source of succour and solidarity.

But this process can contemporaneously act as an impediment to the integration of a minority community into mainstream society. Over time, this can become an impregnable barrier whose ultimate end state is one of isolation and insularity. For society at large, we make the explicit value judgement that this is not a healthy outcome, and indeed is regressive. This suggests the conclusion that strong religious-ethnic identities foment psychic detachment and divisiveness and are, therefore, an unalloyed social ill. The next section (and its two chapters) focuses on aspects of a community that has indeed fomented a very strong religious identity and, in recent years, aroused enormous attention and interest, that is, the Muslim community. As we shall see, the implications of multicultural policies in this regard are again highly disquieting.

PART II

FOCUS ON KEY 'MUSLIM ISSUES'

Chapter 4

The misplaced doctrine of 'Islamophobia'

Examining the doctrine

Since 11 September 2001, the epithet 'Islamophobia' has increasingly come into vogue[*] – not only with Muslims but also in society generally, especially with liberals and those who would consider themselves to be on the left. The justification for this appellation rests on crucial foreign policy issues: the US-led invasions of Afghanistan and Iraq as part of its 'war on terror', the West's firm support for Israel's long-standing oppression of Palestinians and the continuous ratcheting up of sanctions and threats of war against Iran. In reality, it is argued, this is tantamount to a war against Muslims and Islam. Because Muslims in the West strongly oppose wars against Muslim states and occupation of Muslim lands, so the reasoning goes, they arouse suspicion by the forces of the state and public, are harassed, and are discriminated against. If they fight back, they are denounced as 'Islamic terrorists'. Furthermore, their religion is disparaged and devout believers are pejoratively referred to as 'Muslim fundamentalists'. In combination, these anti-Islam/Muslim views and actions provide unambiguous evidence of 'Islamophobia'. Though the literal meaning of the term is 'irrational fear of Islam', the intended meaning is hatred or dislike of Muslims and Islam.

In October 2006 the then Mayor of London, Ken Livingstone, issued a press release to mark the seventieth anniversary of the Battle of Cable Street by asserting: 'We should say bluntly today the same methods are being used against Muslims as have always been used against Jews. Today's fascists feed on the daily drip of Islamophobia

---

[*] The extent of its usage (especially in the UK) can be gauged by conducting a Google search of the term.

in the media given legitimacy by mainstream politicians pandering to prejudice' (Mayor of London Press Release, 8/10/2006).

The following month, on 18 November, Livingstone, along with others, including left-wing Labour MP John Cruddas, sent a letter to the *Guardian* to protest against the 'sowing of hatred of Muslims'. The letter called on readers to attend a rally against Islamophobia in Westminster two days later. Such sentiments have been entirely the norm among the British left, and not for one moment has any serious examination of the supposed phenomenon of Islamophobia been undertaken within its ranks. Some Muslims, such as Mohommed Naseem, Chairman of Birmingham Central Mosque, have 'likened the plight of Muslims in Britain to that of Jews in Nazi Germany'. Moreover, he thinks that 'the UK was becoming a police state and accused the government of "picking on" the Muslim community to pursue a political goal' (Tempest, 2007). The conclusion is unmistakeable, that there is a close similarity between anti-Semitism (irrational hatred of Jews) and Islamophobia (irrational hatred of Muslims).*

The policy prescription for Islamists and their apologists is clear: criticisms of Islam and of Muslims must be disallowed as it is deemed to be Islamophobic, and Muslims should be offered protection as a distinct ethnic group, in the manner of Jews and Sikhs (see Chapter 1). What is, therefore, being asked is *de facto* censorship, especially self-censorship in the media, press, academia, and the arts. To an astonishing degree this has, indeed, been achieved. Jo Glanville (2008), Director of the Index on Censorship, pointed out that 'Islamophobia' has come to carry nearly the same moral and political clout as the supremely potent charge of 'racism'. But the argument presented in this chapter is that this reasoning is flawed and is not backed up by sufficient evidence. Moreover, rather than improve matters for Muslims in the West, it has accentuated their alienation from the rest of society that we have already highlighted. Let us examine the evidence.

---

* For an attempt to tease out similarities and differences between anti-Semitism and Islamophobia, see Meer and Noorani (2008) – though these authors more sensibly refer to 'anti-Muslim sentiment'.

Following 9/11, The European Monitoring Centre on Racism and Xenophobia (EUMC) recognised that there may be a negative impact on attitudes to Islam and Muslims in EU member states. Accordingly, it monitored the situation and collated data into a Summary Report on Islamophobia in the EU after 11 September 2001, compiled by Christopher Allen and Jorgen Nielsen (2002). The report's findings are summarised as follows (*ibid.*, p. 7):

Acts of violence/aggression:

> Relatively low levels of physical violence were identified in most countries, although verbal abuse, harassment and aggression was much more widespread. Muslims, especially Muslim women, asylum seekers and others, including those who 'look' of Muslim or Arab descent were at times targeted for aggression. Mosques and Islamic cultural centres were also widely targeted for damage and retaliatory acts.

Measures of anti-Islamic actions and reactions:

> The picture remained mixed, where in a number of countries latent and/or pre-existent Islamophobia was seen to find expression in the [above]-mentioned acts of violence/aggression. This was reflected in the increase of activity by far-right and neo-Nazi groups. Other forms of nationally determined ethnic xenophobia were also given a greater impetus. A renewed interest in Islamic culture was identified, although this did not necessarily equate to an increased acceptance.

Good practice to reduce prejudice:

> Numerous inter-faith initiatives, especially between the Abrahamic traditions were undertaken as were similar initiatives emanating from Muslim communities themselves. Academic institutions and other organisations aided the situation with events, debates, semi-

nars and meetings to discuss relevant issues. A number of campaigns for intercultural tolerance and awareness were launched.

Reaction by politicians and other opinion leaders:

> The role of national politicians, both governing and in opposition was considered where the vast majority offered conciliation and solidarity with Muslim communities. Some however chose to remain silent whilst a few made unfortunate and somewhat unnecessary statements. Some NFPs [National Focal Points] noted that political capital was made where immigration and September 11 became entwined. Increased attention by the media was identified by the NFPs as being both positive and negative, largely depending upon the respective country. Instances of sensationalism and stereotypical representations of Muslims were noted.

In Britain:

> Political leaders from all sides, including Prime Minister Tony Blair, immediately expressed their condemnation [of anti-Muslim behaviour] with messages calling for restraint and differentiation ... The Prince of Wales called for peace and tolerance on visiting the UK's largest mosque and held a reception at his official residence for young Muslims. The Archbishop of Canterbury, George Carey called for calm and invited an international seminar on Christian-Muslim relations, with the support of the prime minister, to be held in January 2002 (Allen and Nielsen, 2002, p. 30).

After the 7 July 2005 bombings in London, the EUMC published a follow-up report (in November 2005) entitled *The Impact of 7 July 2005 London Bomb Attacks on Muslim Communities in the EU*. The Executive summary provides the main thrust of the findings (EUMC, pp. 4–5):

Although it is still early to draw final conclusions regarding the impact of the London events on the life of Muslim communities in Europe, the National Focal Point reports indicate that there were incidents against members and property of the Muslim community, but that these tended generally to be sporadic and isolated. The situation in different parts of the United Kingdom (UK), according to official and unofficial reports, indicates a pronounced short-term increase in the number of incidents in the immediate aftermath. The relatively minor level of incidents across the EU could be attributed to a variety of factors such as the swift responses by governments, politicians and opinion formers, supported by the police, who made serious efforts to distinguish clearly between the action of the bombers and Islam as a whole. In addition, there was a strong and immediate reaction by Muslim representatives who unequivocally condemned the bombers. The lesson of 7 July is that strong, co-ordinated action by all stakeholders works effectively. Out of concern about possible anti-Muslim incidents, the UK Government promptly highlighted its support for the legitimate aspirations of the Muslim community. The Police made clear that reprisals against members of the Muslim community would be dealt with harshly. In all EU Member States, governments and political parties responded to the attacks with statements of condolences, and in many Member States a careful distinction was drawn between the bombers and the Muslim community in general.

In the week following the bombings, the media in all Member States generally went to great lengths to appear balanced. The media in the UK underlined the point that the perpetrators were not acting on behalf of the Muslim community. Once the bombers were identified as British Muslims, there was however a distinct change in reporting in the UK and the focus shifted to broader issues about the Muslim communities and prevention of future incidents. Some media focused on the place of Muslim communities in British society, in particular the evidence of alienation of young Muslim males. In other Member States some media raised the issue of regulating immigration, while others focused on the radicalisation of Muslim youth linking it to inadequate integration processes. In most cases the media were careful to distinguish clearly between terrorism and the Muslim faith.

In general terms, according to the National Focal Point reports, there was no significant increase in incidents directed against the Muslim communities in most EU Member States during the reporting period. However, in the UK the number of reported incidents against members of the Muslim community and their places of worship increased almost immediately. In the five weeks after the bombing attacks, the Metropolitan Police in London recorded a sharp rise in faith hate crimes as compared to the same period in 2004. These attacks were directed predominantly at British Muslims. Reports from other parts of the UK, including from NGO sources, confirmed that the Muslim communities had become targets of increased hostility in the wake of the London bombings. However, at the time of writing, the overall assessment for hate crime incidents is that after the rise covering the period between 7 July to beginning of August they are moving back down towards levels similar to those experienced in 2004. In the UK, the temporary increase in racist incidents has made minority groups – and particularly British Muslims – feel vulnerable. The fear of reprisals correlated with rising prejudices perceived by members of the Muslim community. In media interviews and call-in programmes, Muslims said that they felt anxious about going out publicly or to work. Various sources reported that British Muslims felt that they were 'under suspicion'.

Both reports clearly show an increase in anti-Muslim hostility and sentiments in the immediate aftermaths of 9/11 and 7/7, including sporadic acts of violence and aggression. There was expected hostility from far-right groups as well as sections of the popular press. Hence, there is no denying this unpleasant reality and, moreover, there was (and remains) no room for complacency. In regard to officialdom, however, the reports provide evidence that great care was taken on the part of political leaders in countering any hostility towards Muslims and of distinguishing ordinary Muslims and terrorists. The media too, overall, showed restraint and acted in a 'balanced' manner. Similarly, the police come out in a favourable light: they are credited with their reassurances to the Muslim community, and intolerance of any violence committed against them (see below for data pertaining to the criminal justice process in England and Wales).

So, can we conclude from this that, post 9/11, there has been a prevalence of Islamophobia? Unfortunately, the EUMC uncritically accepts the notion and legitimacy of the phenomenon of Islamophobia, flying in the face of the evidence in both its own reports that clearly suggest otherwise. Hence, contrary to the fear-mongering by the likes of Naseem, we are certainly not dealing with a situation remotely comparable to the Jews under the Nazis in the 1930s, nor even of Muslims in the Indian state of Gujarat, which is ruled by a Hindu chauvinist regime with a history of repression and unspeakable violence against its Muslim citizens.* If the situation had been akin to these examples, then we would surely have witnessed a mass exodus of Muslims to Islamic countries. This has patently not been the case. In fact, the reality is quite the opposite: large numbers of people from many Muslim-majority countries have sought, and continue to seek, asylum in Britain and other Western countries. As they say, 'the proof of the pudding is in the eating': clearly, for large numbers of Muslim asylum seekers and would-be migrants, the alleged Islamophobia in the West's 'pudding' appears to be of little or no concern. Contrast that with Nazi Germany: no Jew or gypsy in their right mind sought entry into Germany during the period of Nazi rule.

Furthermore, there is evidence to suggest that the hostility towards Black people in Britain in the late 1950s, and towards all ethnic minorities in the 1970s, when the fascist National Front was becoming a real menace, was probably greater than that faced by Muslims in the 2000s. Peter Fryer points out:

---

* See, for example, the report by Human Rights Watch: 'India: Gujarat officials took part in anti-Muslim violence', 2002.

stimulated by fascist propaganda urging that black people be driven out of Britain, racist attacks were by 1958 a commonplace of black life in London ... By the end of August, brawls, disturbances, and racist attacks were a daily and nightly feature of life in north Kensington. A Jamaican was shot in the leg. Petrol bombs were thrown into black people's homes, including the homes of pregnant women. Such attacks were often preceded by a threatening letter or a shouted warning ... Crowds hundreds strong shouted abuse at black people' (Fryer, 1984, pp. 378–379).

Right through the 1970s, Britain's black communities had been under attack from fascists and police. Between 1976 and 1981, 31 black people in Britain had been murdered by racists (*ibid.*, p. 395).

But the increase in suspicion, discrimination, and the temporary, sporadic, surge in violence and aggression towards Muslims post 9/11 has to be seen in context, given that there is no evidence of prior systematic antipathy towards Muslims such that it is appreciably greater than for other ethnic minority groups. Part of the explanation, therefore, of the increased scrutiny of Muslims is that actual and planned terrorist attacks since 9/11 have almost solely been the work of Islamists. Had such attacks been conducted by those of another religious-ethnic minority say, for example, by Sikhs, then we would expect Sikhs, rather than Muslims, to be more the object of suspicion and discrimination; and doubtless Sikh organisations and apologists would have labelled this as 'Sikhophobia'.

What we have, in fact, is a political phenomenon with well-known antecedents rather than one based on any imputed 'phobia'. A truly egregious example of the repression of a minority group, in the aftermath of a political crisis, is that of the Japanese-American population after the Japanese attacks on Pearl Harbour in December 1941. Jeffrey Hummel (1986) has described the nature and extent of this:

> Within seventy-two hours of the attack, the FBI had 3,846 Japanese, German, and Italian immigrants in custody. A grand total of sixteen

thousand were seized throughout the war and about four thousand of them were held for the duration ... The 'enemy' aliens who were parched [sic] or who remained at large suffered numerous other infringements of their liberty. The national government forced more than ten thousand to leave their homes near defense installations, and it imposed rigid curfews upon others. They all needed permission to travel or move and could not possess firearms or short-wave radios ... Many people were more than anxious to accept columnist Walter Lippmann's strained explanation for the complete absence of any act of sabotage by Japanese-Americans. According to Lippmann, this merely indicated that they were waiting with Oriental patience for the propitious moment to commit some massive coordinated atrocity ... The Army therefore forbade any more voluntary evacuation. Instead, it forcibly collected at race tracks, fairgrounds, and other makeshift assembly points all persons of Japanese ancestry residing not only within the original restricted zone but anywhere within California, Washington, Oregon, southern Arizona, and Alaska. Evacuees could only take clothing, bedding and utensils ... After they left, their leases expired and their farms were generally confiscated. Japanese-Americans suffered an estimated $350 million loss in property and income ...

The War Relocation Agency (WRA) ... erected ten semi-permanent relocation centers in inhospitable regions of seven western states. By September, the army had turned over 110,000 Japanese-Americans to these camps. Nearly two-thirds ... were native-born American citizens. Anyone with simply one Japanese great grandparent qualified for internment ... The relocation centers were, as F. D. R. [President Roosevelt] admitted in a slip of the tongue, 'concentration camps' ringed with barbed wire and armed guards ...

This level of repression was altogether of a different scale compared to that of Muslims in the USA post 9/11, but was not designated as '*Japano*phobia'. Indeed, the treatment of Chinese-Americans has been no better as has recently been highlighted by Paul Fong, a member of

California's state assembly, who has asked the federal government to apologise formally for mistreatment of the Chinese in the manner of apologies given by seven US states to Blacks for slavery. The demand is based on the fact that Chinese-Americans 'were subject to special taxation, forced out of towns and denied the rights to own property, marry whites, or attend public schools. They were also the targets of the first law limiting immigration based on race or nationality, the Chinese Exclusion Act' (*Independent*, 19 June 2009). Again, however, there is no claim to this being a manifestation of '*Chino*phobia'.

There certainly was (and to some extent remains) systematic harassment and discrimination of Muslims (especially of Arabs) in the immediate aftermath of 9/11 (note that the Guantanamo Bay concentration camp was for non-US 'enemy combatants' mostly snatched in Afghanistan) but this cannot be described as 'Arab-phobia' let alone Islamophobia. There were relatively few physical attacks, including fatalities. Indeed, in the immediate aftermath of September 11, when hostility towards Muslims was perhaps at its greatest, there was just one reported murder of a person in either the UK or US who was thought to be a Muslim: this was, in fact, a Sikh man, a petrol station owner in Arizona, Balbir Singh Sodhi, who was shot dead on 15 September, because he wore a turban in the manner of Osama Bin Laden.

In Britain, during the IRA's bombing campaign of the 1970s, there was intense suspicion and harassment of Irish people, especially those from an Irish Catholic background, including the wrongful arrest and imprisonment of innocent Irish people in England (such as 'The Birmingham Six' and 'Guildford Four'). Mary Hickman and Bronwen Walter's research for the Commission for Racial Equality on anti-Irish discrimination provides numerous insightful findings. They make the following stark observations:

> Anti-Irish hostility was dramatically increased by IRA bombings in Britain ... the main changes were:

Intensification of pre-existing stereotypes portraying all Irish people, from North and South, as violent, mindless terrorists.

Easier justification of anti-Irish discrimination and racism. It now appeared self-evident that the Irish should be treated with dislike and contempt (Hickman and Walter, 1997, pp. 203–204).

Following the IRA bombing in 1974 of a Birmingham pub, when twenty-one people were killed (including nine Irish), there was intense hostility towards the Irish in that city, which had a large Irish population. The authors summarise this as 'the British reaction was an outpouring of hatred against Irish people as a whole, which ranged from physical attack to shunning …' and provide testimonies from Irish people of the backlash that ensued in workplaces, neighbourhoods, and in public areas such as shops and pubs. Three examples are provided below to give a flavour of the reality that confronted the Irish in Birmingham. The first is from a man from Sparkbrook in East Birmingham:

> There was a lot of hostility. I worked in Typhoo then. The management and unions met to discuss it. We [the Irish] were told to keep our heads down and not get excited.

The second is from a woman who lived in Erdington, in North Birmingham:

> I was working at Rover and the Director rang to enquire if I was being harassed, that I should be allowed to go home … The Rover workers in the factories marched out to campaign to send the Irish back home.

The third is from a woman in Sparkbrook:

> This was a terrible time. All the Irish community was in shock and people reacted to them. I took my children to school and an English

woman gave us verbal abuse. She said 'Why don't you fucking go back?' (Hickman and Walter, 1997, pp. 204–206).

Now imagine replacing 'Irish' with 'Muslim' in the above examples – for many, this would be demonstrable evidence of unbridled Islamophobia. Yet, throughout the 1970s and 1980s, terms such as 'Irish-phobia' or 'Catholophobia' were never deployed to explain state repression of, and hostility towards, the Irish, not even by the Catholic Church and Irish and Catholic civil organisations, or indeed by anti-racist campaigning groups.

Without extensive, systematic, comparative research, it is not possible to reach definite conclusions regarding anti-Irish discrimination in the 1970s as compared to anti-Muslim discrimination in the 2000s, but from the evidence available, we could conjecture that the former was probably worse. Notwithstanding the increase in suspicion and discrimination, there has not been any systematic targeting of Muslims by state institutions in the manner of the Irish in the 1970s and this perhaps helps to explain why there have, hitherto, been no cases of miscarriages of justice similar to that of 'The Birmingham Six'. Moreover, the only person so far killed by the police in Britain in an anti-terror operation was that of a non-Muslim Brazilian, Jean Charles de Menezes, who was shot dead in a London underground station in July 2005.

* * *

Evidence against Islamophobia
Nonetheless, many Muslims and all Islamist organisations continue to assert that there is manifest Islamophobia,* of which the war on terror is the clearest expression. But such reasoning overlooks some uncomfortable realities of Western relations with the 'Islamic' world.

---

* See, for example, the responses by Inayat Bungawala of the Muslim Council of Britain and Abdul Wahid of Hizb-ut-Tahrir in response to Kenan Malik's article 'The Islamophobia Myth' in *Prospect Magazine* in March 2005. Malik provides an excellent, concise, summary of the weakness of the arguments for Islamophobia in Britain.

Perhaps the most striking is the close relationship between many Western states, especially the UK and US, and the Saudi regime. Saudi Arabia has the most sacred sites of Islam and any instance of Islamophobia should surely reveal some animosity towards this fundamentalist Islamic state. But protests by Western governments against the brutality and oppressiveness of this barbaric society are conspicuous by their absence. On the contrary, the regime is treated with great respect, and is viewed as a strong ally, as was amply demonstrated in the autumn of 2007 when the Saudi monarch was granted a state visit by the British government, including a royal welcome by the Queen. This was at a time when evidence had been accumulating of Saudi money being used to fund a form of Jihadist 'Wahhabi' fundamentalist Islam that was fuelling Islamist terrorism (Ruthven, 2007).* A similar 'Saudiphilia' prevails in the US: for example, Craig Unger (2007) has demonstrated the extraordinarily close relationship between the House of Saud and the Bush family. Though George W. Bush, a devout Christian, did refer to his war on terror as a 'crusade', we cannot infer from this any systematic hostility to Islam and Muslims. Caught out by the carelessness of this remark, doubtless provided for him by one of his speechwriters, he subsequently ceased using it. That he did not have any great animosity towards Muslims *per* se was made clear in his highly symbolic and well-publicised visit to the Grand Mosque in Washington D.C. after 9/11, which was a call for tolerance and the avoidance of scapegoating of Muslims.

Other examples abound, the most important of which involve the provision of extensive military and intelligence support to, and actions ostensibly in defence of, Muslim countries, a subject upon which purveyors of Islamophobia tend to keep silent. Three examples will suffice. The first is that of the US arming, training, and funding the Islamic fundamentalists of the Afghan Mujahidin in the 1980s in their fight against the Soviet invasion. This included nurturing one Osama Bin Laden (see Cooley, 2000). After the removal of the

---

* A Channel 4 documentary 'Undercover Mosque', broadcast in January 2007, provided much evidence of Saudi-funded Jihadist literature permeating mosques in Britain.

Soviets and civil war, the US did not offer any cogent criticisms of the coming to power of the Taliban – the creation largely of Pakistan, another strong ally of the US, which proclaims itself as an avowedly 'Islamic Republic' (see Rashid, 2000).

The second example is that of the US-led coalition's war against Iraq in 1991 to 'liberate' Kuwait, an Arab Muslim country, with the help of practically all the Gulf states. The third is that of the US and its NATO allies, in the spring of 1999 (just two and half years before 9/11), launching a war against Serbia (which Muslim organisations overwhelmingly supported)* to 'liberate' Kosovo – a predominantly Muslim province, from the yoke of 'Christian' Serbia. The ex-Serb President Milosevic was later put on trial in the International Criminal Court in The Hague for 'crimes against humanity' (specifically, against Kosovar Muslims). Moreover, it was Western countries that subsequently pushed for Kosovo's independence – against unrelenting opposition not only from the Serbs, but also from the Russians. Curiously, however, very few Arab/Muslim countries have recognised the independence of Kosovo.

There are other examples of very warm relationships between the US and Islamic countries. Egypt is the second largest recipient of US aid (after Israel) and the US has strongly supported Turkey's application to join the EU. Though Turkey is nominally a secular state, its population is almost entirely Muslim. Other examples can also be provided, but this seems sufficient evidence to rebut the charge of a 'war on Islam'. It is not for nothing that leaders of Muslim countries rarely talk about 'Islamophobia'. Moreover, it is a rarely stated fact (again which purveyors of Islamophobia keep silent about) that Muslims, say from the Indian sub-continent or East Asia, are likely to experience much harsher treatment and discrimination at the hands of 'fellow Muslims' in Arab (especially Gulf) countries than they are in the West (see for example, Amnesty International,

---

* As Anthony McRoy notes: 'no British Muslim group objected to Britain and America bombing Serbia during the Kosova crisis in 1999 without UN authorisation; the *Muslim News* supported this action, describing it as "a welcome move"' (McRoy, 2006, p. 20).

2000; Jureidini, 2005). In a similar vein, the treatment of Muslims in the Darfur region of Sudan by the Muslim Sudanese government and its militia allies can be deemed genocidal, but those incensed by 'Islamophobia' keep studiously silent on this subject, suggesting that, for them, any ill-treatment of Muslims is the sole prerogative of Western or other non-Muslim countries.

The ineluctable truth, however, is that the US and its Western allies have no real interest in the religion of a country: what is key are domestic political considerations, and economic and geo-political strategic interests. They have long supported the most reactionary, dictatorial regimes in the Muslim world, such as Saudi Arabia, for precisely these reasons. But if any ally should fall out of line, as with Saddam Hussein's Iraq, then it is likely to incur the full wrath of the US, and risk being overthrown by a military invasion. By the same token, however, previous enemies who change course, recant, and toe the US line (the Gadaffi regime in Libya is a recent case in point) can be brought back into the fold and have their status altered from 'enemy of freedom', 'evil regime', or 'terrorist' to 'ally'. At most, therefore, we could say that there has certainly been a degree of Anti-Arab hostility post 9/11, a corollary of which has been anti-Muslim sentiment. But this does not alter that fact that there is simply no material basis to support evidence of an 'Islamophobic' foreign policy by Western states, including the US-led war on terror.

Turning now to the evidence of Islamophobia in regard to *domestic* policy, this should show a disproportionately high level of harassment of Muslims by state authorities; in Britain this should be particularly so after the 7 July 2005 suicide bombings in London by young British Islamists. Accordingly, we need to examine the statistics in the ensuing period. Table 5.1 provides data on the criminal justice process broken down into ethnic groups for England and Wales in 2005/6.

Table 5.1: Proportion (%) of ethnic groups at different stages of the criminal justice process, England and Wales, 2005/6

Ethnicity	White	Black	Asian	Other	Unknown
General population (aged ten and over) @ 2001 Census	91.3	2.8	4.7	1.2	0.0
Stop and searches (1)	72.2	15.4	7.9	1.6	2.9
Arrests (2)	83.8	9.1	5.1	1.3	0.6
Cautions (2)	83.5	6.3	4.5	1.4	4.4
Youth offences (4)	87.6	6.0	3.2	0.3	2.8
Tried at Crown Court (3)	76.3	12.6	7.3	3.9	*
Prison population (4) (5)	75.5	15.6	6.8	1.3	0.9

Notes:
(1) Stop and searches recorded by the police under section 1 of the Police and Criminal Evidence Act 1984 and other legislation.
(2) Notifiable offences.
(3) Information on ethnicity is missing in 19% of cases; therefore, percentages are based on known ethnicity.
(4) To make the data in this row consistent with the rest of the table the proportion for Mixed has been excluded because this information is not available for stop and searches, arrests, cautions and Crown Court.
(5) Sentenced.
Source: Ministry of Justice (2007).

Unfortunately, as the data are not disaggregated in terms of religious identity, we do not have accurate figures for Muslims. However, given that a significant majority of Muslims in Britain are Asian, we can use the data for Asians as a reasonable surrogate. For evidence of Islamophobia, we should therefore expect to find a disproportionately high incidence of Asians in the criminal justice process. In regard to 'stop and search' by the police, whilst Asians are *twice* as likely as Whites to be stopped and searched, Blacks are an astonishing *seven* times more likely than Whites. The equivalent figures for *arrests* are 3.5 for Blacks and 1.2 for Asians; for *cautions*: 2.5 for Blacks; 1.1 for Asians, and the rate of *imprisonment*: 6 for Blacks and 1.9 for Asians.

In regard to stop and searches under the Terrorism Act of 2000, there was a very high increase in 2005/6 compared to the previous year: searches of Whites increased by 24 percent, of Blacks by 51 per cent, and of Asians by 84 per cent. The Ministry of Justice report (2007) acknowledges that such large increases are explained, in part, by the 7 July 2005 bombings. We can, with confidence, assume that in this category, a high percentage of searches of Asians would have been conducted in areas with a high Muslim population; a consequence of the fact that the 7/7 bombers were Muslim. Despite this sharp increase, however, the likelihood of Blacks and Asians being searched under the Terrorism Act was, remarkably, the same for both at 4.3 times that of Whites (Ministry of Justice, 2007, p. 24; table 4.6, p. 34).

Finally, we examine deaths stemming from police contact – again evidence of Islamophobia should show a high proportion of Asians in this category. Table 5.2 provides the data from 2001/2 (the post 9/11 period) to 2007/8.

Table 5.2: Deaths during or following contact with the police for England and Wales by Ethnic Origin, 2001/2 to 2007/8

Ethnic Origin	2001–2	2002–3	2003–4	2004–5	2005–6	2006–7	2007–8
White	63	82	90	96	101	65	61
Asian	2	4	2	3	5	7	1
Black	4	17	7	4	7	9	7
Other	1	1	1	3	5	1	6
Total	70	104	100	106	118	82	75

Note: General population (aged ten and over) @ 2001 Census: White (91.3%), Asian (4.7%), Black (2.8%), Other (1.2%)
Cause of deaths: road traffic fatalities, fatal shootings, deaths in or after custody, deaths during or after other contact
Source: IPCC for 2001/2–2003/4; Ministry of Justice for 2004/5–2007/8

For Asian deaths, only in one year (2006–7) is the figure proportionally higher than the population size – the 7 deaths for that year is 8.5 per cent of the total (contrasting with the Asian population of 4.7 per cent). In all other years, deaths of Asians are proportionately lower. We may have expected an upsurge in police-related fatalities in the immediate aftermath of 9/11 (2001) and 7/7 (2005) but this was not the case. In stark contrast are the deaths of Blacks – the absolute numbers are greater than Asian deaths for every year; accordingly, the proportion of Black deaths is far in excess of the population size (from 4 to 16 per cent whereas the population is 2.8 per cent).

From these data of state discretionary and repressive powers there is no demonstrable evidence of disproportionate harassment of Asians and, by implication, of Muslims. It is certainly true that, in truly egregious cases such as the arrests of Muslim men at Forest Gate in East London during a terror raid by the police in June 2006 (Casciani, 2006), the 'Ricin terror plot', and the arrests of a dozen Pakistani nationals in north-west England in April 2009 to thwart a 'terror attack', there appeared to be systematic targeting of Muslims. But in these, and other cases, there was no evidence whatsoever of any malfeasance. These outrages of individual liberty have been a natural consequence of the criminal 'war on terror', and served only to alienate Muslims and all opposed to this Bush-led imbecility. But examples such as these cannot, nevertheless, be taken as the norm, as demonstrated by the data provided. Indeed, what is truly striking about the data related to the criminal justice process is the consistently and proportionally very high rates for all indicators *for Blacks*: excepting the searches under the Terrorism Act in 2005/6, they are proportionally far higher than for Asians. It therefore seems that rather than Islamophobia, there is *prima facie* evidence of the systematic targeting and harassment by the police of Blacks. This could be referred to as an indicator of 'Blackophobia' by the state yet, just as with 'Irish-phobia' and 'Catholophobia', this epithet is never used.

Let us now turn to the likelihood of victims of crime to see if Asians/Muslims are inordinately being targeted. The Ministry of Justice Report (MOJ, 2007) summarises the findings as follows:

> The 2005/6 BCS [British Crime Survey] showed that people from Mixed and Asian ethnic backgrounds (31% and 26% respectively) had a higher risk of becoming a victim of crime than people from White (23%), Black (22%) or Chinese and Other (21%) ethnic backgrounds. There were no statistically significant changes in the risk of victimisation for any of the ethnic groups since 2004/5 ... the differences between the Mixed and other ethnic groups reflect differences in the socio-demographic profiles of the groups rather than ethnicity. In particular, the proportion of young people in the Mixed ethnic group is large in comparison to other ethnic groups and young people are at a higher risk of victimisation ...

This suggests that, in regard to being victims of crime, though the rate for Asians is higher than that for Whites and Blacks, it is still not the highest – that is for those of Mixed ethnicity. Therefore, we cannot conclude from the data that Asians/Muslims are at the receiving end of exceptionally high rates of crime. The MOJ report also provides data on *racially motivated crime*:

> The 2005/6 BCS found that the risk of becoming a victim of a racially motivated crime was low across all ethnic groups. Less than 1% of the White population had been victims of racially motivated crimes compared with 2% of people from Asian, Black and Chinese and Other ethnic backgrounds, and 1% among people from Mixed ethnic backgrounds. The risk of becoming a victim of a racially motivated crime showed no change for any ethnic group between 2004/5 and 2005/6.

Thus, the probability of a Black or Asian person being the victim of a racially motivated crime is about the same and we deduce from this that the rate for Muslims will not be inordinately higher than this though, in the absence of data by religious categories, we cannot be absolutely certain about this.

In regard to homicides, over 2,300 murders were recorded by the police in the years 2003/4 to 2005/6. The ethnic breakdown was 74% White; 10% Black, 7% Asian, and 4% Other (MOJ, 2007). Thus, the likelihood of a Black person being murdered is nearly five times that of a White person; that of an Asian is twice that of a White person. These are broadly in line with other indicators we have examined, confirming once more the inordinately high rate at which Blacks suffer from being victims of crime in comparison with other members of society.

In 2005 a Black teenager by the name of Anthony Walker was murdered in an unprovoked attacked by two young Whites in his home town in Merseyside. There was an understandable outcry as this was a clear case of a racially motivated murder – but again there was no assertion by any organisation or person of this being a case of 'Blackophobia' in Britain. If, however, the murdered teenager had been a Muslim, there would doubtless have been an orchestrated trumpeting of the crime being attributable to rampant Islamophobia. However, as the BBC reporter Jon Williams pointed out: '… murder in the UK is still relatively rare – racist murders more so. Anthony Walker was the exception rather than the rule' (Williams, 2005). Though this is true, it is, nonetheless, important to stress that murders of Muslims are even more exceptional than that of Blacks.

A Gallup poll on British Muslims in 2007 also provided evidence that challenges the doctrine of Islamophobia. The findings of the poll showed that 'Fifty-seven per cent of the Muslims polled said *they identified strongly* with their country, compared with 48% of the general public. Muslims were also more likely to *express confidence in the police* (78% to 69%), national government (64% to 36%), the justice system (67% to 55%) and elections (73% to 60%). Nearly three-quarters of the Muslims said they felt loyal to the UK' (BBC News, 2007). Plainly, even if we allow for the fact that this poll may not be an accurate portrayal of views,* these findings do not portray a group that considers itself under siege and subject to rampant discrimination.

Despite the weak evidence, it was the perception of a rising tide of Islamophobia in Britain that led to pressure for legislation to criminalise 'religious hatred' (which would include Islamophobia) and for Muslims to be accorded the same protection as Jews and Muslims. But, as Polly Toynbee pointed out, if the government was 'advocating equality between all religions, they would repeal the blasphemy laws that only cover Christians (which were indeed subsequently repealed), remove the Bishops from the Lords and abolish religious state schools: 30% of state schools are religious, almost all Christian controlled' (Toynbee, 2005). In general, critics argued that this legislation was akin to extending, by stealth, the blasphemy law and as such was a dangerous curtailing of the right of freedom of expression. However, the Labour government rejected this allegation and, clearly bowing to the will of the religious (especially Islamist) lobby and worried about the haemorrhaging of votes in the midst of the wars in Afghanistan and Iraq, in constituencies with a large Muslim population,† proceeded to draft and pass the Racial and Religious Hatred Act 2006, which came into force on 1 October 2007. It argued that the tough

---

* This is because, in the post-9/11 climate, many Muslims may feel the need to display greater loyalty to the UK than they truly feel. Though such poll findings can cast doubt on systematic 'Islamophobia', they will not necessarily refute the arguments for high levels of psychic detachment which we made in the previous chapter.

† This was made clear, for example, in a letter sent out (with an Urdu translation) by Steve McCabe, Labour MP for Hall Green, Birmingham on 14 March 2005, to those perceived to be Muslim constituents. This stated that 'the government has decided to make changes to the law to ensure that Muslim people have the same protection as other groups like Jews and Sikhs'. The letter states that the intended law has the support of the [avowedly Islamist organisations] the Muslim Council of Britain and the Islamic Human Right Commission. It further added that '[t]his government is determined to treat all people fairly and to respect all law abiding British people whatever their religious beliefs [and] that is why we support Muslim schools ...' This naked appeal to 'Muslim voters' is hardly the sentiment of an 'Islamophobic' politician.

conditions of the Act, where an offence must be deemed 'threatening' (and not merely 'abusive' or 'insulting'), and with the 'intention' of stirring up religious hatred, protected freedom of expression. This much is true as proponents of the law wished to outlaw all abusive remarks and insults aimed at religions – but as comics such as Rowan Atkinson forcefully pointed out, this would be a serious threat to freedom of expression in general and artistic freedom in particular; and perhaps their intervention did influence the legislators (Rojas, 2006). Future data collated under this offence, and the testing of it in courts, will provide a valuable insight into whether this act is merely symbolic, put on the statute book with the principal aim of placating the religious/Islamist lobby, or whether it marks an important breach of freedom of expression in regard to religious beliefs and practices. What is surely unmistakable is that a government wishing to target and criminalise sections of the Muslim population would hardly have resorted to such legislation.*

Islamophobia as an offspring of multiculturalism

The use of the term Islamophobia came into the public terrain during the 1990s, in the aftermath of the furore surrounding the Rushdie/*Satanic Verses* affair. Muslims of a fundamentalist persuasion were convinced that it was only the prevalence of widespread Islamophobia in British society and the state that allowed the book to remain in print, and Rushdie to go unpunished. They were not at all convinced by arguments relating to freedom of expression. Precisely similar sentiments were again revealed during the controversy surrounding the publication of cartoons of the prophet Muhammad in a Danish newspaper in September 2005. Nonetheless, the decisive

---

* Another widely-publicised example is that of the government refusing entry to the right-wing Dutch politician, Geert Wilders, in February 2009 (BBC News, 12/2/2009). Wilders had made the controversial anti-Islamic film *Fitna* which is freely available to view on Youtube. The government argued that his presence would be a threat to public security – though no evidence was provided as proof. But it was clear that this did appease Muslim groups, and provided further proof against any official Islamophobia.

factor behind this appellation receiving a semi-official imprimatur was the publication, in 1997, of a report by The Runnymede Trust's 'Commission on British Muslims and Islamophobia' entitled *Islamophobia: a Challenge for Us All* (Conway, 1997). The *raison d'être* of the report flows from its definition of Islamophobia (p. 4):

'The term Islamophobia refers to an unfounded hostility towards Islam. It refers also to the practical consequences of such hostility in unfair discrimination against Muslim individuals and communities, and to the exclusion of Muslims from mainstream political and social affairs'.*

The reason why it is a 'phobia' is because of *unfounded* hostility – which approximates to the more conventional 'irrational fear'. But there can, of course, be a *rational* basis for a fear or a well-founded hostility, which the report does not allow for. Therefore, its thrust is that *any* hostility towards Islam and Muslims is deemed unfounded and, therefore, Islamophobic. It is this reasoning that makes the term so problematic and misplaced in grappling with the realities in their multitudinous forms. The hostile attitude of Islamists when confronting their critics betrays a desire for censorship which must be intolerable to advocates of freedom of expression.

The laudable concerns of the Runnymede Trust – notably, 'unfair discrimination', and 'physical violence and harassment' – should apply to *all*, regardless of religion. Moreover, there are laws which outlaw discrimination and violence, so legal recourse to such breaches of the law is available to all citizens. In regard to 'exclusion from mainstream political and social affairs', we have stressed how multiculturalism has accentuated segregation and psychic detachment and, therefore, been an important, if unwitting, contributor to such an exclusion. This suggests a wider agenda behind the report, which is evidenced in its philosophical and normative stance. That this is so is clearly revealed

---

* The report's following two sentences are important to note: 'The term is not, admittedly, ideal. Critics of it consider that its use panders to what they call political correctness, that it stifles legitimate criticism of Islam, and that it demonises and stigmatises anyone who wishes to engage in such criticism' (*loc. cit.*). This is absolutely correct and is in accordance with the views of the present author.

in regard to the summary of Chapter 7 (Making the nation: inclusive education for an inclusive society):

> ... we recommend that social inclusion and cultural pluralism should be included centrally in citizenship education, that formal policies and guidance be developed on meeting the pastoral, religious and cultural needs of Muslim pupils in mainstream schools, and that there should be state funding for Muslim schools' (*ibid*, p. 3).

All this is familiar: for 'cultural pluralism' read 'multiculturalism'. Accordingly, the cultural relativist reasoning behind the report is unmistakeable, so that we may think of the use of 'Islamophobia' as a defence shield to ward off criticisms of Islam and Muslims. Clearly, then, the thinking underpinning the purveyors of Islamophobia stems from the source of multiculturalism, and we can justly assert that Islamophobia is an offspring of multiculturalism.

The debilitating aspect of cultural relativism is the heightened sensitivity it arouses in religious-ethnic minorities, none more so than among Muslims. From Rushdie's *Satanic Verses* to the Danish cartoons, there has been an outcry on the part of large numbers of Muslims on the grounds that their faith and identity have been maligned. So every slight it seems – whether intentional or not – is tantamount to Islamophobic 'misrecognition' giving rise to egregious offence, harm, and a damaging of identity. A physical equivalent would be to conflate a pin prick to a lethal injection. This tactic serves well in warding off would-be critics.

With respect to US/UK-led foreign policy, it is curious why so many Western Muslims – especially young Muslims – have formed such a close emotional affinity, sense of solidarity and identity with fellow Muslims in other parts of the world and become radicalised by gross injustices inflicted by Western powers on Arab/Muslim countries and regions (to which the majority, born and brought up in the West, have probably never visited). Precisely why this is so is not entirely clear but any convincing explanation must encompass the strong alienation from mainstream society and attendant 'parallel' existence, compounded by a manifestation of the primacy of a religious identity. Moreover, the capacity for significant numbers of Muslims to be mobilised on strictly communal grounds has entrenched the power and influence of the religious traditionalists who have relentlessly utilised the 'Islamophobic ploy'.

Hence, the increasing adherence to their religion has led many (perhaps the vast majority) of British – indeed Western – Muslims to view their concerns via the prism of the Islamic faith and communal identity. These concerns can be categorised in terms of domestic and international issues. In regard to the former, they can be deemed largely reactionary, being based on a 'Maginot-like' defence of their religion that profoundly informs their traditions, customs, and culture. Thus, issues related to women's oppression (including veiling), gender segregation, the strict enforcement of the Muslim faith on children and the concomitant curtailing of an array of freedoms available in the mainstream society, ritual slaughter etc. are all deemed out of bounds, no-go areas for critics. The Rushdie Affair was the first and most important challenge to freedom of expression by British Muslims – and even though the authorities stood firm and did not ban the *Satanic Verses*, right-wing and deeply conservative forces within Muslim communities obtained much confidence from their campaign of censorship. One can argue that, since then, this aggressive strategy has proved to be extremely effective in silencing criticism or serious engagement with Islamic beliefs and practices. Indeed, it appears that Muslim organisations have looked with great envy at how Jewish and Pro-Israel organisations have relentlessly and, to astonishing effect, played the 'anti-semitic card' to silence any criticism of the state of Israel. A grouping such as the Muslim Public Affairs Committee (MPAC) has avowedly named, and to some extent modelled itself upon, the notorious and supremely powerful American Israel Public Affairs Committee (AIPAC). One can, therefore, certainly understand why Muslim organisations wish to adopt a similar approach and, even if they manage to achieve (as they appear to be doing) a small fraction of the success of the Israel lobby by playing the 'Islamophobia card', then they should undoubtedly consider this a resounding success. But it remains the case that this is a wilful distortion of the truth.

As we noted at the beginning of the chapter, one of the animating features of Muslim angst and sense of victimhood is the perennial plight of the Palestinians. Most Muslims support the cause of Palestinians; *ipso facto*, they oppose their oppressors, the state of Israel. Equally, Zionists strongly identify with, and support, Israel; *ipso facto*, they oppose those who criticise Israel or challenge its legitimacy. Accordingly, Muslims and Zionists, on this issue, are diametrically opposed. One unfortunate consequence of this has been that, hitherto, a substantial proportion (though by no means all) of critiques of Islam have emanated from Zionist sources. In the British press, for example, these include commentators such as David Aaronovitch, Nick Cohen, Howard Jacobson, and Melanie Phillips. In the USA, such critiques are at the heart of the work of an assortment of neocon 'think tanks' (a veritable industry) which are strongly pro-Israel.[*] In the virtual absence of liberal/left critiques of Islam[†], by default, opposition to the notion of Islamophobia is seen largely as the product of neocon Zionist commentators. This has facilitated the dismissal of those who dare to resort to critiques of Islam as 'neocon/Zionist Islamophobes', and helped to sow the idea of Islamophobia as a clear and present danger which should be vigorously challenged in the manner that racism is.

This attempt at conflating racism with Islamophobia has also proved effective. We argued in Chapter 1 that some adherents of multiculturalism often display a pervasive fear of being charged with racism by non-White ethnic minorities. Within this group, one

---

[*] Examples include American Enterprise Institute, Center for Security Policy, Hudson Institute, Project for the New American Century, and Washington Institute for Near East Policy

[†] A rare presence is Polly Toynbee of the *Guardian*. However, for her powerful and principled critiques of Islam Toynbee was designated one of the 'Islamophobes of the year' in 2004 by the Islamic Human Rights Commission.

can locate those who refrain from offering criticisms and critiques of Islam on the grounds that to do so would be Islamophobic, that is, it would represent (or be deemed to be) racism against Muslims. The purported legitimacy of this reasoning stems from the fact that though 'Muslim' is not a racial category, nonetheless, in the Western context, Muslims are overwhelmingly non-White, so that *any* criticism of such citizens can be associated with racist connotations. A second order defence – but far less satisfactory – for this conflation raises the status of identity to that of 'race' so that religious identity in particular assumes the same characteristic and importance as 'race' or ethnicity: accordingly, criticisms of this identity, its misrecognition, warrant the same censure as racism.

As already noted, these lines of reasoning have close parallels with the fear of being labelled 'anti-Semitic' in regard to a critical stance on Israel. Accordingly, just as there is, and has long been, considerable self-censorship in regard to criticising Israel or Zionism, so there has now come to pass similar self-censorship in regard to Islam and Muslims (although it is not necessarily of the same magnitude). It is indubitably the case that the charge of Islamophobia does not have the emotional, 'guilt-tripping' cogency of anti-Semitism; nevertheless, its invocation has proved extremely effective as a prophylactic given that anti-racists are deeply sensitive to the charge of racism. But the conflation of any hostility to Islam's beliefs, practices, and ethical code with Islamophobia, which is then further conflated with racism, is a sleight of hand that is rarely exposed and opposed.* This, for example, is precisely the assumption behind the following assertion by Modood (2007, p. 9): 'And also like its neighbours, Britain has to address an anti-Muslim cultural racism as Muslims become a

---

* At the Edinburgh TV Festival in August 2007, I attended a panel discussion 'Don't mention Islam'. Included on the panel were spokespersons from the Muslim Council of Britain and the Islamic Human Rights Commission. Both systematically conflated racism and Islamophobia, and invoked the discourse of anti-racism from the 1970s. However, my impression was that the bulk of the audience were not at all convinced by their appeal to anti-racism to block off criticisms of Islam – the reason for this of course being that they were not convinced by this conflation.

significant feature of its cities ...' We rejected the legitimacy of 'cultural racism' in Chapter 1 – indeed it is an oxymoron. Accordingly, a more accurate terminology is 'anti-Muslim prejudice' (which requires evidence, as well as an explanation as to why such a prejudice exists, if indeed it does) but this clearly lacks the same cogency as the invoking of the 'race card'. So what we have here is religious ideology being baldly and falsely equated with imputed racial characteristics.

A further difficulty for would-be critics of Islam – and a gift for the Islamists – is that the US-led 'war on terror', with the decimation of Afghanistan and Iraq is, as we have seen, considered by many sympathetic to the notion of Islamophobia to be in essence a 'war against Islam'. Again, this conflation is possible because of the imputed racist undertones of the war – an assault and invasion by White imperialist powers (let us leave aside the fact that about a third of the US army is comprised of Black and Hispanic soldiers) of the lands of non-White Muslims. Given this international dimension, which has led to an increase in the scrutiny and harassment of Muslims, the argument goes, indulging in criticisms of Muslims or Islam is, in effect, no matter how objective and valid, contributing to Islamophobia. A typical illustration of this reasoning is that of *Guardian* columnist Madeleine Bunting's interview with Ed Husain, author of *The Islamist*. She concludes her piece:

> One suspects the naivety which took him into [the Islamist organisation] Hizb-ut-Tahrir has blinded him as to how his story will be used to buttress positions hostile to many things he holds dear – his own faith and racial tolerance, for example. A glance at the blog response to a Husain piece in the *Telegraph* reveals how right-wing racism and anti-Islamic sentiment are feasting on his testimony (Bunting, 2007).

This is the naked advocacy of self-censorship – with the implicit assumption that right-wing racist arguments cannot be adequately and contemporaneously rebutted whilst maintaining the right to criticise

Muslim belief and practices. What Bunting forgets is that Islamic thinking is itself deeply conservative and right wing: indeed, in most respects, Western conservative thinking, in comparison, is decidedly liberal. Therefore, she can be hoist by her own petard: Bunting's reasoning provides right-wing Islamists with useful scaremongering arguments to call for a halt to critical inquiry or satirising of Islam, Muslims, and Islamic organisations.

In multicultural and multifaith thinking much emphasis is put on 'inter-cultural' and 'inter-faith' dialogue and understanding. The assumption is that it is the lack of knowledge of other cultures and faiths by Westerners that can give rise to disrespect and misrecognition. Cultural relativism, therefore, needs to be supplemented by greater respect and understanding of the beliefs and traditions of religious-ethnic minorities. This reasoning has been utilised by Islamists – an oft-repeated grievance of theirs is that non-Muslim Western critics do not know much about Islam, having only a fleeting and usually false impression. Invariably unaware of it, this is the utilisation of the fallacy of *argumentum ad ignorantium* (argument from ignorance).

There is certainly an element of truth in this but, excepting Christianity, this is also the case for other religions. However, the charge of ignorance is invariably exaggerated or asserted so as to deflect criticisms away, which is to say, it is used as a ploy so as to avoid entering into a debate on substantive issues. Moreover, we are certainly not likely to accept such a ploy in regard to other religions or bodies of knowledge, so it would not do to accept it in regard to Islam. For example, to reject criticisms of Hinduism on the grounds that it is an ancient religion with an enormous body of scriptural texts and historical development will not suffice as a deflective tactic for a critic who admittedly has only a rudimentary knowledge of the texts, has not studied, for example, the Vedas and Upanishads, but does know that it has its foundations in the caste system. For such a critic, this is sufficient knowledge to attack the whole edifice of Hinduism, and Hindu apologists cannot, therefore, utilise the charge of the fallacy of *argumentum ad ignorantium* to rebut such a criticism. Moreover, in this regard, they are themselves resorting to the 'argument from scripture fallacy', that is, only those who have studied the scriptures have the right to utilise them. This is a subset of the fallacy of *argumentum ad verecundiam* (argument from authority) thereby making this defence untenable.

However, the charge of ignorance of Islam and of Muslims is invariably overblown. Given that millions of Muslims have lived in the West for decades; that countless articles on Islam have been written in the press, magazines, books; and documentaries have been made for TV and radio (often serving up apologetics), we can assume that ordinary people will, at least, have a rudimentary understanding of some of the basic tenets and practices of the religion. It was on this premise that Paul Sniderman and Louk Hagendoorn (2007) conducted their research on the views of Dutch people in regard to Muslim residents in the Netherlands (who, in the main, originate from Morocco and Turkey). Their findings showed that over half the Dutch population thought that 'Western European and Muslim ways of life are irreconcilable'. More specifically, 'nine out of every ten agree that Muslim men in the Netherlands dominate their women ... Three out of every four Dutch agree that Muslims in the Netherlands raise their children in an authoritarian way' (Sniderman and Hagendoorn, 2007, p. 23). It seems clear that striking statistics such as these inspired the title of their book: *When Ways of Life Collide*.

The authors do not think these stark findings arise out of ignorance or Islamophobia on the part of the Dutch population, but rather that they are based on informed opinion gleaned from living in a country with a large Muslim population. As we shall see in the next chapter, opinion polls in France show a majority opposing the Islamic veil. The explanation of this is similar: that people do have some understanding of this Islamic attire and do not like it as it connotes women's oppression and subjugation under Islam. Moreover, widespread Muslim hostility to issues of freedom of expression regarding Islam (such as Rushdie's *Satanic Verses* or the Danish cartoonist's depiction of the prophet Muhammad), further provide explanation as to why ordinary Westerners are not enamoured by a religion that arouses such intense intolerant passions among the faithful. Given such views, what is striking is how relatively few substantive critiques there are of Islamic beliefs and practices; the charge of Islamophobia certainly serves well in hindering any such endeavour.

But, the point that needs to be stressed is that for socially-engaged people, often of a progressive bent, knowledge about Islam has long been available, enabling them to arrive at firm reasoned judgements. An important example is Mary Wollstonecraft, a pioneer for women's equality and emancipation. In two of her most influential works, Wollstonecraft explicitly made severe and fearful references about Islam (or what she termed 'Mahometism') as part of her attack on bigoted views towards women that were standard fare in Western Europe in the late eighteenth century. In *A Letter to the Right Honourable Edmund Burke*, written in 1790, in the passage 'what is truth?', she powerfully asserts:

> To argue from experience, it should seem as if the human mind, averse to thought, could only be opened by necessity; for when it can take opinions on trust, it gladly lets the spirit lie quiet in its gross tenement. Perhaps the most improving exercise of the mind, confining the argument to the enlargement of the understanding, is the restless enquiries that hover on the boundary, or stretch over the dark abyss of uncertainty. These lively conjectures are the breezes that preserve the still lake from stagnating. We should be aware of confining all moral excellence to one channel, however capacious; or, if we are so narrow-minded, we should not forget how much we owe to chance that our inheritance was not Mahometism; and that the iron hand of destiny, in the shape of deeply rooted authority, has not suspended the sword of destruction over our heads (Wollstonecraft, 1995 [1790], p. 19).

She provides similar sentiments in her most famous work, *A Vindication of the Rights of Woman*, written two years later:

> In a treatise, therefore, on female rights and manners, the works which have been particularly written for their improvement must not be overlooked; especially when it is asserted, in direct terms, that the minds of women are enfeebled by false refinement; that the books of instruction, written by men of genius, have had the same tendency as more frivolous productions; and that, in the true style of Mahometism, they are treated as a kind of subordinate beings, and not as part of the human species, when improveable [*sic*] reason is allowed to be the dignified distinction which raises men above brute creation, and puts a natural sceptre in a feeble hand …
> Thus Milton describes our frail mother, though when he tells us that women are formed for softness and sweet attractive grace, I cannot comprehend his meaning, unless, in the true Mahometism strain, he meant us to deprive us of souls, and insinuate that we were beings only designed by sweet attractive grace, and docile blind obedience, to gratify the senses of man when he can no longer soar on the wing of contemplation … (Wollstonecraft, 1995 [1792], pp. 74, 87).

These are very harsh sentiments indeed, which many a modern reader will doubtless find discomfiting, but they are redolent of the rational, emancipatory ideas and ideals of the Enlightenment that were raging in the context of the French revolution, ideas that were vital to future social progress of women in particular, and society at large. Clearly, Wollstonecraft uses Islam as an example of a value-system in antithesis to Enlightenment ideals – a *de facto* bogeyman. Hence her assertion that Islam confines women to a 'subordinate being'. But are these strident criticisms and fear-mongering that of an 'Orientalist', born out of wilful ignorance and prejudice? One avers not, as the knowledge of one of the world's major religions that had already been in existence for some 1,200 years at the time of her writing was, even then, readily available to the educated, inquiring mind. For Wollstonecraft (who also made several disparaging comments on the Harems of the Muslim Ottoman rulers), such evidence was plain and incontrovertible: she was terrified of the Islamic Sharia Law that confines women to second class status and, in the frankest of terms, was thankful that England/Britain had not perchance taken this path ('we owe to chance that our inheritance was not Mahometism').

Yet, if she had written such lines in the current context, imbued with multicultural, mutifaith, mindsets, she would roundly be denounced as an Islamophobe. One suspects that her rejoinder would have been equally uncompromising and principled – and backed up by hard evidence. That said, it is an odd, somewhat inexplicable, observation that modern feminists, often inspired by Wollstonecraft's path-braking works in the cause of women's rights, remain silent in regard to women's oppression under Islam. This is, of course, because of their fidelity to the precepts of multiculturalism and the attendant fear of the charge of being designated Islamophobic. The indubitable (and sad) fact is that if such sentiments were aired by a woman living in the Islamic world of today, she is very much likely to be *more than* just denounced as an Islamophobe; a powerful indicator of the very long road still ahead for campaigners for women's equality and rights in these countries.

We conclude this chapter by arguing that 'Islamophobia' can legitimately be considered an offspring of multiculturalism and its successor, multifaithism. It emanates directly from cultural/religious relativism and facilitates the collapsing of identity into one supremely dominant (that is, Islamic) category which is defended with great vigilance and diligence by those who strongly identify with the faith. Moreover, at the turn of the twenty-first century, any slight to Islam and Islamic identity is seen as an affront to the whole person and wider community, and invariably elicits a sharp rebuke from its moral guardians. In essence, this is the politics of perpetual victimhood and the accentuation of a victim identity that is immediately triggered because of any perceived misrecognition. In the absence, however, of demonstrable evidence of victimisation of Muslims in

Britain and other Western countries, perceived victimhood is often seen as feigned and unwarranted by large sections of mainstream society and also by other religious-ethnic minorities. This has led to a further consequence, that is, the increased alienation of non-Muslims from Muslims in general which, in turn, further entraps Muslim communities in an isolated, victimised mentality. We can concede that this was unintended but is nevertheless a decidedly negative outcome whose full implications have certainly not been carefully thought through by multiculturalists in general, and purveyors of Islamophobia in particular.

Chapter 5
Reflections on the Veiling of Muslim Women in Western societies

Background

In the autumn of 2006, Leader of the House of Commons Jack Straw made a statement that caused an enormous stir in Britain. He made public that when Muslim women wearing the full veil (*niqab*) visit his constituency surgery in Blackburn, north-west England (which has a large Muslim population), he asks them to remove the part that covers the face. His reason for this request was that face-to-face conversations were of 'greater value' and 'seeing peoples' faces is fundamental to relationships between people'. To this point about facilitating communication between people, Straw suggested that veiling accentuated 'separateness' and that he was concerned about 'parallel communities' in which people did not mix. With this, he brought into the public domain in Britain an issue (the veiling of Muslim women) that, hitherto, had largely been neglected by leading politicians. But the effect of Straw's initiation of this debate was by no means positive: he was denounced by the Lancashire Council of Mosques for his 'very insensitive and unwise statement'. The Council went on to claim that 'many of these women find Mr Straw's comments both offensive and disturbing', though none were named and one can reasonably assume that this organisation is dominated in its entirety by men. Straw countered that no one had refused his request and most 'seemed relieved' (Sturcke, 2006).

However, an obvious truth regarding Jack Straw went largely unmentioned at the time. Despite the importance of the arguments he was making, Straw suffered from an almost complete lack of credibility among the vast majority of Muslims in Britain, and indeed also among those who would consider themselves to be of a liberal/left persuasion. The reason for this was unambiguous – Straw had been Tony Blair's Foreign Secretary in the run-up to the US/UK invasion of Iraq in 2003, an invasion which he vehemently supported. But the war was vociferously and resolutely opposed by large sections of British society, including the Muslim community in its entirety. Right from the first day of the invasion, the ringing sentiment was that this was an illegal unjustified war, that war crimes were being committed and, accordingly, perpetrators of these crimes should be indicted in the International Criminal Court in the Hague – including Blair, Straw, and other senior ministers. Given this monumental backdrop, it was not at all surprising that the opinions and musings of Straw would most likely be held in contempt by large sections of British society. So, though Straw was the first senior UK politician to lift the veil, so to speak, over the implications of the veiling of Muslim women, it was profoundly unfortunate that this was done by someone suffering from such a credibility gap.[*] Moreover, he made his remarks during the height of the furore over 'Islamophobia', as elaborated upon in the previous chapter, further adding to the difficulty of discussing this issue in a reasoned manner. Whilst *ad hominem* attacks can never be a substitute for reasoned argument, in this case, nonetheless, they seemed entirely explicable.

Be that as it may, the veil debate ignited by Straw brought to prominence an issue with profound implications for multiculturalism. Moreover, the former Foreign Secretary's argument received wide support. One, somewhat unlikely, source was the Muslim Labour peer Lord Ahmed who forthrightly argued that the veil was a 'mark of separation, segregation and defiance against mainstream British culture'. But, as we shall see, he was mistaken in his belief

---

[*] Around the same time as Straw's remarks, the issue was given further prominence when a Muslim teaching assistant (Aishah Azmi) refused to remove her veil in class in a Dewsbury school when asked to do so because the pupils – mainly from an Asian, Muslim background – could not understand her. The local MP, Shahid Malik, supported this decision (Meikle, J., 2006). Subsequently, she was sacked by the school after an employment tribunal ruled against her claim of religious discrimination.

that this was a 'purely cultural' phenomenon, rather than a religious compulsion (Herbert, 2007). The issue of veiling is not just peculiar to Britain – indeed it has aroused much discussion and controversy in other European countries with significant Muslim populations, above all in France (as discussed below). There is certainly a sense that this is a religious/cultural manifestation too far. Why this is so is explored in this chapter.

The veiling of women is associated with all three Abrahamic faiths (Judaism, Christianity, and Islam), ostensibly denoting respect, modesty, and propriety. In the modern world, veiling by Christian and Jewish women is rare and not considered a religious duty in ordinary life by any of the major traditions of these two religions. But there are religious occasions when it is deemed appropriate for the woman to adopt some form of veil: for a Jewish bride at her wedding ceremony, for example, or for a Christian woman attending church, where some minor form of veiling (that is to say the covering of the head by a hat) is considered respectful. Extensive veiling (where, excepting the face, all of the body is covered) only applies to nuns pursuing a monastic life – and not necessarily to nuns who are not confined to a nunnery.

In Islam, by contrast, under most interpretations, the necessity for veiling by women is an obligation outside the home and even at home, with the exception of certain close family members, as provided in the Koranic sura below. It is this phenomenon, which has become highly prevalent not only in Muslim-majority countries but also among Muslim women in the West, that has aroused much controversy and debate.

The stricture concerning veiling of women in Islam is given in the Koran, in the following key verses (though there are others) in suras 24. 31 and 33. 59:

> And say to the believing women, that they cast down their eyes and guard their private parts, and reveal not their adornment save such as is outward; and let them cast their veils over their bosoms, and

> not reveal their adornment save to their husbands, or their fathers, or their husbands' fathers, or their sons, or their husbands' sons, or their brothers, or their brothers' sons, or their sisters' sons, or their women, or what their right hands own, or such men as attend them, not having any sexual desire, or children who have not yet attained knowledge of women's private parts ... (Koran, 24. 31).

> O Prophet, say to thy wives and daughters and the believing women, that they draw their veils close to them; so it is likelier they will be known, and not hurt ... (Koran, 33. 59).

Because there is some ambiguity in this (leaving alone inherent problems in translation), some Muslims do not accept that this implies veiling in the manner of the *burqa* or even *hijab*, and so many devout Muslim women do not veil themselves. Yet, the demand for modesty is very great, so much so that sura 33. 34, addressed to the wives of the prophet, proclaims: 'Remain in your houses; and display not your finery, as did the pagans of old'. A strict interpretation of this would be that, if this injunction applies to the prophet's wives, then so it must for *all* Muslim women. What is unambiguous is that by modesty is meant that women should remain covered and hidden to a very great extent. And among Muslims across the world, including in the West, there does indeed seem less and less ambiguity, given that increasing numbers of Muslim women are wearing some kind of veil. There are many reasons why this is so. We shall presently attempt to differentiate these, bearing in mind that, in Britain, there has been scant research on this issue.

Because the Koran does not require men to wear the veil, it is inherently discriminatory; nonetheless, its understanding of male biology is fundamental to the stricture on the veiling of women. This can be inferred in regard to the *justification* for the veiling of women which can easily be gleaned from this revealing passage in sura 24. 31 cited above: '... or such men as attend them, not having any sexual desire, or children who have not yet attained knowledge of women's private parts …' This clearly posits *sexual temptation* on the part of men – and its prevention – as the rationalisation for women's veiling; though one needs to be cognisant of the caveat that religious texts (with the Koran being no exception) do not necessarily provide rational, carefully reasoned explanations for their edicts.

Fatima Mernissi has cogently drawn the logical conclusion from this justification:

> The Muslim woman is endowed with a fatal attraction which erodes the male's will to resist her and reduces him to a passive acquiescent role. He has no choice; he can only give in to her attraction, whence her identification with *fitna*, chaos, and with the anti-divine and anti-social forces of the universe.
>
> If a woman could dismiss her husband at will, then she possessed substantial independence and self-determination. The Muslim social order was vehemently opposed to self-determination for women and declared that only men could repudiate their spouses. The fear of female self-determination is basic to the Muslim order and is closely linked to fear of *fitna*. If women are not constrained, then men are faced with an irresistible sexual attraction that inevitably leads to *fitna* and chaos by driving them to *zina*, illicit copulation. The prophet's own experience of the corrosive attraction of female sexuality underlies much of the Muslim attitude towards women and sexuality. Fear of succumbing to the temptation represented by women's sexual attraction – a fear experienced by the prophet himself – accounts for many of the defensive reactions to women by Muslim society' (Mernissi, 1985, pp. 41, 53–54).

Mounira Charrad locates the veil as a crucial element in ensuring male dominance and social control over woman:

> Part of a complex system of social control, veils and walls ensure a separation of the sexes. They also serve to keep women within their

kinship network. The continued responsibility of men toward their kinswomen, the value of ird,* the importance of women's behaviour for family honor, and the veiling of women constitute social norms that have converged toward facilitating the control of women by male members of the kin group (Charrad, 2001, p. 67).

In 1982, Judge Bertrand Richards at Ipswich Crown Court adjudged that a teenage hitchhiker, who had been raped by the driver, was 'guilty of a great deal of contributory negligence' by the very fact of her seeking and accepting a lift from the man in question (Boseley, 1989). Naturally, this caused great astonishment and anger. In a similar vein, another judge, James Pickles, has caused much consternation in regard to women and female attire. He makes the argument (which we presume informed his judgments) that 'if she [a bra-less woman] seems to want sex but does not [*sic*], a man who tries to grab it from her cannot be excused but she must share the blame' (Pickles, 1993, p. 138). We can argue that the notion of 'contributory negligence' is very much at the core of the Islamic injunction on veiling because it is not women's *intentionality* that is key but rather their very *appearance*: women *qua* women are deemed problematic. Indeed, this reasoning forms the thinking and assumption made – in a stark, vulgar, and misogynistic manner – by Sheikh Aldin al Hilali, the Grand Mufti of Sydney Mosque in Australia. In a sermon in September 2006 that gained international notoriety, he posited this crude analogy:

> if you take out uncovered meat and place it outside … and the cats come to eat it … whose fault is it, the cat's or the uncovered meat's? The uncovered meat is the problem. If she was in her room, in her home, in her hijab, no problem would have occurred (Tran, 2006).

Though Hilali recanted somewhat, in another setting – say in a mosque in a Muslim-majority country – he could reasonably have attempted to defend his analogy through recourse to Koranic verses

* *Ird* 'refers inclusively to the honor or moral purity of a group, its prestige in the community, and its strength' (Charrad, 2001, p. 63).

and the *hadith*. Let us further explore the implications of this because it provides a theory of not only characteristics of women, but also of men; and the relations between the two sexes. We can summarise it thus: women have to be veiled because men's sexual passions are considered out of control. The doctrine not only assumes that women are sexual temptresses but also that men are habitually tempted by unveiled women. The prescription for what may be considered 'nature's problem' or, more accurately, 'God's problem' is, in effect, to make women hidden by veiling (in Arabic, *hijab* means a 'curtain' between men and women), thus enabling men's fiery sexual passions to be brought under control. In regard to the type of veil that should be worn, the justification suggests that a blanket covering of the woman's face and body (in the manner of the *niqab*) would be most effective; in contrast, the partial *hijab* (covering only the head) by no means removes the contours of a woman's body and so is much less effective in acting as a constraint to men's sexual passions.

So what we have here is a model of human sexual behaviour that is not only misogynistic, but also misanthropic given that it assumes that men are, by their very nature, akin to beasts full of unbridled sexual fervour, unable to exercise self-control at the sight of a woman who is not covered by some kind of cloth. The stark, and by no means outlandish, inference from this is that they are considered rapists-in-waiting. Perverse assumptions can beget perverse prescriptions. A truly perverse, bogus assumption of male behaviour has given rise to the perverse, oppressive injunction of veiling for women as an aid to gender segregation. A moment's reflection shows how utterly absurd – and without any empirical validation – is this feral-like view of men.

All around the world, and for the vast majority of humanity's existence, women have been unveiled, yet the world has not descended into *fitna* as assumed by Islamic doctrine: men simply do not attack unveiled women as cats do uncovered meat. Indeed, on the relatively rare occasions when they do, these are rightly considered outrageous crimes and punishable as such.* Indeed, the paradoxical and perverse

---

* We cannot include mass rapes which sometimes occur during wars as being induced by unveiled women – these are overwhelmingly *political* acts.

aspect of Islamic veiling is that because it is deemed an unalloyed good by virtue of its conferring 'modesty' onto veiled women, *ipso facto,* unveiled women are deemed 'immodest' hence may (for some at least) be considered legitimate targets for sexual harassment. It must surely be the case that non-Muslims who become aware of this perverse justification for veiling will recoil from it and ought to reject it.

Lest one forget, the right of women to *unveil* has been an important social advance for women in many parts of the world. In the West, a high degree of bodily covering had long been the social norm: social acceptance of women publicly exposing parts of their bodies by the wearing of skirts and short-sleeved shirts appears only from the beginning of the twentieth century. This was an important part of the struggle for emancipation. A more recent phenomenon has been the right to breastfeed in public places. Yet, this eminently sensible and most natural of human acts, which medical opinion holds to be beneficial to babies, is a complete taboo under the strictures of veiling for Muslim women.

In other parts of the world, however, including in many tribal societies, such a right did not have to be fought for as women have always been unveiled, with their 'adornments' on display in full glory, that is to say, bare heads and bare breasts in public have long been considered entirely normal. Such is the case, for example, with women of the Aborigine community of Papunya that aroused controversy in 2004. They were stopped from dancing topless by the police in a public park in the city of Alice Springs, Australia. The women and the Aboriginal community responded by pointing out that dancing topless was part of Aboriginal culture dating back thousands of years (BBC, 2004). What is true is that such unveiled women were/are not attacked by men driven to a sexual frenzy in their presence.

Similarly, in recent decades, in countless beaches and swimming pools around the world (including in Australia and even in some resorts in Arab countries), women (like men) are practically naked. The Greek Orthodox Church, for example, long resented and protested against topless bathing on Greek beaches on the grounds of decency. But the sheer numbers of, in particular, north European women persisting in exercising their right to reveal their adornments, and their refusal to comply with religious edicts, eventually forced the church to concede defeat. The practice has now become entirely normal, so much so that hitherto socially conservative Greek women also, in increasing numbers, resort to topless bathing. No doubt, Muslim religious leaders would rail against the Greek Church's spinelessness in allowing such a morally corrupt practice to be conducted – and would fight to the death to prevent the same from occurring in 'their' countries. But, contrary to what they believe and would doubtless like to imagine, men are not driven to lustful frenzy by the sight of naked female adornments in such close proximity, and nor has society degenerated into *fitna*. Quite the contrary: the unpalatable truth for adherents of the Islamic strictures on veiling is surely that, where and whenever such 'corrupting practices' occur, it actually marks a significant step forward for the status of women in society. Islamic rules on veiling, therefore, represent a complete rejection of the emancipatory impulse in regard to women's rights.

The use of an extract from a vulgar sermon by an imam might be deemed uncharitable but, nonetheless, we should ask what guidelines an imam should give to his flock in regard to veiling. A charitable – liberal – approach might be to take a neutral position, on the grounds of textual ambiguity. However, this would be problematic for it collides with the *literal* approach, with little scope for ambiguity that tends to be *de rigueur* for imams, who are the defenders and purveyors of the faith. Just as with so many theological issues in Islam, the literalists voice their views with crystal clarity and maintain a fortress-like stance over their detractors. Indeed, this is the problem that avowed Muslim 'reformers' in the West such as Tariq Ramadan and Ziauddin Sardar encounter: their attempts to provide alternate, less illiberal, interpretations of Islamic doctrine that are more amenable to modern, largely secular societies invariably clash with the immutable, timeless interpretations of the 'true believers'. At least, outside the Muslim world, their case can, with reasonable freedom, be aired in public, including in the mass media. In contrast, reformers in the Islamic world – especially in countries where the legal code is modelled on the Sharia – are not suffered so gladly; moreover, they are invariably routed by the fundamentalist orthodoxy for whom the Sharia provides a clear distinction between what is *halal* and *haram*.* Consequently, for the orthodoxy, attempts to reform the Sharia would be deemed *haram* and automatically dismissed. It is for this reason that Muslim reformers store great hope in liberal, secular, Western Europe as the fount for an Islamic Reformation (see, for example, Ramadan, 2005).

As we have noted, what is not in doubt is that the tide of global Islamic opinion regarding the veil has been flowing against the notion of ambiguity. Accordingly, veiling is increasingly considered compulsory for girls and women – and any 'debate', if we can deem it to be so, is over the kind of veil (full or partial) that should be worn. Outside the Muslim world – particularly, but not only, in the secular West – unflinching Islamic doctrines and practices come into much sharper collision with ideas, mores, attitudes, and laws that have, over centuries, pushed back the boundaries of religion. Laws have long been passed without recourse to religious texts or bodies (nonetheless, exemptions to the law – or more accurately, privileges as we argued in Chapter 1 – are frequently provided on the grounds of freedom of religious expression). Not surprisingly, therefore, in the secular West, the terrain for the 'Maginot Islamists' is much more hostile. The response to this 'misrecognition' (which they do not encounter in Muslim majority countries) is frequently met with accusations of Islamophobia, intimidation, and threats to the point of actual acts of violence.

Be that as it may, arguments raised *against* veiling by 'moderate' or 'reforming' Muslims have been, to all intents and purposes, nil. This accords with their general weakness vis-à-vis their fundamentalist brethren. The situation of moderates re the Islamic faith was

---

* What is permitted and prohibited under Islamic law.

starkly expressed by Sardar (2006) in his assertion that 'all Muslims are fundamentalists' given that for them the Koran is the literal word of God – a remarkably honest position from someone who has gained considerable media coverage for his reforming views.* When such a concession – one might say capitulation – is made, the distinction becomes that of 'moderate fundamentalist' and 'uncompromising fundamentalist'; and where the two are in conflict, the latter will invariably trump the former by pointing to the scriptures which all Muslims have to accept as the 'literal word of God'.

Why the shift to veiling in the West?
A woman's right to choose?
Up until quite recently, the veiling of women in the UK went largely without serious comment, let alone critique. We can postulate that this is partly because the practice overwhelmingly occurs in close-knit Muslim communities and so is, to some extent, 'hidden' from the rest of society; but also because there has been – and remains – a profound reluctance on the part of mainstream society (including what remains of the 'women's liberation movement') to comment critically upon religious-ethnic minority communities. Consequently, Muslim women who wear the veil and the men who strongly advocate it have not had to provide careful explanation or defence of the practice – save that it is obligatory in Islam, hence is beyond reproach. This is, of course, entirely consistent with multiculturalism and multifaithism.

However, even prior to Jack Straw's comments, one could gauge murmurs surrounding the practice – albeit subtle and non-interventionist. This led some politically active veil-wearing Muslim women to provide a defence beyond the simple 'right to religious expression'. One such – perhaps the main – defence appeals to the right to 'freedom of choice', viz. that Muslim women have an absolute right to choose to wear the veil, full or partial. The irony can surely not be lost on erstwhile feminists given that this was, of course, the clarion call of

* Ziauddin Sardar's presentation at conference on 'Fundamentalisms', University of Brighton, May 2006.

the pro-choice campaign for abortion rights and a fundamental plank of the women's liberation movement (see, for example, Rowbotham, 1973, chs. 14 and 22). In regard to clothing, the right of freedom of dress has been granted for only the past one hundred or so years – in the Victorian age, for example, women were forbidden to expose their legs. However, we cannot think of the veil as a fashion choice or just a form of attire; nor is it, as in the case of the *hijab*, a simple piece of cloth covering the head. It is steeped in religious obligation and symbolism, which is readily acknowledged by women who wear it. Therefore, appealing to the 'right to choose' defence is inappropriate and indeed can be construed as doubly perverse – not only is it an abuse of a profoundly emancipatory political demand (the right to abortion) for oppressive purposes, it is being done so under the edict of a faith in which there can *not* be any freedom of choice; that is to say, Islam disallows a buffet type 'pick and mix' approach, and devout Muslims understand this very well.

Given this doctrinal reality, the freedom of choice argument appears to be a clever ruse to deflect criticism away from the practice of veiling. In effect, proponents of veiling are saying that in a society where freedom of religious expression is enshrined in the law, the constitution, and various rules, regulations, and charters, the right to veil should be protected and guaranteed. *Prima facie*, this is a powerful argument and it appears that many are swayed by it: indeed it is precisely the position of Shami Chakrabarti, Director of Liberty, one of Britain's foremost guardians of civil liberties.[*] Contrast this with what we examined in the previous chapter, viz. that robust criticisms of Muslim beliefs and practices are deemed to be Islamophobic. A variant on this theme is the argument that the right of veiling is simply analogous to the freedom to don some forms of 'Western' attire, such as of miniskirts[†] (Al-Hibri, 1999, p. 44). But this argument is so crass that it does not at all deserve to be taken seriously for

---

[*] Chakrabarti spoke at the European Social Forum in London on 16 October 2004 on a panel entitled 'Hijab: a woman's right to choose'.
[†] Like so many phenomena that are qualified with the epithet 'Western', the wearing of miniskirts occurs/has occurred in many non-Western countries.

the obvious reason that one is a symbol of fashion whilst the other a religious imperative for life.

But, rather than this being a defence of existing freedoms (in this case, of religious expression), in reality it is tantamount to the *defence of women's oppression and subjugation*. Freedom of religious expression cannot be, and in liberal democracies is not, granted *carte blanche* – we need to carefully weigh up such freedoms with attendant 'unfreedoms' or, more explicitly, oppression. If we can apply the freedom of choice defence to veiling then could we not also do the same, for example, to other cultural and religious practices? How would those advocating this defence respond to women wishing to exercise the same for practices such as clitoridectomy, footbinding of Chinese women until the 1949 revolution, and *sati* (immolating on a husband's funeral pyre) by widowed Hindu women? To deny the freedom of choice for these three practices but approve it for veiling plainly involves a double standard and consequently necessitates a more robust defence than the freedom to choose, or indeed freedom of religious expression. The only *rational* argument would be that veiling, unlike the other three, is not harmful. But my contention is that this is false – veiling is indeed harmful in many ways, as is discussed below.

There are no comprehensive surveys in the UK regarding the reasons Muslim women have taken up the veil in recent years. What is not in doubt is that the instance of veiling has risen markedly. We can, with some degree of confidence, postulate that around the time of the Iraq war of 1991, veiling of Muslim women was still the exception, rather than the rule, in towns and cities in Britain with large Muslim communities, and the same may be applied in other west European countries with significant Muslim populations. By the time of the invasion of Iraq in 2003, however, we can assert that the situation had reversed – the practice had very much become the norm.* A number of more specific reasons can be postulated as to why

---
* Indeed, my own close observation of 'Muslim areas' of Birmingham (such as Sparkbrook, Alum Rock, and Bordesley Green) in the early 2000s, suggested that it was a rare occurrence to see *un*veiled women: one could reasonably conjecture that unveiled Asian women in these areas were likely to be non-Muslim.

so many Muslim women in the West have taken up the veil, which we now examine.

Assertion of religious identity
The rise in veiling has, it appears, coincided with the rise in religion as the most important determinant of identity of British Asians so much so that we can hypothesise that very significant numbers of Muslims see themselves primarily as 'Muslims' rather than other identities. In Britain, as we discussed in Chapter 1, this has increasingly led to the abandonment of previous identity descriptors, namely, 'Asian', 'British Asian', and 'Black'. Moreover, the religious identity for Muslims especially is not a private matter of belief, but instead a public expression. That is to say for significant numbers, the appearance of being a Muslim is of profound importance. Nothing is more explicit in this shift in self-identity than the veil, given that this mode of attire is solely worn by Muslim women (excluding the very small numbers of nuns). In her research on Pakistani women in England in 1993/4, Claire Dwyer (2008, p. 144) discovered that 'clothes become powerful representations of identity for young Muslim women – wearing 'English' clothes is a signifier for active sexuality, rebelliousness and modernity while 'Asian' clothes suggest morality and ethnic integrity'

The formation of large, segregated neighbourhoods of Muslims more easily enables the preservation of very distinct cultural and religious norms, customs and traditions – including codes of dress in accordance with religious strictures, such as the wearing of the veil, that are enormously at variance with those seen in the wider society. This has provided a fillip to the assertion of religious identity and tribal loyalty. For an adult woman, adopting the veil can stem from the genuine desire to assert her identity as Muslim woman; moreover, the veil enables a constant, public expression of fidelity to the faith and community. But it can also be coercive because *not* visibly appearing as a Muslim woman and member of the religious tribe might risk censure and accusation of disloyalty. Indeed, in this context, choice in any meaningful sense is a chimera. This has been a crucial argument made by the French North African feminist group, *Ni Poute Ni Soumises* in debates on veiling in France (see below).

Some reasons for taking up the veil can only be described as a form of perverse identity. Take the following example of a young French Muslim woman taking up the veil: 'I feel completely liberated by the veil. As soon as I put it on, I felt as if I'd blossomed. The veil allows a woman no longer to be a slave to her body. It is the belief that a woman can go far through means other than using her body' (cited in Parekh, 2000, p. 252). Now let us reword this slightly and replace 'the veil' with 'the prison': 'I feel completely liberated by the prison. As soon as I entered it, I felt as if I'd blossomed. The prison allows a woman no longer to be a slave to her body'. Without dismissing the sincerity of this woman's beliefs, nonetheless, on any rational, humane, basis, one would think that something had grievously gone awry in her attitude to life and self-identity. Indeed, there is very good reason to think that she is in need of psychiatric attention. Yet this analogy and reasoning would doubtless be vehemently ridiculed and challenged by multiculturalists. But, pray, on what basis? Is there such a distinction between volunteering to hide in a prison (leaving aside, for the sake of argument, that this is a legal impossibility) and hiding beneath a veil? The only material difference is that the latter stems from an edict from one of the world's major religions whereas the former does not. Moreover, this is not such a trivial or absurd analogy. In Japan, there is a phenomenon (*hikikomori*) of some one million boys and young men who lock themselves in their bedrooms, hiding from society and its expectations (see Zielenziger, 2006).* This is not excused away under any freedom of choice but is rightly considered a social and psychological problem. So, why cannot veiling also legitimately be considered as such?

International political events

The 'war on terror' and invasions of Afghanistan in 2001 and Iraq in 2003, by the US and UK (plus other much smaller forces of the

---

* The poignant and accurate title of Zielenziger's book is *Shutting Out the Sun* – which, of course, is precisely what fully veiled women do.

'coalition of the willing'), has intensified a global Muslim identity. The natural affinity immigrants feel for their countries of origin and its attendant faith and culture tends to intensify when these countries come under attack, especially by the government of the adopted country. Such intensification of feelings towards 'home' countries can manifest itself in a fierce attachment to their cultural and religious mores, including donning the veil. This appears to have happened since 9/11 for many Muslims in the West – notwithstanding the fact that the countries that have been attacked are the countries of origin for only a minority of such Muslims. The fact that they are Muslim-majority countries suffices in this identity attachment, which can be considered as being loyalty to the global *umma*. Conversely, had the attacked and invaded countries not been Muslim, one would simply not have seen much concern from Muslims.

Racism and isolation
If mainstream society is racist or hostile (or considered as such) to an individual or community's religion, culture, and traditions, then the individual or community can seek refuge in the safe haven constituted by its own group and, by so doing, turn inwards and adopt with increased vigour these identity-defining attributes, and seek comfort in other customs and values of the 'home country'. This is analogous to the situation obtaining in the USA during the 1960s and 1970s. Then, some elements of the civil rights movement, described as 'cultural nationalists' or 'Pan-Africanists', looked to Africa which they perceived to be their 'homeland', and, by so doing, came to adopt customs and practices of Africans, including codes of dress and changing of names. This was a mark of their avowed rejection of the racist American society that refused to treat black people with equality and dignity (Marable, 1991, pp. 107–108; 134–137). A similar rationale is doubtless a factor in some Muslim women taking up the veil, though this is not attributed as cultural or religious nationalism – but the *umma* can be considered a form of 'nation' for Muslims, and the identification with it a form of religious nationalism.

Coercion and manipulation
Whilst recognising that many women do choose to cover themselves in a veil – for the various reasons cited – others indubitably do so because of coercion or manipulation. This can emanate from religious and cultural zealots frequently influenced by their brethren in Muslim countries who have an evangelical zeal; a zeal they conscientiously emulate. These 'leaders' hold great sway in isolated, ghettoised communities which provide fertile ground for their views – and powerless, marginalised women are unable to offer much resistance to them. Hence, to their demand: 'God wills that you veil', they meekly submit.

Absence of a challenge to veiling
Though Jack Straw's remarks were supported by other ministers, including Tony Blair, nonetheless in Britain there has not been any systematic critique of the veil by government, public authorities and institutions – this is a logical outcome of multicultural thinking and assumptions. The practice – if not entirely welcomed – is certainly tolerated and accepted. The exception is the occasional complaint made against schoolgirls wearing the veil in its full form (the *niqab* or *jilbab*). To my knowledge, no complaints have been made against the *hijab* by any school, state institution, or mainstream NGO (see below). Not surprisingly, Muslim organisations in their entirety are in favour of veiling of girls and women. Given the absence of secular voices of any significance within the 'Muslim community', these organisations have encountered no opposition, be it from political, or community representatives, or from media commentators and academics from an Islamic background. This leaves the 'freedom of religious expression' and the 'right to choose' arguments unchallenged and, by default, accorded unanimity and legitimacy.

Nor has there been opposition to veiling from non-governmental organisations given that under the multicultural imperative, there is a widespread tolerance of ideas and customs of ethnic minorities. One can postulate that what is really behind this laissez-faire approach, as we have seen, is the fear of being labelled 'racist' – and, regarding Muslim beliefs and customs, 'Islamophobic'. This is the manifestation of what can be termed 'white liberal post-colonial guilt' (discussed in the following chapter). The remnants of the feminist/women's liberation movement remain silent, invariably adopting an accomodationist, multicultural stance. For example, the foremost feminist organisation in the UK, the Fawcett Society, does not have a position on the veil. It did, however, convene a conference on the issue (in December 2006)[*] which included representatives from Islamist groups with pretty unsavoury records on women's right, but not one woman from an Islamic background who opposed the veil.

There appears, therefore, to be a real sense of current feminist thinkers and activists viewing women from ethnic minorities as being part of the estranged 'other', even though they reside in the same country. Consequently, the political, ethical, and social compass that has been developed over decades in the West for women's rights and against discrimination seems not to apply to Muslim women – so their oppression does not warrant much concern, genuine debate and critique, policy development, or need for campaigning. Indeed any comment regarding their condition within *their own* communities is a taboo. The huge lacuna in feminist thinking in Britain is that, even if Muslim women voluntarily take up the veil, this is, we maintain, a clear manifestation of their *internalising* their oppression. Obviously, gender inequalities can take various forms, including mode of dress. From this perspective – which the present author adheres to – even if the veil is voluntarily taken up, for example, as a mark of resisting oppression on racial grounds, it is an *oppressive response to oppression*.

Equally, however, Asian women's organisations (such as Newham Asian Women's Project and Southall Black Sisters) who generally have a brave and principled history of tackling manifestations of cultural and religious oppression have also not taken a stance on the veil but,

---

[*] This was entitled 'The veil, feminism and Muslim women: a debate'.

by their silence, have given it tacit support. Indeed, the entire political spectrum in Britain – from the right to far left, including ethnic minority groups – have adopted a position of multicultural accommodation on the issue. This (we might say conveniently) obviates the need for a principled critique, being quietly subsumed beneath the twin umbrellas of cultural relativism and the freedom of religious expression. This is certainly in stark contrast to the robust debates on the issue in France, across the entire political spectrum, to which we now turn.

Veiling and *laïcité*: the debate in France
In regard to veiling in society and veiling in schools in particular, by far the most extensive debate in the Western world has occurred in France. John Bowen (2007) has provided a comprehensive survey and discussion of this issue, which this section draws on.[*] French concern about veiling in schools came to a head in 1989 when three schoolgirls of North African descent arrived at their school wearing the *hijab*[†] and 'refused the principal's request to take off their scarves in class and were expelled, on the grounds that the scarves infringed on the "laïcité and neutrality of the public school"'. Soon after, this became a national incident (Bowen, 2007, pp. 83–84). Similar episodes occurred in 1993 and 1994, and then again in 2002, and it was these that compelled the Chirac government to take some sort of action on the issue.

---

[*] Though Bowen, an American anthropologist, attempts to be objective and 'neutral' in his discussion and analysis, it is quite clear that he adopts a critical stance against those who are avowedly opposed to veiling; in stark contrast, he empathises and sympathises with especially those girls and women who wear the veil. That said, the book is perhaps the best survey of the issue in the English language. Dominic McGoldrick's *Human Rights and Religion: The Islamic Headscarf Debate in Europe* is also an informative work, from a legal perspective which examines the debate on the veil in a number of countries. By comparison, Joan Scott's *The Politics of the Veil* adopts a brazenly hostile stance against *laïcité*. As such, it does not properly engage with the arguments and views in France and other countries with an avowedly secular approach, so is a rather weak, jejune exercise.
[†] In France, the terms *foulard* and *voile* are used instead of *hijab, niqab, burqa* etc.

At the core of the debate in France, and the widespread hostility to the veil which compelled government action, lies the principle of *laïcité* (that is, the separation of the church [religion] and state; in English, the closest term is 'laicization' or, better, 'secularism').* Bowen explains the origin and significance of this principle:

> From the 1880s to mid-1920s, the Third Republic succeeded, through a series of decrees, laws, and negotiation, in removing the Church from the public schools and depriving the Church of its public status, a dual victory that was *later* to be summed up with the single word *laïcité* ... This legacy of combat against the Church in the name of the Republic has been handed through civic instruction, popular media, and teacher-training courses. The legacy helps to explain the degree to which many teachers and intellectuals see the contemporary presence of Islam in the schools as threatening to turn back the clock on at least two struggles: the fight to keep religion from controlling young minds, and the struggle to forge a common French identity ... [including] the struggle for gender equality in public and private life (*ibid.*, pp. 12, 25).

The key law on the relationship between the state and religion in France is that of the law of 1905 which guarantees 'freedom of conscience and the free exercise of organized religions', but which also proclaims that the state 'neither recognizes, nor pays the salaries of, nor subsidizes any religion'. But this law does not refer to *laïcité* as such. It was the Constitution of 1946 which made the explicit reference: 'France is an indivisible, secular [*laïque*], democratic, and social Republic' (*ibid.*, pp. 26, 29).

---

* The importance this principle holds in French society, and the general hostility there to the veil, is little understood. This ignorance is graphically shown by Bhikhu Parekh who, as we have seen, is one of the foremost exponents of multiculturalism: '[s]hould French schools allow Muslim girls to wear headscarves? Yes, say multiculturalists, because these do not subvert the tradition of *laïcité* ...' (Parekh, 2002, p. 147). This could not be further from the truth: the whole drive to remove headscarves (and other religious symbols) from the school was precisely because it was felt that these *did* subvert *laïcité*.

But, neither the 1905 law (nor other related laws) nor the 1946 Constitution provided unambiguous guidelines in regard to the wearing of religious attire in public schools. Some argued that their prohibition was a logical inference, whilst others could provide legitimate grounds for disagreement. Hence, pressure was building up for a new law to clarify matters, which is to say, to outlaw religious symbols in schools. Despite protestations from Muslim groups – backed up by Catholic and Jewish organisations – President Chirac authorised a commission in September 2003 (The Independent Commission of Reflection on the Application of the Principle of Laïcité in the Republic – or, simply 'The Stasi Commission' named after the Chair Bernard Stasi) to report, and make recommendations, on issues related to *laïcité*, though the focus was very much on religious symbols in school, especially the *hijab*.* The Commission duly reported in December 2003, its key recommendation being:

> In schools, middle schools, and high schools, appearances and signs displaying a religious or political affiliation be forbidden, conditional on respecting the freedom of conscience and the specific nature of private schools under contract with the state (*ibid.*, p. 123).

The members of the Commission understood that there was considerable support for a new law – indeed, apart from Muslim organisations and other religious groups there was overwhelming support for this across the political spectrum (including the governing right UMP and the opposition Socialist Party). One week before the report was published an opinion poll by BVA (on 3 December 2003) showed that 72 per cent favoured a ban, whilst a poll in *Elle* magazine showed that 49 per cent of *Muslim* women supported such a law, whereas 43 per cent opposed it (*ibid.*, pp. 124–125).

---

* There was also a committee created by the National Assembly to deliberate on the same issue. This was the Parliamentary Information on Religious Signs, chaired by the Speaker, Jean-Louis Debré. This recommended a prohibition on all 'visible' signs (*ibid.*, pp. 106, 139).

Armed with this knowledge, a law based on this recommendation was overwhelmingly passed by both the Assembly and Senate. The Education Ministry expressed this in an administrative order in May 2004, which came into effect at the start of the school year in September 2004:

> the signs and clothing that are forbidden are those where the wearing can be immediately recognized for a religious affiliation, such as the Islamic voile, by whatever name, the [Jewish] kippa, or a cross of excessive large size (*ibid.*, p. 140).*

A surprising opponent of the law was Nicholas Sarkozy (then the Interior Minister): he had argued that such a law would humiliate Muslims and lead to radicalisation on both sides of the debate (*ibid.*, p. 119). We have earlier asserted that those with a strong religious identity can claim misrecognition (including 'humiliation') whenever their beliefs are challenged – so this warning by Sarkozy can be rebutted on this basis too. Be that as it may, did reality confirm Sarkozy's fears? The answer must be a decisive 'no' given that compliance with the law has been achieved without much dissent: in the first year of the new law, only 47 pupils were expelled from school because of their refusal to remove religious signs, whilst a further 550 incidents were resolved through dialogue, and 96 had left school for private schools, distance learning, or to enrol in another country (*ibid.*, pp. 150–151). Nor was there any evidence of rising radicalisation, such as a flurry of protests against the new law, as there had been prior to its introduction. Anecdotal evidence suggests that radicalisation of young Muslims has been much greater in Britain, which has been so accommodating to the Muslim faith. That said, a vital reason for this radicalisation is undoubtedly attributable to UK foreign policy, especially the invasion of Iraq – which France did not partake in.

---

* The full title is 'Law no. 2004-228 of March 15, 2004 concerning, as an application of the principle of the separation of church and state, the wearing of symbols or garb which show religious affiliation in public primary and secondary schools'.

Indeed, the move towards the law generated arguments, clarified principles, and provided evidence of the utmost import in regard to veiling in general, and its impact on society, which have not even been touched upon, let alone deliberated upon, in countries such as Britain. Though the British government has, of late, been attempting to forge a 'British identity', inculcating values associated with 'Britishness' with the aim of enhancing 'social cohesion', it has not instigated anything like an honest debate in regard to how strong religious, communal identities nurtured under multiculturalism run in direct opposition to these aims. Contrast this with the array of firm but principled positions adopted in France, including by those with a history of opposition to colonialism and racism.

Thus, the anti-colonial revolutionary, Régis Débray, a member of the Stasi Commission, described 'those who would allow girls with headscarves into classrooms' as 'counterrevolutionary' (*ibid.*, pp. 82–83). Another member of the Commission, sociologist Alain Touraine (of a conservative disposition, and who was initially opposed to the law, but voted for it) argued that 'we do not want communalism, that rational thinking exists, that equality between men and women exists, that citizenship exists' (*ibid.*, p. 124). Hanifa Cherifi (originating from the Kabyle region of Algeria), the Education Ministry Mediator for headscarf cases, asserted that 'although previously many claimed that the voile gave girls a space of freedom between the family and society, "we have neglected the intrinsic significance of the voile: to remind women, starting at puberty, that [with echoes of both Mernissi and Charrad] Islamic morality forbids mixing of the sexes in all public spaces, including the school"' (*ibid.*, p. 93). Teachers who were in favour of a law explained that 'sometimes, for adolescents, the voile is at one and the same time a family obligation, a sign of identity, and protection against what they feel as aggression by boys' (*ibid.*, p. 121).

This last observation regarding 'protection against aggressive boys' was highlighted by the movement for women's rights of North African origin, *Ni Putes Ni Soumises* (Neither Whores Nor Doormats),

whose founder, Fadela Amara, argued that 'the scarf was one element of a misogynist mind-set that had to be changed' (*ibid.*, p. 215).*
Another leading proponent of the ban, Samira Bellil (deceased in 2004), of Algerian origins (who was raped twice as a teenager in the Paris suburbs by Muslim boys), provides a graphic example of some of the reality in French ghettos (*banlieu*) (see George, 2003). She argues that girls are being pressurised to wear the *hijab*, as much to protect themselves from the casual violence of the ghetto (including gang rape or *tourantes*), as by their families or religious leaders. In other words, there is the belief that she wouldn't have been attacked and raped if she had been wearing the *hijab* instead of flaunting herself 'bare-headed' in a Westernised manner. She campaigned against this idea of women as objects, being told what to do and how to dress by men in 'Muslim' communities, and she understood the challenge to reactionary male attitudes within Muslim communities that the ban should bring. Indeed such reasoning is why French North African women's groups generally supported the ban.

Unlike their counterparts in Britain and the US, French feminists who had been active during the 1970s opposed wearing the veil on the grounds that it was 'a sign of sexist discrimination incompatible with a secularist and egalitarian education', a sign 'of the oppression and constraining of Muslim women'. Bowen points out that the strongest denouncers of scarves remained those women who most ardently fought for women's rights (*ibid.*, p. 210, 218). The feminists Anne Vigerie and Anne Zelensky, in an article in *Le Monde*, acknowledged the argument (which we noted above) that women and girls who wear the veil do so in the name of freedom of religious expression. But they counter this in a firm and unambiguous manner:

> wearing the voile is not only a sign of belonging to a religion. It symbolizes the place of women in Islam as Islamism understands it. That place is in the shadow, downgraded and submitting to men. The fact that some women demand it does not change its meaning.

---

* It is disappointing (and indicative) that Bowen did not interview any member of this important group – or adequately summarise its politics.

We know that dominated people are the most fervent supporters of their domination (*ibid.*, p. 229).

The last line is obviously an exaggeration so the 'are' should be replaced with 'can be'.

Despite the evidence and forthright views, Bowen thinks that rather than veiling being an obligation or choice, it is 'a subtle dance among convictions and constraints' (*ibid.*, p. 81). This is partly true: it applies to a subset of veiled women. But the indubitable reality is that for a large percentage – perhaps a majority – the constraints (arising from coercion, manipulation, exhortation, guilt-inducing sense of obligation etc.) are so overbearing that a 'subtle dance' is well nigh impossible, meaning that there is simply no real choice or conviction in the matter. For the remainder, the balance of what they think and what they are forced to think is such that some freedom of choice does remain. But some of these will do so, as we have argued, because of social conditioning and internalisation. Moreover, for many young Muslim women in segregated neighbourhoods, the veil has become a form of 'symbolic capital', that is to say a symbol of chastity and submissiveness, which is highly prized by many Muslim men.* Others will do so (again, as we noted earlier) to assert an Islamic identity as a reaction against racism and rejection by mainstream society, or of global events such as the war on terror. The fact that these are ostensibly 'free acts' does not detract from the oppressive nature of veiling that is absolutely clear in the Koranic passages referred to above. In the case of social conditioning, this is oppression garbed as

---

* Pierre Bourdieu elaborates upon 'symbolic capital' in his analysis of 'cultural production'. It refers to 'degree of accumulated prestige, celebrity, consecration of honour and is founded on a dialectic of knowledge (*connaisance*) and recognition (*reconnaissance*)' (Bourdieu, 1993, editor's introduction, p. 7). In Bowen's discussion with three young Muslim women regarding the veil, all 'agreed that [Muslim] men were less likely to harass a woman wearing a headscarf'. One commented that 'when I began to wear it they proposed marriage. And I know one or two women who put on the voile in order to get married' (Bowen, 2007, p. 80). In its role as an impediment to unwanted advances and as a facilitator of marriage, we can think of the veil as a form of symbolic capital.

conviction. In the case of assertion of identity, this is an oppressive response to oppression that is internalised as an expression of pride in one's religion and community. Certainly, the injunction for veiling is intolerable on the basis of human emancipation and gender equality.

It is of vital importance to recognise that, with respect to the veiling of young *girls*, there cannot be any real choice – as young children are plainly unable to carefully evaluate religious or ideological choices. This means that veiling, which usually starts at the age of 3 or 4 must, *ipso facto* be the result of *coercion*, rather than socialisation. Those who reject this view should bear in mind that it is extremely rare to find girls from a non-Muslim background *choosing* to don the *hijab* – possibly out of fun, or in sympathy with girls from Muslim families who are required to wear it. It seems that even very young girls can clearly sense an oppressive infringement in regard to attire. This absence of veil mimicking is far from being a unique phenomenon given that precisely the same applies to boys regarding the Sikh turban or Jewish yarmulke. There appears, therefore, to be a kind of iron law which holds that children, playful by definition and often so adventurous, have an aversion to donning religious attire out of their own volition, thus confirming coercion as the decisive factor for those who do so. As such, this must be tantamount to a fundamental breach of the rights of a child (some go so far as to argue that veiling of children is, in fact, a form of child abuse – see, for example, Namazie, 2007). What is incontrovertible is that equality with non-Muslim girls is denied to girls born of Muslim parentage who are coerced into wearing a veil. But what if a child *chooses* to wear a veil? We can respond to this by use of an analogy: suppose a child chooses to work as a stripper or, assuming the law permits this, to work in a brothel. What kind of morality justifies this as acceptable under the doctrine of freedom of choice? If the latter are deemed intolerable under a moral code, then why can not the former? In fact, the remark made by the judge regarding the Shia self-flagellation case, noted in Chapter 1, 'the law recognises that children and young persons may wish to take part in some activities which it considers they should not. It is sometimes expressed as protecting themselves from themselves', is also apposite in the case of the veil.

In regard to veiling of girls in schools, given that it is a *religious* practice, it is clearly in breach of the principle of secular education that follows from the separation of state and religion. Consequently, advocates of secular schooling must disallow veiling of girls, as with other religious symbols and practices, in schools.

The argument that the systematic racism and discrimination against non-white minorities that is still so prevalent in France demonstrates the weakness of the French model of *laïcité* will not do. Indeed, the widespread racism is a severe breach of *laïcité* that stems from the republican ideals of *liberté, egalité*, and *fraternité*. The point is cogently made in regard to Algeria by Yazid Sebag (of Berber origins and later appointed by the government to oversee equal opportunities): 'France established in Algeria a social and interethnic organization based on communalism and discrimination, ignoring its own republican principles' (cited in Bowen, 2007, p. 36). Moreover, in the debates on the veil, there was often acknowledgement that France had failed in integrating significant numbers of its citizens from Muslim backgrounds – an issue that came to the fore with a vengeance during the urban riots of autumn 2005 (McGoldrick, 2006, pp. 56–59).

In recognition of this failure, a number of measures have been implemented, including the setting up of a High Authority against Discrimination and for Equality (*ibid.*, p. 58). In December 2008 President Sarkozy openly denounced the sharp contradiction between reality and republican principles: 'How can we talk about a republic when your success at school and in professional life depends not on … merit but largely on your social origin, the neighbourhood where you live, your name or the colour of your skin?' he asked. He said the republican principle of equality had become 'more myth than reality' (Chrysafis, 2008). What is patently clear is that abandoning *laïcité* and republican ideals is not at all likely to make the situation better but, instead, will probably make matters worse.

It needs to be stressed that France is not unique in banning religious symbols in schools on the basis of *laïcité*: indeed, Muslim-majority countries such as Tunisia and Turkey do precisely the same. In Turkey's case, the *hijab* is banned not only in schools but also in government offices and universities (McGoldrick, 2006, p. 171).* Moreover, the issue and importance of secular schooling is also being considered in other European countries. This does not just relate to religious attire of pupils, but also of buildings and accoutrements therein. For example, in the Spanish city of Valladolid, a judge (Alejandero Valentin) 'ordered the Macias Picavea School to remove religious symbols from classrooms and public spaces, arguing that the presence of these symbols where minors are educated can promote the idea that the state is closer to Catholicism than other religions'. The basis for this ruling was the 'secular' and 'neutral' character of the Spanish state. This has naturally upset the Catholic Church with a Spanish cardinal describing this as 'Christophobic' (obviously paralleling the 'Islamophobic' charge used by Islamists) (CNA, 2008).

Possibly inspired by the debate in France, there have also been calls for the banning of the veil by parliamentarians of a Muslim background in some European countries. For example, in October 2006, Green MP Ekin Deligöz, along with other public figures of Turkish descent in Germany, published an article in the *Bild am Sonntag* newspaper calling on all Muslim women in Germany to stop wearing the headscarf. Deligöz labelled the garment as a 'sign

---

* The origins of this policy go back to the founder of modern Turkey, Kemal Atatürk, as part his drive to modernise Turkey and lift it from the backwardness of Ottoman rule. The emancipation of women was central to this. In 1925 he made the following observation: 'In some places I have seen women who put a piece of cloth or a towel or something like it over their heads to hide their faces, and who turn their backs or huddle themselves on the ground when a man passes by. What is the meaning of this behaviour? Gentleman, can the mothers and daughters of a civilized nation adopt this strange manner, this barbarous posture? It is a spectacle that makes the nation an object of ridicule. It must be remedied at once' (cited in Kinross, 1993 [1964], p. 420).

of oppression for Muslim women', adding that, 'those who require women to cover their hair with a veil, make it a sex object,' (Murray and Verwey, 2008, pp. 6–7). Similarly, Nyamko Sabuni, Zairian-Swedish Member of Parliament and Minister for Integration and Gender Equality since October 2006, has supported a motion to ban all women under the age of fifteen from wearing the headscarf (*ibid.*, p. 17).

Social and health consequences of veiling
Though incontrovertible evidence is not available for this assertion, my position is that veiling acts as a barrier to the flowering of meaningful dialogue, social interaction, and formation of friendships between veiled Muslim women and non-Muslims. Anecdotal evidence suggests that it is relatively rare to witness veiled and non-veiled women (of any ethnicity) fraternising. It necessarily follows that veiling accentuates the psychic detachment already prevalent in segregated communities. Moreover, veiling tends often to be the precursor of other forms of oppression: the drive to gender segregation, restrictions of veiled girls partaking in physical education, especially swimming, or in dancing etc. Furthermore, some parents might go further and persuade their daughters to completely veil themselves, that is, to wear the *jilbab* or burqa. If this were unacceptable to some ('a step too far'), then why should the *hijab* be deemed acceptable given that the reasons underpinning both are the same, that is, stemming from Koranic strictures?*

What is not in doubt is that fully veiled women are prevented from fruitfully engaging in non-verbal communication, including both facial expressions and bodily gestures. There can be no mean-

---

* In John Bowen's interview with three young French Muslim women, one who wore the *hijab* commented that 'One day I heard a girl in *niqab* talking this way and that. That clashed!' Another *hijabi* replied 'it shocked me; I consider them to have a stricter interpretation than I have ... They are not necessarily more pious'. The first then makes an important admission: 'I find myself vis-à-vis someone wearing the *niqab* like someone who does not wear the foulard [*hijab*] vis-à-vis those of us who do wear it' (Bowen, 2007, p. 80).

ingful eye contact and physical gestures are heavily constrained thereby obstructing the communication of the full range of emotions such as happiness, unhappiness, sadness, anger, joyfulness, surprise, shock, fear, disgust etc. In the case of mother and child, the veil inevitably hinders the development of their relationship given the importance of non-verbal communication to a child's process of knowledge acquisition and acculturation into society, and also that 'the acquisition of nonverbal communication skills provides an important foundation for the emergence of language in atypical as well as typical development' (Mundy *et al.*, 1995). Accordingly, the conclusion that must be drawn is that veiling diminishes the quality of being fully human and, therefore, is dehumanising. If we think that forced veiling is wrong in countries such as Afghanistan, Iran, and Saudi Arabia, because this is an imposition that degrades and dehumanises women, then why is a woman who chooses to veil not considered also as degraded and dehumanised? Surely, the end result is precisely the same? Reprising the analogy utilised earlier, if someone is sent to prison whilst another volunteers to be imprisoned, the result in both cases is imprisonment. Adding the qualifier 'self' does not alter this reality.

Research also shows that the veil has negative health effects. For example, a study by a Manchester University team (Roy *et al.*, 2007) on young Asian women (aged between 18 and 36) of a Pakistani background showed 'a high prevalence of hypovitaminosis D ... A significant proportion (approximately one quarter) had [a] marked deficiency. The data also indicate the adverse impact of vitamin D insufficiency on bone mass particularly at the hip and wrist' (*ibid.*, p. 202). One of the researchers, Alan Silman (Medical Director of the Arthritis Research Campaign) provides a clear explanation for this:

> the problem for South Asian women is that they cover themselves up and are not exposed to sunlight. As a result they have to rely on their diet. But if you have a diet that is low in dairy and meat, which many Asian women have, you will not get what you need ... The combination of covering yourself up and not exposing yourself to

sunlight, and not getting enough vitamin D in your diet, is a kind of double whammy. What is needed is dialogue between health educators and the Asian community to see whether there is a level that would be culturally acceptable but which would provide sufficient exposure. We do need some urgent action, and I think it is an issue of health education (Dobson, 2007, p. 334).

The study, unfortunately, does not make clear whether the women in the study wore some kind of veil. But, given the very high prevalence of the wearing of the *hijab* among Pakistani Muslim women in Britain, we can assume that a significant proportion did so, thereby further minimising exposure to sunlight. Similar research in Turkey of veiled women found an increased incidence of osteoporosis (Bahceci *et al.*, 2006). In regard, therefore, to the indubitable harmful social and health effects of veiling, multicultural apologists for the practice again offer no comment.

If veiling can be defended on the grounds of either a broad freedom of choice or narrower freedom of religious and cultural expression, then why is the scarring of the face, as is the custom in some African tribes, not granted the same freedom? In fact this practice is illegal in the UK – an eminently sensible restriction (and in accordance with other self-harming activities, including suicide) but by being outlawed it is, nonetheless, a breach of the freedom of cultural expression. Invoking the same freedom for the veil and not for other cultural and religious practices suggests a privileging of Islamic practices. There is certainly the sense that the major religions in Britain are accorded a privileged status over other supernatural belief systems; a point emphasised in Chapter 1. But in each case the freedom of choice argument should be trumped by the guaranteeing of human rights: hence, freedom *from* cultural and religious oppression becomes a fundamental plank in defence of human rights. Choices are, of course, not made in a vacuum and, in regard to the adoption of oppressive cultural and religious practices, these are internalised from the formative years by, as already noted, a combination of careful and systematic social conditioning, indoctrination, inducement of guilt, manipulation, coercion, and threat of sanctions including, and not always as a last resort, violence. In sum, there is often no *real* choice – and this is most certainly the case with the veil. A simple test confirms this: remove these pressures, as is the case for non-Muslim women, and one finds that veiling practically never occurs (apart from a few women who convert to Islam).

Secularist Arab women's groups and individuals in France, notably *Ni Putes Ni Soumises,* have pointed out how the pressure to veil intensifies in Muslim neighbourhoods; this was, as we have seen, one of their key arguments for removing the veil from schools. Surveying areas of high Muslim population, we can see the same phenomenon – indeed we may have reached the stage where girls and women in 'Muslim areas' of British towns and cities find it impossible *not* to cover their heads should they so choose. Those brave enough to try are likely to gain very little support from inside their 'community'. One argument, as noted earlier, often used in defence, if not in justification, is that this is a response to women feeling sexually harassed (which can be considered a reflection on the systematic segregation of the sexes that can generate frustration and harassment of women, especially on the part of some adolescents and young men). But, importantly, this actually represents a *defeat* for their liberation (in the manner in which black people have to hide from white society in 'no go areas' for fear of harassment and racist attacks).

Islamic morality is clear: unveiled women lack modesty, *ipso facto* are temptresses who must, therefore, be considered 'immoral'. Moreover, it is precisely the gains made by women over the past two centuries that are central to the labelling of these gains as 'decadent' by defenders of veiling under Sharia law. These include freedom to lead an independent life, to marry or not to marry – and whom to marry, liberal attitude to sex, especially pre-marriage, freedom of dress, and equality with men in all spheres of life. Those accustomed to such freedoms ought naturally to oppose and reject a morality that sharply collides with these – one which seeks to prevent women from an Islamic background from acquiring them. Despite there being no campaign by any political party or women's group to outlaw it, there is evidence to show that significant opposition to veiling exists, especially in schools.* This provides reason to think that, when presented with the arguments, a majority (perhaps significant) as in France is likely to oppose veiling not only in schools but in society in general.

During the debate in France, Prime Minister Jean-Pierre Raffarin made the interesting observation that 'the voile is a symbol for those who wear it, but also for those men and women who oppose it' (Bowen, p. 104). In Chapter 1, we commented on how certain cultural and religious customs (such as female genital mutilation, polygamy, *sati* etc.) were unacceptable even to multiculturalists. The arguments of freedom of cultural and religious expression and freedom of choice are deemed inadmissible on the grounds that even if these customs are practised on the basis of autonomous choice they are, nonetheless, considered truly egregious and simply beyond the pale. Under multiculturalist reasoning it is unclear where precisely is situated the line between acceptable and unacceptable practices, and on what moral or ideological basis it might rest. That said, it is nonetheless the case that adherents of multiculturalism find veiling, including veiling of schoolgirls, to be on the acceptable side of the line. Those who oppose veiling do so because it falls on the unacceptable side, and what pushes it into unacceptability is precisely its meaning and symbolism, namely women's oppression.

In the final chapter of *The God Delusion* (in a section entitled 'The mother of all burkas'), Richard Dawkins describes that:

* For example, an opinion poll (in November 2007) for the London *Evening Standard* showed that 'nearly 90 per cent of respondents say that Muslim teachers should not be allowed to wear a veil at school … and 84 per cent say that Muslim pupils should not be allowed to wear a veil at school' (Bentham, 2007). A poll carried by *YouGov* in October 2008 found that '46 per cent of primary and secondary school teachers suggested that allowing pupils to wear religious symbols went against British values. They also feared it would undermine the drive to promote religious and racial harmony in schools' (Kenber, 2008).

> One of the unhappiest spectacles to be seen on our streets today is the image of a woman swathed in shapeless black from head to toe, peering out at the world through a tiny slit. The burka is not just an instrument of oppression of women and claustral repression of their liberty and their beauty; not just a token of egregious male cruelty and tragically cowed female submission.

He then proceeds 'to use the narrow slit in the veil as a symbol of something else' and argues that: 'what science does for us is widen the window. It opens up so wide that the imprisoning black garment drops away almost completely, exposing our senses to airy and exhilarating freedom (Dawkins, 2006, p. 362).

This was a brave and principled stance, particularly in the context of the hue and cry over Islamophobia around the time the book was published. Our hope is that in this chapter, we have provided sufficient evidence and arguments for this stance also to be viewed as being truthful. We now end this chapter by again drawing on morality expounded by Mary Wollstonecraft over 200 years ago because it continues to shed a piercing light on the modern world – especially on those parts still trapped in a benighted pre-modernity. Those who defend Islamic veiling on whatever grounds, particularly those who consider themselves to be concerned with women's rights and liberation, should take heed of this uncompromisingly principled stand:

> I wish to sum up what I have said in a few words, for I here throw down my gauntlet, and deny the existence of sexual virtues, not excepting modesty. For man and woman, truth, if I understand the meaning of the word, must be the same ... I mean explicitly to say that they [women] must only bow to the authority of reason, instead of being the *modest* slaves of opinion (Wollstonecraft, 1995 [1792], p. 124).

Regarding 'opinion', we can be more explicit and, for our purposes, rephrase it as '... slaves of religious and cultural opinions and edicts', a codicil that Wollstonecraft would surely have approved of. The gauntlet that this author wishes to throw down is that women's *physical* liberation is also a *sine qua non* for their emancipation. Just as the right to be unveiled or the removal of footbinding in China were decisive progressive steps forward in this supreme endeavour, so too must the removal of the veil, a practice that is propounded on the basis of a misanthropic understanding of human sexuality and misogynistic notions of female 'modesty'.

PART III

OBSTACLES AND SOLUTIONS

Chapter 6

Obstacles

From the preceding chapters, there should be no doubt that this book's overall thesis is that multiculturalism has become an obstacle to the goals of integration and social cohesion which the government and probably a large majority of the British population now wish to see, and with some alacrity. We now focus in this chapter on three issues that can be thought of as being particularly problematic, that is to say, are significant obstacles to achieving these salutary goals. These are, first, the existence of segregated schools and the threat of an explosion in minority-faith schools; second, the prevalence of what we term 'White post-colonial liberal guilt'; and third, the weakness of secularism. Each is examined in turn.

Segregated schools and the threat of minority-faith schools
A key argument of this book has been that multiculturalism has contributed to the segregation of communities and accentuated strong religious-ethnic identities. These, in turn, have generated self-segregation whereby 'choice' factors in regard to residence appear to have become more important than 'constraint' factors.

But does a low level, or even absence, of residential segregation increase social cohesion? Not necessarily, though a reduction in segregation is likely to reduce or offset inter-ethnic tensions. This, however, assumes that racism is not so prominent a factor as to compel religious-ethnic minorities to live in close proximity in order to provide mutual protection. That is to say, constraint factors in regard to residential choice are minimal. That said, one possibility is that even where members of minorities do not live in segregated neighbourhoods they nevertheless have meaningful contacts only with those of their own group. To some – indeed significant – extent, this is often the case with middle class minority citizens. We saw in Chapter 3 how high levels of psychic detachment can arise even where the predicted social distance is low and we argued that this can especially emanate from strong religious identities. But this is not at all conducive to cohesion – in other words, pockets of isolated families detached from those in their midst is not too far removed from a mindset that is obtained from living in segregated areas.

Leaving aside this possibility, we can defend the general principle that a society with low levels of segregation of religious-ethnic minorities is likely to be more socially cohesive than the converse. As a value-judgement, this is much the more preferable societal outcome. This has, in fact, also been the conclusion of reports on riots and social disturbances in northern towns in England, for example, the Bradford Race Review (2001) and the Cantle Reports (2001, 2006). Indeed, as far back as 1985, the Swann Report on education (1985, pp. 767–776) highlighted the dangers of 'separate schools' for ethnic minorities. This was made explicit in the following recommendation:

> 6.7 The establishment of 'separate' schools would fail to tackle many of the underlying concerns of the communities and might exacerbate the very feelings of rejection which they are seeking to overcome.

Two decades later, the same sentiment was expressed by the Commission for Racial Equality. At a seminar on segregation in April 2007, CRE Policy Director Nick Johnson warned that Britain risks becoming a 'mini America' dominated by racially determined schools, pointing to research which suggested that segregation was increasing in schools and called for urgent action to reverse the trend. He stated: 'If a Muslim child is educated in a school where the vast majority of other children are also Muslim, how can we expect him to work, live and interact with people from other cultures when he leaves school? This is a ticking time-bomb waiting to explode' (BBC News, 2007).

This reasoning and warning is absolutely correct and a natural consequence of residential segregation has indeed been that schools have also become segregated. Given the enormous importance of the formative years in life, this phenomenon can have a highly significant and lasting effect on how children from different backgrounds relate to each other. Put bluntly, there is likely to be a deleterious impact on integration and cohesion from heightened levels of segregation of children and this surely does not at all augur well for the goal of a socially cohesive society. If segregation of communities is not a desirable outcome and is an obstacle to improving social cohesion, then it is certainly also true for children in schools.

Longitudinal studies of segregation have been hampered by a lack of data. No one can, however, deny the *existence* of segregation in many towns and cities that has arisen over the past five decades. Nonetheless, there is research which suggests that residential segregation has not increased between the 'census years' 1991 and 2001 (as has been suggested by, for example, the Commission for Racial Equality), and is not as great as in US cities. One implication of this is that the problem of segregation has been overblown. For example, Ludi Simpson (2004, p. 9) has argued that, with respect to Bradford, 'South Asian population growth alone has added to existing areas of settlement, causing both overcrowding and a change in the ethnic group composition of local communities … more localities have become mixed, more have a South Asian majority, and fewer are predominantly white. This change is a result of growth in the South Asian populations, not of segregation'. Accordingly, Simpson is critical of the findings of reports such as the Bradford Race Review (2001) and Cantle Report (2001) on Oldham. But this is complacent reasoning – the fact that the growing South Asian population in Bradford is 'natural', arising from population growth, does not detract from the *fact* of increasing concentrations of mono-religious-ethnic populations. This is precisely what has occurred in many US inner cities, which are rightly deemed to be 'Black ghettos'. Similarly, the phenomenon in Bradford can be more accurately described as increasing ghettoisation of Muslim South Asians. In any case, Simpson's methodology and findings have been challenged by Johnston, Poulsen, and Forrest (2005). Using an alternative conception of residential segregation, they show that segregation of South Asians in Bradford did *increase* over the period 1991–2001. Nonetheless, without extensive data sets for, say, the past five decades, a definitive conclusion on the dynamics of segregation cannot be made. Be that as it may, our value judgement is that the reality of present *levels* of segregation and ghettoisation is, nevertheless, very worrying – especially in schools – and needs to be tackled by robust measures.

Research by Johnston, Burgess, Harris, and Wilson (2006); Burgess, Wilson, and Lupton (2005) and Burgess and Wilson (2004) provides unambiguous evidence for the existence of segregation in schools and neighbourhoods in England (given that the vast majority of religious-ethnic minorities reside in England, the absence of data for other parts of the UK is not of material importance). As an example of the link between residential segregation and school segregation, Johnston *et al.* provide the examples of ethnic Indians in Leicester, Pakistanis in Bradford, and Bangladeshis in Tower Hamlets, East London:

> Leicester, for example, has one of the largest concentrations of students from Indian ethnic backgrounds; they formed 31 per cent of all students entering primary schools there in 1997 and 37 per cent of those entering secondary schools in 1998. If these students were evenly distributed across the city's schools, therefore, one would expect to find Indians comprising about one third of the entry-cohort at each level. Almost half of all Indian secondary students entered schools where Indians comprised at least 75 per cent of the cohort, however, with a further third entering schools where they formed 50–74 per cent of the cohort – *much greater segregation than a random allocation of students to schools would generate* – a function of the residential segregation of the country's largest ethnic minority groups and its reflection in school ethnic composition ... Similar levels of segregation characterised both Pakistanis in Bradford (where they formed 25 per cent of primary and 26 per cent of secondary school students in those intake cohorts) and Bangladeshis in Tower

Hamlets (an LEA within Greater London where they formed 57 per cent of the borough's primary schools' entry cohort and 60 per cent of the secondary schools') (Johnston *et al.*, 2006, p. 6).

Burgess *et al.* (2005) used the 2001 Schools Census and Population Census data to compare patterns of segregation* across nine ethnic groups, and across Local Education Authorities in England. Their results show that at both schools and neighbourhoods, there are *high levels of segregation for the different groups*, along with considerable variation in segregation across England. There is consistently higher segregation for South Asian pupils than for Black pupils. The data also suggest that segregation tends to be *lower* for Black pupils where they are relatively numerous, but for pupils of South Asian origin segregation is *higher* where they are relatively numerous. Interestingly, the data show that children are more segregated in school than in their neighbourhood. But there is variation: it is more the case with Black Caribbean ethnicity, children of Indian ethnicity, Pakistani ethnicity and Bangladeshi ethnicity, but less true of children with Black African ethnicity. The ratio of school to neighbourhood segregation increases with the population density of the area (Burgess, Wilson, and Lupton, 2005, p. 41).

Using London as a sample – this being the one UK city which has significant percentages of all ethnic minorities – Burgess and Wilson (*ibid.*, p. 14) discover some striking findings in regard to how pupils from the different ethnic groups are segregated from each other. These show that Black pupils with African heritage and Black pupils with Caribbean heritage are not segregated from each other, whereas pupils of Indian ethnic origin and Pakistani ethnic origin are more highly

---

* The degree of segregation is measured by utilising the indices of 'dissimilarity' (which measures the distribution – or degree of evenness – of social groups in a geographic space) and 'isolation' (the degree of potential contact – or exposure – between members of different social groups within an area). The former is interpreted as the fraction of students of a group that need to be moved to different schools in order to make each school have the same composition in terms of that group. The latter is the average probability of meeting another of the same ethnicity (Burgess and Wilson, 2004, pp. 2, 4).

segregated from each other. Second, pupils of Bangladeshi origin are highly segregated from all other groups. Third, Asian (that is, the sum of Indian, Pakistani, and Bangladeshi pupils) and Black pupils are highly segregated from each other. Importantly, Black pupils are more highly segregated from Asian pupils than they are from Whites. Fourth, Whites are least segregated from Chinese students, then Black, Indian, Pakistani and Bangladeshi students.

These findings provide sound evidence for the arguments we have stressed in this book. They clearly demonstrate that segregation of schoolchildren is a reality but which affects Asian children the most – above all the Bangladeshis.

More recent data acknowledging the problems of segregation in schools have been highlighted by the Department of Education and Skills (now the Department for Children, Schools, and Families). It has produced data which show that in many towns (especially in Northern England), the majority of pupils have little contact with children from other ethnic backgrounds, which is to say that Asian school children in particular are largely marooned from non-Asians – this is especially true for children of a Muslim background. Given that Asians comprise less than 5 per cent of the population, and Muslims less than 3 percent, this is a most unhealthy situation. The preponderance of Asians in schools is resulting in 'White flight', a phenomenon that should not be understood merely as a form of reflexive racism; on the contrary, White parents legitimately and understandably wish for their children to be taught in schools where the ethnic and religious mix reflects that of society at large. What is, however, neglected is that a similar sentiment applies to religious-ethnic minorities who are not in 'their' own areas – for example, schools which are largely comprised of pupils from a Muslim background will see the flight of non-Muslim Asians from its catchment area. At its extreme, this gives rise to ghettoised neighbourhoods, a phenomenon we have stressed in previous chapters, with mono religious-ethnic schools.

Thus, in Blackburn and Darwen in Lancashire (with a 70.5 per cent White and 26.5 per cent Asian population), 4 out of 9 secondary schools have more than 90 per cent pupils from just one ethnic background; in Bradford (63 per cent White and 33 per cent Asian), 10 out of 28 secondary schools have more than 90 per cent of pupils of one ethnicity (the most extreme example being that of Belle Vue Boys school with nearly 96 per cent Asian and a mere 1.2 per cent White) (Watt, 2007). Similarly, in Oldham, one secondary school – Grange School – has 98.5 per cent pupils from a Bangladeshi background; a percentage that has risen exponentially since the early 1980s when it was only 10 per cent (Herbert, 2007).

It is clear that the sharp segregation in schools is a manifestation of segregation in towns and cities that has become fortified over the decades. The Northern mill towns clearly provide a high concentration of Asian migrants so that their population is far higher than the overall proportion of the Asian population in Britain. Speaking to the *Observer* newspaper, former schools minister Stephen Byers, using phraseology first used by Commission of Racial Equality Chair Trevor Phillips, stated that:

> in parts of the country we are sleepwalking towards the segregation of schools on racial grounds. With no public debate, we are enshrining division and discrimination at an early age. Separate communities are growing up alongside each other with little or any common point of reference (cited in Watt, 2007).

All this is very true except that it is not 'sleepwalking' but a long walk by various governments with eyes very much wide open to a *de facto* US-style ghettoisation that Phillips (2005) had warned about as being 'our nightmare' (implying that levels of segregation in Britain had fortunately not yet reached those of Black ghettos in US cities).

In the face of this very serious situation, the responses from the government and opposition parties have generally been weak. None of the major political parties attempt to deny the reality, but neither do they offer a systematic setting out of policies to tackle the problem. The previous Education Secretary, Alan Johnson, has argued that the government is indeed tackling the problem by 'bringing in a new duty to promote community cohesion. Faith schools and also non-faith schools will have to undertake action to enhance community cohesion. This can involve twinning and sharing teachers so that this kind of problem can be tackled' (Watt, 2007). If ever there was sticking a plaster over a gaping wound this it. Research by Irene Bruegel in twelve primary schools in England conducted in 2003–05 found evidence that rebuts these simplistic solutions: 'Primary school twinning had little positive effect on White children's attitudes, fuelling indeed their community's sense of losing out on investment'. Moreover, 'shared out-of-school facilities and enhanced teacher contact may bring younger children together, but that will largely be an unintended consequence of such policies. In the context of the fissiparous processes of competition between schools and between pupils they can be likened to masking tape, not the social glue, relevant to a multi-ethnic society'. Her crucial finding is that 'Day-to-day contact between children has far more chance of breaking down barriers between communities, than school twinning and sporting encounters. This is in line with the thrust of social psychology research on prejudice which emphasises the importance of establishing contact between equals' (Bruegel, 2006, pp. 2, 4).

What the government has neglected to consider is the fact that twinning and sharing out-of-school facilities (such as sports), as means to enable religious-ethnic minority school children to meet with their White counterparts, is a drastic sign of societal failure, a *de facto* admission that segregation in schools is rife and unacceptably high. Yet little serious attempt is given to examining and tackling the *causes* of this most serious of social problems which, as we have seen, go back to decades of neglect in regard to integrating religious-ethnic minorities. With respect to 'faith schools taking action to enhance community cohesion', any actions they may undertake are likely to be fruitless (as discussed below).

The response from the Conservative opposition has been no better – though one can perhaps be thankful that they have shown an interest in an issue which, hitherto, they have usually ignored or downplayed. Shadow Home Secretary David Willets's suggestion of targeting academies and ensuring that they have an intake from 'both' (presumably meaning White and non-White) communities is, quite frankly, no solution at all. Instead of tackling segregation in existing schools, this appears to be a thinly-veiled plug for city academies (Watt, 2007).

We highlighted in Chapter 1 that, in accordance with the principle of 'group rights', multiculturalism permits, indeed even advocates, separate facilities and resources for different religious-ethnic minority groups. This is deemed to be a celebration of 'difference'. In the transformation of multiculturalism into multifaithism, we have seen these minorities increasingly being divided into 'faith communities'. A natural corollary of this process has been the ever-increasing demands for 'faith schools', which are taken to mean separate religious schools for each minority 'faith community'. Moreover, a strong religious identity leads parents to argue that their children should be taught within their own faith schools – for to deny this would be to deny their identity. If unchecked, this phenomenon will continue to have profound consequences for society, especially in the intensification of segregation and divisiveness of school children. The Labour government has stressed social cohesion as a major societal goal yet, concurrently, has not only strongly supported existing (predominantly Christian) faith schools, but also advocated their expansion for minorities – as made clear in the report *Faith in the System* (DCSF, 2007). The problem is that the two pull in opposite directions. Our argument is that genuine moves to cohesion require the prevention of the expansion of minority-faith schools and faith schools *per se* being phased out. In this regard, Amartya Sen's powerful caveats are perfectly sound:

> In Britain a confounded view of what a multiethnic society must do has led to encouraging the development of state-financed Muslim schools, Hindu Schools, Sikh Schools etc., to supplement preexisting state-sponsored Christian Schools, and young children are pow-

erfully placed in the domain of singular affiliations well before they have the ability to reason about different systems of identification that may compete for their attention. Earlier on, state-run denominational schools in Northern Ireland had fed the political distancing of Catholics and Protestants along one line of divisive categorization assigned at infancy, and the same predetermination of 'discovered' identities is now being allowed and, in effect, encouraged to sow even more alienation among a different part of the British population (Sen, 2006, p. 13).

Nonetheless, there is a reasonable defence for faith schools by minority-faith communities on the grounds of precedent and equity. Given that Anglican, Catholic, and Jewish schools have long existed,[*] not to allow similar schools for other faiths is *prima facie* unjust. Unsurprisingly, this reasoning has relentlessly been used by those in faith communities seeking to establish faith schools; the validity of which the government has, by its actions, accepted. Moreover, the granting of minority-faith schools can potentially have a positive electoral effect in parliamentary constituencies with significant faith communities as was evidenced by the letter sent by Labour MP Steve McCabe to his Muslim constituents in Birmingham, noted in Chapter 4. We again stress that this is not just simply an accommodation to deeply-felt religious/faith minority identities but a conferral of a privilege that is in breach of the egalitarian principle. Further, given the acute levels of segregation within many schools, the creation of minority-faith schools is akin to throwing fuel onto a fire.

Tables 6.1 and 6.2 provide a breakdown of faith schools. There are 6,785 faith schools in the state sector, the bulk of which (92%) are primary schools; the vast majority of these (97%) are either Church of England or Roman Catholic schools. Faith schools make up a third of all maintained schools. To this can be added 890 faith schools in the independent (private) sector – which represent 37 per cent of private schools.

---

[*] For a history of faith schools, see Gates, 2005.

Table 6.1: Faith Schools in the State Sector

Religious Character	Voluntary aided Primary	Voluntary aided 2ndary	Voluntary controlled Primary	Voluntary controlled 2ndary	Foundation Primary	Foundation 2ndary	TOTAL
Christian	4	14	8	4	0	2	32
Church of England	1946	132	2425	49	42	9	4603
Greek Orthodox	1	0	0	0	0	0	1
Hindu	1	0	0	0	0	0	1
Jewish	29	9	0	0	0	0	38
Joint Christian Faiths	25	12	19	2	1	0	59
Methodist	2	0	24	0	0	0	26
Muslim	6	5	0	0	0	0	11
Quaker	0	0	1	0	0	0	1
Roman Catholic	1677	330	0	0	0	1	2008
Seventh Day Adventist	0	1	0	0	0	0	1
Sikh	2	1	0	0	0	0	3
United Reform Church	0	0	1	0	0	0	1
TOTAL Faith Schools	3693	504	2478	55	43	12	6785

Source – Edubase (March 2009), provided by the Department of Children, Schools and Families to the author.

Table 6.2: Independent schools with Religious Ethos

Religious ethos	Schools
Buddhist	1
Christian	349*
Church of England	267
Jewish	38
Muslim	115
Roman Catholic	116
Sikh	1
Hindu	2
Greek Orthodox	1
Total Religious ethos	890 (37 per cent of independent schools)
No religious character	1,490**
Total	2,380

Notes:
* Includes 26 schools that belong to the Focus Learning Trust.
** Includes two schools that claim a religious ethos as 'scientology'; however, this is not a religious ethos recognised by the Department of Children, Schools and Families.
Source: Department of Children, Schools and Families (provided to the author)[*]

The astonishingly high numbers of faith schools is now totally out of kilter with the characteristics of the British population. The *British Social Attitudes Report 2006* (NCSR, 2007) shows:

- that there has been a major decline over time in religious identity, defined as belonging to a religion or attending religious services:
- In 1964, a quarter (26%) either did not belong to a religion or never attended a religious service. Now [2006] the same is true for over two-thirds (69%).
- Even people who belong to a religion are less likely to attend services regularly, down from around three-quarters in 1964 to half now.

---
* It is curious that data on faith schools is not available on the website of the Department of Children, Schools and Families.

Table 6.3 clearly shows the sharp decline of religious belonging: the most striking statistic is the rise of the category 'does not belong to a religion' from 3 per cent in 1964 to 38 per cent in 2005.

Table 6.3: Religious belonging in Britain 1964-2005

	1964	1970	1983	1992	2005
Belongs to a religion, attends services	74	71	55	37	31
Belongs to a religion, never attends services	23	24	30	31	31
Does not belong	3	5	26	31	38

Source: Heath et al., 2007, table 1.3, p. 9

An important point to consider, though accurate data for this is not available, is that a proportion of 'belongs to a religion, never attends services' may in fact be *non-believers*, sometimes referred, oxymoronically, to as 'Godless Christians', for whom a religious (Christian) identity is a *de facto* ethnic or cultural identity.[*] Indirect evidence for this can be gleaned from a Eurobarometer survey in 2005 which showed that only 38 percent of the UK population 'believed in God', which is in line with other West European countries (Social Trends 38, 2008, table 13.19, p. 190); whereas the 2001 Census showed that 72 per cent (in England and Wales) described themselves as 'Christian'. This clearly suggests that many who 'do not believe in God', nevertheless, identify themselves as Christians. Voas and Bruce (2004, p. 28) argue that this seeming anomaly is explained by the fact that the 'census results ... represent increasing anxiety about national identity rather than increasing commitment to the Christian faith'.

---

[*] For example, on Channel 4 News on 27 March 2009, the historian David Starkey described himself as an 'Anglican atheist'. This is on cultural and political grounds for he believes that the disestablishment of the Church of England can be damaging to England and its sense of 'decency' and 'calmness'.

There is further indirect evidence from Christian Research, the statistical arm of the Biblical Society, which has forecast that Church of England Sunday Services will, by 2050, fall to *less than a tenth* of what they are now (from just under a million to 88,000) (Doward, 2008). It is not implausible to think that, by then, 'Godless Christians' may be numerically greater than believers in the faith. In line with decline in attending services has been a decline in church weddings: only one in three marriages (77,000) involved a religious ceremony, a 50 per cent drop since 1991 (McSmith, 2009).

The predicted decline in religious belonging is attested by research which shows that two-thirds of 12- to 19-year-olds do not regard themselves as belonging to any religion, an increase of ten percentage points in as many years (from 55 per cent in 1994 to 65 per cent in 2003) (Park *et al.*, 2004, p. 10). In an ICM poll for the *Guardian* in August 2005, a similar percentage (64 per cent) thought that *'schools should be for everyone, regardless of religion and the government should not be funding faith schools of any kind'* (Guardian Opinion Poll, 2005). One presumes that those favouring faith schools were, in the main, those who had children attending them. Therefore, the expansion of faith schools is occurring at a time of steep decline in adherence to a religion, above all of Christianity, and when a significant majority opposes them. This is brazenly undemocratic and tantamount to state-sanctioned religious indoctrination at the tax payers' expense.

Naturally, therefore, faith schools for each 'faith community' are/will be a huge fillip and prize to community and religious leaders, invaluable as they are in ensuring that, from the formative years, children are indoctrinated into the religion of their parents and 'faith community'. Indubitably, their critical faculties will be severely impaired and in particular the casting of doubt, of critiquing, or debating the tenets of the faith will be discouraged. Indeed, any deviation from such mandatory allegiance is not at all likely to be tolerated. Given this, it is no exaggeration to assert that such children are deemed to be the property of their parents and community, and not considered as autonomous persons in their own right. Moreover, parents with strong religious identities will seek to 'protect' their children – especially girls – from Western secular influences, which they find immoral. Such 'protection' is indeed likely to be on offer as minority-faith schools vigorously police the behaviour of pupils strictly in line with religious doctrines. This confirms the point stressed earlier that the power and influence of traditional, invariably reactionary, community and religious 'leaders' will be strengthened; a power they will doubtless use to exclude from 'their schools' non-believers or those deemed not to be sufficiently observant. An inescapable outcome is the accentuation of divisions along religious lines. This is not only profoundly unjust and anti-egalitarian, but flies in the face of the stated goal of increasing social cohesion.

A vital question – alluded to above – is whether minority-faith schools will be exclusively for those who are observant of the faith or also for those who are not at all observant but, nonetheless, are considered part of the relevant faith community. In regard to school children (universally so for those in primary schools), we argued in Chapter 5 that they have not reached an age of sufficient maturity to make reasoned decisions regarding belief systems. The same reasoning can also reasonably be applied to the majority of secondary school children. Accordingly, there is necessarily a coercive element in regard to the instilling of religious beliefs in children and this is surely the *raison d'être* of faith schools. The decision, therefore, in regard to whether a child attends a faith school or not is that of the parents – and we would expect that devout believers are more likely to take this option for their children if it is available. In regard to this issue, with respect to Muslim schools, Keith Porteous-Wood (2007, p. 9) of the National Secular Society argues that 'the more Muslim schools there are, the more the latter category parents [who are not observant] will be pressured into sending their children to Muslim schools, and it should be asked … whether this is in the interests of cohesion'. It should indeed be asked and the answer must be a resounding 'no'. He further cautions that:

The mass conversion to the maintained sector of what we understand to be little-inspected independent Muslim schools runs the risk of institutionalising a very much more theocratic school model than any Anglican or Roman Catholic school. The areas of major difference are likely to be over:

a. the amount of time spent on religious studies;

b. whether the curriculum and opportunities are the same for both sexes;

c. whether male teachers are permitted to teach female pupils and/or if whole sections of state funded schools are going to be off limits to one sex or the other;

d. physical education;

e. the insinuation of religious dogma into every subject, including biology and other science subjects (*loc. cit.*).

All this is undeniably true. For example, in *Sex education: The Muslim Perspective,* Sarwar argues that: 'the need for sex education is not in doubt. The debate is concerned with where, how and by whom this education should be given' (cited in Parker-Jenkins *et al.*, 2005, p. 138). The reality however is that in Muslim schools, this 'debate' will be so heavily dictated by the religious governors that it becomes a dead letter. Similarly, in regard to the teaching of evolution, the Muslim Islamia School's (one of the first to be granted voluntary aided status) approach is likely to provide the standard: 'we approach Darwinism theory [*sic*] in a phenomenological way. We say, 'there is a theory believed by some, that we are descended from apes. It's just one idea among many."' In regard to the teaching of other faiths, the head teacher states: 'we can practice any religion we like. We pray five times a day, we learn the Koran in the traditional manner – but

---

* In regard to the teaching of creationism, the National Secular Society's riposte is salutary: 'Mr Blair's enthusiasm for faith schools will give the green light to every crackpot religious group to start peddling their own fantasies in schools that are paid for by the taxpayer' (Parker-Jenkins *et al.*, 2005, p. 141). But this caution must also apply to private schools that are not required to follow the National Curriculum so that children attending these are not force-fed such 'fantasies'.

with translation, explanation and discussion. One thing we never do is celebrate Christmas ... the school looks at other religions, but we examine the historical aspects quite critically. Was Jesus really born on December 25?' (*ibid.*, p. 140, 132). Make no mistake: such a 'critical examination' will not take place in regard to any Islamic doctrine or historical fact.

But the more theocratic school model also applies to other minority religious schools. For example, at the Guru Nanak Sikh Secondary School, religious *instruction* and collective worship are taught in all classes, and take place alongside Sikh studies (*ibid.*, p. 133). At the Jewish Hasmonean High School in North London, the Head teacher explains: 'in biology, we tell students that, in true Judaism, reproduction takes place only within marriage. If a biology book shows the nude female form that is one reason why a page might be removed. We should rather use line drawings' (*ibid.*, p. 138).

And we can find a plethora of examples for all the differences highlighted by Porteous-Wood in minority-faith schools. But he further makes the compelling point that attempting to minimise these inevitable problems by the imposition of quotas of those from a different faith background or none is likely to be ineffectual as hardly any parent from outside the minority faith concerned would wish to send their children to such schools (Porteous-Wood, 2007, p. 10). Given the 'White flight' from segregated areas which comprise faith communities, the pool of those not of the faith is likely to be very small. In any case, the governing bodies of such faith schools and many of their children's parents are likely to fiercely resist any such 'dilution' of their schools. The inevitable consequence is the creation of a mono-ethnic, mono-faith schooling environment for the children forced into such schools.

Research by Rupert Brown, Adam Rutland and Charles Watters on young children (aged 5–11 years) from immigrant backgrounds and their peers from the White majority in south of England, examined the development of children's identities and acculturation orientations. Their findings and conclusions are clear and similar to those of Bruegel:

> ... the effects of school diversity were consistent, most evidently on social relations: higher self-esteem, fewer peer problems and more cross group friendships. Such findings show that school ethnic composition can significantly affect the promotion of positive intergroup attitudes. These findings speak against policies promoting single faith schools, since such policies are likely to lead to reduced ethnic diversity in schools (Brown *et al.*, 2008, p. 9).

We noted in Chapter 2 that religion is far more important to the identity of Asians than for other ethnic groups. Their religions have not been subjected to the incessant challenge and resistance from Enlightenment and secular ideas going back centuries, so have not been tamed in the manner of Christianity in Europe. Left unchallenged, they have accumulated enormous power and influence in South Asia, including in India, which nominally has a secular constitution. They thereby remain extraordinarily doctrinaire and authoritarian in character. The crucial point is the very real danger of such traits characterising minority-faith schools in Britain given that their staff will comprise, almost in their entirety, those from within the faith. The oft-quoted quip 'schools are for teaching and not for preaching' will fall on deaf ears: such schools will think they have a licence to preach to 'their' children and will do so with gusto.

The push to expand faith schools in Britain is particularly odd for it suggests wilful neglect or disregard of the sobering example of Northern Ireland (highlighted by Sen in the above quotation), where state schools are divided on the basis of faith; as such they are sectarian in character and have long been a powerful incubator of the schism between Catholics and Protestants.[*] An educational policy whose aim is cohesion and inclusion would take serious note of this

---

[*] In 2001/2, only 4% of schools in Northern Ireland (primary, secondary, and grammar) were 'Integrated' whereas 48% were Protestant and 47% Catholic (Gallagher, 2005, table 14.1, p. 161).

tragic, divisive phenomenon, learn the lessons, and ensure that it is not repeated in any other part of the country. But the lessons have not (as yet) been learned and there is a real danger that the same mistake will be made in regard to minority-faith schools. As Barry Sheerman, chairman of the Commons Education Select Committee, warned in 2005: 'Do we want a ghettoised education system? ... Schools play a crucial role in integrating different communities and the growth of faith schools poses a real threat to this. These things need to be thought through very carefully before they are implemented' (cited by Taylor, 2005). Alas, they have not been thought through carefully at all, otherwise the divisive, segregationist dynamic of faith schools would be acknowledged and acted upon – and this would, at a minimum, mean a halt to their expansion.

Back in 1931, R. H. Tawney argued that 'the two most massive pillars of indefensible disparities of income and opportunity consist, as before the war, of inherited wealth and the educational system'. In regard to the latter he asserted that 'the hereditary curse upon English education is its organization along lines of social class' – by which he meant the Public, that is private, schools (Tawney, 1964 [1931], pp. 142, 223). It is true that these two pillars still stand unshaken but we can now add to these a further 'hereditary curse' for so many schoolchildren: faith schools. But the point that Tawney passed over, perhaps for reasons of realism, is that none of these are hereditary in any natural sense. What is needed is political will buttressed by firm political principles that all these pillars are harmful to society. Moreover, public schools and faith schools accentuate inequality so that one means of reducing this is to create schools founded on the principles of equality broadly defined. This, in turn, requires the abandonment of divisive schools which is precisely what public and faith schools are. Using the yardstick of realism, the easier of the hereditary curses to remove is that of faith schools; to ensure that these do not become as rigid and potent as public schools it is imperative that they do not take deeper root and cause further harm.

The difficulty of 'White Liberal Post-colonial Guilt'

A key motif of this book is that multiculturalism and cultural relativism give rise to cultural and religious laissez-faire so that there is the presumption of toleration and accommodation of, excepting some truly egregious cases, the whole gamut of beliefs, customs and traditions of religious-ethnic minorities. The assumption is that these exceptions are relatively few and marginal, so should not detract from the laissez-faire principle. But, we argue, this operative principle provides an illegitimate excuse for not engaging in critiques of the mode of living of religious-ethnic minorities, a cover that is not available to the majority society. In reality, we can make the case that there is in fact another powerful dynamic at play, which was discussed in Chapter 4: that is, the fear of being labelled racist, Islamophobic, or bigoted whenever and wherever critical observation and analysis is made of religious-ethnic minorities. These fearful rejoinders hang like a Damocles sword over liberal-minded, progressive Whites (including almost the entirety of the 'left'), which has a debilitating and muting affect on their critical faculties. Self-censorship and non-intervention becomes the order of the day. We can term this phenomenon 'White liberal post-colonial guilt'; one important effect of which is to buttress multiculturalism. As such, it is another significant obstacle in the move to an integrated, socially cohesive society.

The ravages of empire and the colonial legacy, steeped in a discourse of racism and White and Christian supremacy, understandably prey very heavily on the minds of those who wish to acknowledge this as a dark chapter in their nation's or culture's history, one which they would indubitably have preferred not to have happened. In a remarkable passage for its time, William Howitt cogently described these sentiments as far back as 1838:

> The barbarities and desperate outrages of the so-called Christian race, throughout every region of the world, and upon every people that they have been able to subdue, are not to be paralleled by those of any other race, however fierce, however untaught, and however

reckless of mercy and of shame, in any age of the earth (Howitt, 1838, p. 9).

Accordingly, it is natural that many seek to make some amends by resorting to a *modus vivendi* that is in direct opposition to their racist, colonial forebears. From this perspective, the *impulse* and motive of *not* partaking in any systematic critiquing of cultural and religious beliefs and practices of non-Whites with antecedents in the former colonies is actually positive. Furthermore, there is cognisance of the fact that these fellow citizens also tend to constitute some of the most deprived sections of society, and suffer from racism, including institutional racism, which feeds into their relative deprivation. The feeling then is that by raking over how these minorities conduct their lives, or how they relate to each other within their communities and families, will only add to their difficulties. So we can observe an almost steadfast refusal, on the part of those who would ordinarily consider themselves to engage critically with society, to expose and challenge myriad oppressive practices within religious-ethnic minority communities. Paradoxically, in the name of liberalism and political correctness, thoroughly *il*liberal practices and beliefs come to be tolerated.*

Since 9/11 White liberal post-colonial guilt has been most clearly seen in regard to Muslims, but it also applies to other religious-ethnic minority groups. In Chapter 4 we observed the similarity of usage of 'Islamophobia' and 'anti-Semitism', with the former applying to Muslims and Islam and the latter to Jews and Israel. The reasons why both of these epithets carry such great force are also comparable. In regard to the charge of anti-Semitism, there is a deeply ingrained feeling of guilt which stems from the failure of Western powers to

---

* It is quite evident that Robert Mugabe understands this well – for that is why he incessantly rails against the crimes of British colonialism whenever criticisms of his despotic regime are made by British politicians and commentators. But this ploy to deflect the disastrous failings of his regime on to the former colonial power has worn thin – and surely to the point where not even the most guilt-ridden post-colonial White liberal is taken in by it.

prevent Nazi state-sponsored anti-Semitism that ultimately culminated in the Holocaust. This can be termed 'Western post-Holocaust guilt'. Arguably, it is most intense in Germany (at least at the level of officialdom) but is highly pervasive in other Western European countries too.* One method of atoning for the neglect and failings of their forebears by post-Second World War generations has been through the adoption of a disciplined self-censorship in regard to Jewry in general and Israel in particular.† A similar dynamic can be discerned in regard to non-Western peoples from the former colonies so that anti-Semitism and the Holocaust are replaced by racism and Empire. There is, however, a key difference: whereas, the entire political spectrum (with the exception of the far right and far left) has internalised the guilt emanating from the Nazi Holocaust, in the case of empire and colonisation, by contrast, this appears largely to be confined to liberal/left politics – hence our insertion of 'liberal' before 'guilt'. Such feelings of guilt can be adduced to base emotions but, nonetheless, beg the question as to why those who had no involvement in the crimes and misdemeanours of their forbears should show remorse and guilt – surely, regret would be a more appropriate impulse.‡

Be that as it may, under the pretext of cultural and religious tolerance, multiculturalism provides an especially fertile terrain for the

---

* Similar sentiments of guilt are largely absent in Russia and Eastern Europe despite their history of widespread anti-Semitism and pogroms. One possible explanation for this is that these countries also suffered enormous death and destruction under the Nazis.

† However, with the perennial oppression of the Palestinians by Israel, such discipline, in the UK at least, no longer appears as strong as it has hitherto been. For example, Richard Ingrams (2009), in the midst of Israel's brutal assault on Gaza in January 2009, points out that 'as can be seen from the correspondence column in this paper (*Independent*), the country's critics no longer feel constrained by possible charges of anti-Semitism'.

‡ Though the discussion of this interesting issue is beyond the scope of this book, the two broad categories of mental types made by William James (1988, [1907], p. 12) – 'tough-minded' and 'tender-minded' – may be pertinent. We could offer the tentative hypothesis that for the latter type, feelings of guilt – whether justified or not – hold great sway.

expression of White liberal post-colonial guilt and self-censorship. What is invariably neglected is a fact of great import: guilt-induced silence and self-censorship can have *damaging effects*, most notably that abuses and malfeasance with respect to the weakest and most vulnerable members of minority groups can be allowed to occur without comment or reprimand.

But we need to escape the clutches of empire and, reflexively but erroneously, of what are perceived to be anti-orientalist politics and beliefs. This mode of thinking has had an inevitable and pernicious effect, namely, the tolerance of intolerant, frequently bigoted and oppressive beliefs and practices within minority communities. Apologetics are incessantly used to excuse or justify oppressive practices used by religious-ethnic minorities as sanctioned by culture, religion, or tradition. Often, in regard to religion, the argument develops along the lines that all faiths have doctrines, sacred texts, and rituals, and acknowledges that some of these are indeed less than savoury. Therefore, to 'pick on' one religion ignores the failings of other religions. This has been a favoured ploy by many Muslims and their apologists in recent years. Moreover – and this is usually thought of as the trump card by all believers – criticisms of religiously-inspired repression ignore the myriad atrocities committed in the name of *non*-religious ideologies, usually in the interests of naked power.

But this is, at best, evasive: one can firmly denounce oppression and atrocities from whatever source they emanate. The point is that reasoned argument is a *sine qua non* to do this. It was precisely reasoned argument, evidence, and use of historical context that was employed by critics of the war on Iraq in the run up to the invasion in March 2003; and the same has relentlessly been used against the occupation. Every reason and defence for the war was rigorously interrogated, and demonstrably shown to be false. In India an elephant-dung sweeper will follow elephants and sweep away the trail of dung with a broom. Similarly, the job of critics of the war has been to closely follow the execrable arguments of the warmongers and systematically sweep them away through use of the highest standards of reason and evidence.*

If reason and evidence are deemed essential for critiquing arguments for imperial aggression then why should one suspend these in regard to atrocities committed in the name of religion? A. C. Grayling cogently makes this point:

> No doubt people will still find reason to quarrel, and peoples will still find reasons to go to war with each other; but in the absence of the portmanteau appeal, the all-trumping, simplistic, total motivation that religion provides to people who think it gives them divine sanction to murder strangers, that indeed makes the murder of strangers a moral good, there will have to be much sounder arguments and much better evidence available for doing evil. At present, all that evil needs is the name of faith (Grayling, 2007).

However, we know that much evil is perpetrated without recourse to faith, as with the Iraq war (nothwithstanding the fact that both Bush and Blair are devout Christians). But the crucial point is that the 'murdering of strangers' in the name of religion does not even require the pretext of sound arguments and demonstrable evidence. The sufficient condition is the justification sanctioned by some religious doctrine – reasoned critique is futile and certainly not a necessary condition. This contrasts sharply with murdering of strangers for political and/or economic interests. For the warmongers, the *casus belli* of the war on Iraq was that Saddam Hussein presented a clear and present mortal danger owing to his possession of weapons of mass destruction. Opponents of the war argued that this, in any case,

---

* Some of the arguments for war, which served Bush, Blair *et al.* well, were made by those with some liberal sympathies (hence they most certainly did/do not suffer from White liberal post-colonial guilt); in the past, this grouping was rightly derided as 'B52 liberals' (named after the US Air Force's B52 bomber). In *The Liberal Defence of Murder,* Richard Seymour dissects their ideas, but they are a small minority and, in reality, not all that liberal. With the notable exception of Christopher Hitchens, a key to understanding their strong pro-war politics is strong Zionist sympathies.

was not a *sufficient* condition for an aggressive war: Saddam Hussein had never attacked any Western country and nor was there ever any likelihood of his doing so. Had he done so, he would have been crushed immediately. But post-invasion, no *evidence* whatsoever was, of course, found so that the case for war, *in their own terms*, was shown to be based on a catalogue of grotesque, barefaced lies. Naturally, this did enormous damage to the integrity of advocates of war. Already, it is clear that much sounder arguments and evidence will be required for future wars – this has precisely happened with the next target of the US neocons: Iran. After a report by the US intelligence agencies which clearly stated that Iran had given up its nuclear weapons programme in 2003, the push for attacking Iran received a severe blow (Dombey and Ward, 2007). Consequently, any war on Iran would not even have the pretext of legitimacy, let alone legality. Perhaps it was this that proved decisive in restraining the Bush regime from launching another unprovoked war of aggression.

A further operating principle in regard to the politics of modern anti-imperialism has been the adoption of that old adage, 'my enemy's enemy is my friend'. This has been the *de facto* stance of the left spectrum (almost in its entirety) in Britain since 9/11, the effect of which – yet again – has been the virtual absence of critical engagement with the beliefs of the mass of Muslims and their organisations, who have vehemently protested against the wars in Afghanistan and Iraq. So, we see the formation of an 'unholy alliance' between liberal/ left White secularists and Islamists (overwhelmingly non-White). The world view of these two groups, in almost every other regard, is in stark opposition, with the latter being deeply reactionary and socially conservative – as such, very right wing.[*] Certainly the views

---

[*] The formation of the *Respect* party, led by former Labour MP and foremost critic of the Iraq war, George Galloway, is perhaps the best example of such an unholy (one could say electorally opportunistic) alliance between White secularists and Muslim organisations and individuals. This represented a historic move away from alliances with non-White *secular* groups to campaign against racism and discrimination, to an alliance with avowedly *religious* groups whose agenda, aside from foreign policy, is focused on demands for separate rights, exemptions, and provisions.

of secular, progressive, critics of political Islam in Muslim countries, which have laid bare its manifold dangers, have been blithely ignored or cast aside.*

White liberal post-colonial guilt not only has a strong tendency to suspend reason and evidence with respect to religious-ethnic minorities, it implicitly assumes a *hierarchy of oppression*; at the top of which is racial oppression (and perceived racism). This is followed by women's oppression (importantly, when it predominantly affects majority White women), gay oppression, disabled oppression etc. What is not in the hierarchy is the oppression suffered by those within minority communities by their *own* (usually male) members and, by extension, the myriad oppressive practices in the developing world. Thus, whereas the first in the hierarchy (racism) is now resisted and challenged with admirable force and conviction, the last are invariably quietly ignored, underplayed, or even supported through a variety of apologetics.

A typical example of such apologetics is provided by Mary Dejevsky in an article on a report by Human Rights Watch (HRW) on Saudi Arabia. She provides this reasoning:

> 'Saudi women,' says HRW's researcher … 'won't make any progress until the government ends the abuses that stem from these misguided policies.' I am sure that HRW thinks it is being moderate and pragmatic in calling for an end only to the 'abuses' rather than the sum of 'misguided policies' this country pursues. In so saying, however, the campaigners are not only judging Saudi Arabia by standards it would consider alien, but demanding that it forsake the

---

* Take, for example, the eminent and uncompromisingly secular Lebanese-Palestinian journalist, Samir Kassir who (prior to being murdered in 2005) argued that 'once the religious veil is removed the societal attitudes of the Islamist movements reveal many similarities with fascist dictatorships. If one is to admit political Islam's claim to be a force of change, therefore, one must accept that the democratic deficit is permanent and that the Arab world will never make its appointment with modernity' (Kassir, 2006, p. 29).

whole philosophical, cultural and social system on which it is built (Dejevsky, 2008).

She then discusses the rapid modernisation of Qatar to draw this conclusion:

> The view that women in a Muslim society necessarily enjoy fewer rights than we do may or may not be true. I am repeatedly told by British Muslim women that the Koran is highly protective of women – interpretation, of course, is all. But when campaigners demand an end to such 'misguided' policies as segregation by sex, what they are actually saying is that Western ways rule. One look at the newly prosperous Gulf states should call that assumption into question (*ibid.*).

Now imagine replacing 'Saudi Arabia' in her suggestion that 'judging Saudi Arabia by standards it would consider alien' with say the 'Confederate states during slavery', or 'Apartheid South Africa'. I imagine no one but the most profound reactionary would wish to defend this. She then attempts to offer a further defence by her statement that the contention that 'women in Muslim society necessarily enjoy fewer rights than we do may or may not be true'. But this brazen apologia shows scant knowledge of reality – which is that 'misguided policies', which are infused with Islamic strictures, are the precise cause of women in Muslim societies having far *fewer* rights. And the effete, lazy, punchline of 'Western ways rule' is, in effect, implying that the whole discourse of human rights and women's liberation is solely the preserve of the West. How utterly contemptible this must be to myriad millions of women of the non-Western the world. As appalling as it is, this serves well to illustrate a poignant and revealing example of the corrosive mix of cultural relativism and White post-colonial liberal guilt which leads to the viewing of Arab Muslim society as truly the 'other', including women who suffer from institutionalised and horrific oppression as the HRW report highlights.

Take another interesting and rather unsavoury phenomenon that occurs in Western societies – though its occurrence must not be exaggerated. This is that of Western women voluntarily espousing a culture or religion (usually of their partners) that, in effect, decries the huge gains that have been made by women in the West over the past 200 years and more. Above all, this is especially true of women who convert to Islam – the injunction for which usually occurs as part of their marrying a Muslim man (non-Muslim men who marry Muslim women are not required to convert). To excuse this under the guise of paying respect on the basis of extant, but radically different, traditions and values is also a reflection of White liberal post-colonial guilt and an affront to emancipatory politics and beliefs. In regard to those who convert intentionally to religions that afford them lesser rights, we can assert that – whilst not impinging on their right to convert to a religion of their choice – it is no less than an abandonment of the gains that have made in the West and beyond for women's rights and equality. As such, it represents a betrayal of all those struggles of yesteryear that brought these gains to fruition. Furthermore, it is also a betrayal of the campaigns and struggles which millions in the developing world are engaged in so as to achieve precisely the same gains. Those whom one would ordinarily expect to vigorously make these points – notably, feminist activists and organisations – resist from doing so. Instead, also being afflicted by this guilt complex, they quietly absent themselves from the debate.

In the same vein, we can point to the use of the term 'borderline racism' that has come in vogue of late. In essence this is supposed to occur when, say, a sharp polemic is levelled at an individual or organisation of a religious-ethnic minority background, but when the critic is acknowledged *not* to be motivated by an overt racism. Even if the polemicist in question is an avowed anti-racist this is, nonetheless, tantamount to 'borderline' racism. Once more, unsurprisingly, this possible rejoinder similarly induces guilt-induced self-censorship and undue caution.

An example of the sort of difficulties placed in the way of open criticism of religious-ethnic minorities was provided by novelist Ian McEwan in an interview given to the Italian newspaper *Corriere della Sera*:

> As soon as a writer expresses an opinion against Islamism, immediately someone on the left leaps to his feet and claims that because the majority of Muslims are dark-skinned, he who criticizes it is racist. This is logically absurd and morally unacceptable. Martin [Amis] is not a racist. And I myself despise Islamism, because it wants to create a society that I detest, based on religious belief, on a text, on lack of freedom for women, intolerance towards homosexuality and so on – we know it well (Popham and Porthilo-Shrimpton, 2008).[*]

Indeed we know it all too well – though Martin Amis is rather an undeserving candidate for McEwan's robust and principled defence of freedom of expression. This defence arose after Amis was quite properly attacked by many who ordinarily defend this precious freedom, in particular by the literary critic Terry Eagleton who described his views as vile.[†] This was legitimate as Amis had not made a reasoned critique of Islamism, of the reactionary oppressive beliefs and practices arising from it, but rather associated, in a crude right-wing, neocon manner, terrorist connotations to the 'Muslim community' in general. One unfortunate outcome of this 'vile' tirade was that it played into the hands of those who are forever worried by 'Islamophobia'.

---

[*] The interview with McEwan is tellingly headed 'Ian McEwan faces backlash over press interview'. The journalists in question already assumed that the author's robust attack on reactionary aspects of Islamism, and on those who would wish to silence the likes of him, would automatically lead to a 'backlash'. Unwittingly, they thereby played into the agenda of self-censorship.

[†] This followed Amis's notorious, intemperate outburst: 'the Muslim community will have to suffer until it gets its house in order. What sort of suffering? Not letting them travel. Deportation – further down the road. Curtailing of freedoms. Strip-searching people who look like they're from the Middle East or from Pakistan ... Discriminatory stuff, until it hurts the whole community and they start getting tough with their children ...'. These were rightly described by Eagleton as vile and obnoxious comments (Eagleton, 2007).

For many a year playing the 'race card' was the prerogative of unscrupulous politicians who used this as an invariably successful tactic to drum up electoral support among the White majority – the most notorious example of which was Enoch Powell's 'Rivers of blood' speech in 1968. However, this crude, racist, electoral device was vehemently challenged and, gradually, within the mainstream political parties, has largely become illegitimate. As the racists' playing of the race card faded, we saw the recourse to a variant of it by anti-racists who strongly espoused multiculturalism, notably those immersed in the race relations 'industry'. Their use, as noted in Chapter 1, became increasingly focused on 'cultural racism' whereby criticisms of a minority's culture were deemed to be a surrogate for racism. What had some legitimacy in the climate of rampant racism in the 1970s and '80s – when racists on occasion crudely used 'culture' as a racist disguise – became a means to muffle legitimate observations and criticisms of the beliefs and traditions of non-White minorities.

Plainly, this coupling of 'race' with 'culture' and, later, 'faith' has proved most effective as a guilt-inducing device. But this is a curious kind of what can be termed 'positive racism'; one which implicitly assumes that religious-ethnic minorities are childlike people whose behaviour and beliefs should be excused away without enquiry. The Asian women's rights group, Southall Black Sisters (1990, p. 16), in the midst of the Rushdie saga in 1990 levelled the charge against the left in particular that multiculturalism (with its tolerance of oppressive practices) and anti-racists (meaning the left) 'collude in practice', amounting to, in reality, a non-interventionist stance. A similar charge was levelled by an Asian domestic violence worker a decade later:

> ... Britain wants to be seen as accepting minority communities ... But who benefits? It's the men. White men colluding with black men ... Community leaders advocate what is needed in terms of service provision; they advocate what our religious views are, how to accommodate Islamic values in British society and how to accept the Asian community. They are always ready to give their views with

one distorted dimension or another which reinforces the control that they want to have over women anyway ... So this is multi-cultural politics! (cited in Beckett and Macey, 2001, p. 311).

This important charge was – and indeed remains – justified, but such unprincipled collusion and non-intervention obtained precisely for reasons of White liberal post-colonial guilt, with its conflation of criticisms of religious-ethnic minority *modus vivendi* with racism.

What those who are burdened by the phenomenon of White liberal post-colonial guilt dispense with or neglect is the guidance available on the matter from progressive thinking and theorising. Take one example, that of the influential political philosopher John Rawls who (1971, p. 217, 220) argued, in regard to religious toleration, that under a just constitution, an intolerant sect has no title to complain if it is not tolerated. In a later work, Rawls (1997, p. 98) also usefully invoked the idea of 'reasonable comprehensive doctrines' so that aspects of those doctrines which are not 'reasonable' should not be tolerated; indubitably, these should include oppressive cultural and religious beliefs and traditions that are steeped in intolerance.*

To reiterate: an important corollary of this reluctance or refusal to criticise is that those religious-ethnic minority citizens who are most subjected to oppression, emanating from their 'own' culture or religion, tend also to be those who are least able to offer effective resistance (that is, girls and young women) and so are, to all intents and purposes, liable to be denied a voice and support. A further and little-acknowledged consequence, but one of grave importance, is that guilt-induced silence in the face of such oppression weakens progressive thinking and activism within segregated communities so that these inevitably become marginalised, thereby leaving obscurantist, reactionary dogma to dominate unopposed. This, in turn, weakens

---

* Note that this need not contradict the famous remark attributed to Voltaire: 'I disapprove of what you say, but I will defend to the death your right to say it'. If what is being said is the advocacy of some sort of oppression, then it must be disapproved of and challenged, but a just constitution will not tolerate its *demand* (such as diminished rights for women etc.).

the ability to resist oppression not only from within these communities, but also from external forces, such as racist scapegoating by far right groups. The upshot of this is that White liberal post-colonial guilt can – and does – have a deleterious impact on the push for integration and cohesion.

The weakness of secularism

A profound consequence of silence in regard to oppressive practices within religious-ethic minority communities has been the abandonment, or the downplaying, of key universalist egalitarian, principles. One such principle, which one might assume to be a cornerstone of those claiming to be rational and progressive, is that of secularism. But commitment to this fundamental principle of organising society and its institutions on the basis of reason, free of superstitions, has simply been disregarded and, as ever, myriad apologia have been used to justify this omission. Can this lacuna be attributed, in any way, to the fact that the UK is not a secular state? The monarch is both head of state and the Church of England; the latter remains the established church and 26 of its bishops have the entitlement to a seat in the unelected parliamentary chamber, the House of Lords. Moreover, the non-secular character of the state is imprinted on the various Education Acts that require a daily act of worship, usually of a Christian character.

Nonetheless, this does not alter the increasingly secular character of British *society*. Indeed, as the data above demonstrate, the secular nature of Britain is intensifying, and its society accords well with the 'secularisation thesis', which asserts that 'modernisation ... brings in its wake (and may itself be accelerated by) the diminution of the social significance of religion' (Wallis and Bruce, 1992, p. 11).[*] It is incontrovertible that, for the mass of British citizens, the social significance of religion has very significantly diminished since the

---

[*] Kaufmann (2006) has, however, conjectured that secularisation in Europe is actually in decline owing to the 'fertility advantage' of the religious over non-believers, in combination with the growth of the Muslim population. Wolfe (2006) firmly rebuts Kaufmann's methodology and conclusions.

Second World War. But what is also clear is that institutions of the state and political organisations of all shades have not properly come to terms with this, and nor have they adapted policies to fit this reality. Tradition and inertia reign supreme: *plus ça change, plus c'est la même chose*. This weakness has had, and will continue to have, a deleterious impact on the move to a more integrated and cohesive society. Yet the government maintains (consonant with the views of its predecessors) that religion is of importance to state and citizens, that indeed the UK is a 'multi-faith society' (as we shall see in the next chapter).

But this cuts against the grain of the desires of the majority of UK citizens. As indicated by the polls on faith schools and on sharply declining religiosity, there is clearly a desire for secular schooling, with the corollary of separation of state and religion. These desires are, however, ignored as there is a profound 'interference' of religion in many aspects of state and public institutions. This includes not only the constitution and schooling, but also the health service (for example, the publicly funded chaplains in hospitals), the provision of certain welfare services by religious organisations (such as adoption agencies), the obligation on the public broadcaster, the BBC, to allocate very significant amounts of time and resources to religious programmes.* There is certainly an element of inertia in this case given that, forty–fifty years earlier, there was much interest in such programmes – but that is now simply no longer true. In Chapter 4 we noted the government's introduction of the Racial and Religious Hatred Act 2006 which we argued is a sop to religious groups. Though the blasphemy law has rightly been abolished, this Act in fact risks by stealth the extension of blasphemy to all religions. A secular constitution and state would ensure that such privileges to religious groups would not arise, and so minimise the danger of attendant pork-barrel politics (whereby there are demands, for example, for provision of non-Christian priests in hospital, for non-Christian assemblies at schools, and for provision of non-Christian programmes on the

---

* It is not too uncharitable to think of these, in essence, as no more than preaching and indoctrination.

BBC); which is to assert that secularism is a *sine qua non* for ensuring equality of treatment.

We can make the case that the foundational doctrines of the belief systems of religious-ethnic minorities are pre-Enlightenment. Infused with obscurantism and superstition, they provide a mode of thinking and world view that are very much at odds with modernity. Moreover, we take as axiomatic that this 'clash of reason and unreason' is counterproductive to the cause of social progress and social cohesion. But for these stated and laudable goals to obtain, a necessary condition is that reason must prevail in public life and institutions – which necessitates a secular outlook and secular institutions. Indeed, the granting of privileges and unwarranted consideration to religious bodies and 'faith groups' is tantamount to giving succour and support to 'unreason'. Quite simply, there are no better adverts for secularism than countries and societies where it is absent or very weak. The vista of strong faith identities, sectarian parties and confessional or semi-confessional states is surely an unedifying one. More than that, a strong secular *culture* is vital to ensuring freedom of expression and debate.

Thus, even in some 'best case scenarios' – such as Turkey and India, with (admittedly problematic) secular constitutions – but with long histories of overbearing religious interference and influence in society, albeit to a different extent, the challenge to religious sensibilities can be met with crude censorship and worse. Regarding these countries, the following two examples highlight the point. In Turkey Richard Dawkins' website has been banned ostensibly because of its unrelenting hostility to the ideas of creationism and intelligent design.[*] This is a pretty damning indictment of Turkey's pretensions to be a secular, democratic state. In India the following experience, incurred by the *Independent* columnist Johann Hari, is sobering and chilling. The following extract is from an article Hari wrote in February 2009:

---

[*] See 'Turkey bans biologist Richard Dawkins' website', http://richarddawkins.net/article,3128,Turkey-bans-biologist-Richard-Dawkins-website,Monsters-and-Critics

... that's why I wrote: 'All people deserve respect, but not all ideas do. I don't respect the idea that a man was born of a virgin, walked on water and rose from the dead. I don't respect the idea that we should follow a "Prophet" who at the age of 53 had sex with a nine-year-old girl, and ordered the murder of whole villages of Jews because they wouldn't follow him. I don't respect the idea that the West Bank was handed to Jews by God and the Palestinians should be bombed or bullied into surrendering it. I don't respect the idea that we may have lived before as goats, and could live again as woodlice. When you demand "respect", you are demanding we lie to you. I have too much real respect for you as a human being to engage in that charade.'

An Indian newspaper called *The Statesman* – one of the oldest and most venerable dailies in the country – thought this accorded with the rich Indian tradition of secularism, and reprinted the article. That night, four thousand Islamic fundamentalists began to riot outside their offices, calling for me, the editor, and the publisher to be arrested – or worse. They brought Central Calcutta to a standstill. A typical supporter of the riots, Abdus Subhan, said he was 'prepared to lay down his life, if necessary, to protect the honour of the Prophet' and I should be sent 'to hell if he chooses not to respect any religion or religious symbol! He has no liberty to vilify or blaspheme any religion or its icons on grounds of freedom of speech.'

Then, two days ago, the editor and publisher were indeed arrested. They have been charged – in the world's largest democracy, with a constitution supposedly guaranteeing a right to free speech – with 'deliberately acting with malicious intent to outrage religious feelings'. I am told I too will be arrested if I go to Calcutta (Hari, 2009).

This example is surely a case of *res ipsa loquitur,* hence does not require elaboration. Suffice to say: to inoculate against these terrible dangers is to ensure that there is a maximum emphasis on secularising state institutions and public life, and of confining religious ideas to the private sphere. Unfortunately, even in Britain, there is little sign of such principled politics emanating from the present government and the main opposition parties. That is a vital reason why secularism remains weak, and is an important obstacle to integration and social cohesion.

Chapter 7

Solutions

Breaking down segregation, increasing integration and cohesion

Surveying parts of modern British cities and towns, it would seem that Kipling's famous ode ('The Ballad of East and West') of 1889 to the supposed irreconcilability of East and West: 'Oh, East is East and West is West and never the twain shall meet', now applies *within* the West also.* Whereas in the days of the British Empire, it was the White colonialists who ensured that they did not socially mix with those of a darker hue, the situation in Britain, in regard to many settlers from the 'East', seems to have been reversed: it is *they* who appear now to be largely responsible for not mixing with those of a lighter hue. This has accentuated a problem that has inexorably deepened over the past five decades: the sprawling, segregated neighbourhoods of religious-ethnic minorities that have arisen throughout the country. We noted that the origins of these lay in a combination of 'choice' and 'constraints' and there is good reason to believe that 'choice', (that is, self-segregation) is now of greater importance. This was borne out by the Bradford Race Review (2001), a crucial finding of which was that 'community and religious leaders' were now perpetuating segregation and, by implication, vigorously enforcing their cultural and religious practices on the young within 'their' community.

We now hypothesise a 'twin movement' that has insufficiently been discussed in regard to relationships between the majority society and ethnic minority groups. First, a movement of 'attraction': this is the coming closer together of migrant settlers and their descendants and the indigenous population. We noted in Chapter 3 that with the passage of time since the early period of migration post-Second World War, the indigenous population by and large has become more willing

---

* However, less famous is the third line which seems to be a negation of the first: 'But there is neither East nor West, Border, nor Breed, nor Birth' (Kipling, 1889).

to accept migrants and their children as legitimate citizens. This is a key determinant for the overall declining levels of racism towards settled communities. But such a generalisation should, however, not detract from the racism and xenophobia that still prevails – plainly, for example, such legitimacy and tolerance is generally not afforded to asylum seekers (as highlighted by, for example, the work of the Commission of Racial Equality in the UK (now Equality and Human Rights Commission) or The European Monitoring Centre on Racism and Xenophobia (now EU Agency for Fundamental Rights).

The second movement follows and counters the first: it is that of 'rejection' *by* certain migrant communities (especially within segregated areas) of the host society, where there has been a decline in points of contact with 'outsiders' – either because of unwillingness or lack of necessity to do so. Moreover, the dynamic of segregation has *increased* – being driven by the aforementioned 'choice' factors whereby migrants *choose* only to live in areas with their co-ethnic or co-religious brethren. This, in turn, engenders alienation on the part of sections of the indigenous White society so that religious-ethnic minorities become the 'other' in their midst, confirming the scenario of Kipling's poem.

Our charge is that this dynamic can be explained by the contributory role played by multiculturalism, and its offspring multifaithism, in the entrenchment of strong religious-ethnic identities, isolation, ghettoisation and attendant psychic detachment. For many Asian (in particular, Muslim) communities, this has led to their being trapped in a mono-cultural, mono-faith straitjacket. It would be the height of irresponsible politics to allow this profoundly disquieting phenomenon to continue unabated. Firm measures need to be taken to reverse the tide – this has become an urgent task of the greatest import. This chapter considers the factors which we consider to be absolutely vital to the achievement of a genuinely integrated and socially cohesive society.

We have acknowledged and highlighted throughout this book that government thinking has, in recent years, veered away from an emphasis on 'difference' between peoples to the objective of integration and community cohesion, with the implicit recognition that the former has become a hindrance to the achievement of the latter. As an element in furthering this new objective, given added urgency by the 7/7 bombs in London, the Department of Communities and Local Government, in June 2006, set up a Commission on Integration and Cohesion (COIC). Its remit was to examine the benefits of diversity as well as the tensions it sometimes engenders, and to make recommendations concerning improving community cohesion, focusing on the local ('community') level. The Commission (chaired by Darra Singh, Chief Executive of Ealing Council) duly reported a year later, in June 2007. The title of the final report 'Our Shared Future' was taken from the first key principle of the Commission:

> The sense of **shared** futures which we believe is at the heart of our model and our recommendations – an emphasis on articulating what binds communities together rather than what differences divide them, and prioritising a shared future over divided legacies (COIC, 2007, p. 7).

Indeed, this is refreshing and positive (despite the clumsiness of expression) – and a recognition that the previous emphasis on 'celebrating differences' between communities, espoused under multiculturalism, is to be downplayed (with the implication that this is/ has been a contributory factor to bringing about 'divided legacies'). Contrast this approach with, for example, the recommendation made by The Parekh Report (The Future of Multi-Ethnic Britain) with its repeated stress on 'differences' and its recommendation that 'the government should formally declare that the United Kingdom is a multicultural society …' (The Parekh Report, 2000, p. 313).[*] So far, so good. But when the Commission's report goes on to recognise that 'diversity can have a negative impact on cohesion, but only in particular local circumstances' – by which is meant those urban areas

---
[*] Note that this report was not commissioned by the government but rather by the Runnymede Trust.

which are starting to experience diversity and ethnically diverse areas experiencing new migration (COIC, p. 9) – it neglects to mention by far the most important local circumstance, namely, the high levels of segregation in towns and cities with long-settled, diverse, migrant communities. This is an astonishing lacuna given that it is the existence of precisely this social reality, and eventual acknowledgement, that prompted the government to begin to take some corrective measures, including establishing the Commission. Furthermore, the definition of integration and cohesion used is problematic:

> Cohesion is principally the process that must happen in all communities to ensure different groups of people get on well together; while integration is principally the process that ensures new residents and existing residents adapt to one another' (*loc. cit.*)

But residents can 'adapt to one another' by simply ignoring each other – as indeed happens in segregated areas. This is not at all what is ordinarily meant by 'integration' and the report's breakdown of what an integrated and cohesive community looks like, unfortunately, does not provide much clarification. For example, 'there is a clearly defined and widely shared sense of the contribution of different individuals and different communities to a future vision for a neighbourhood, city, region or country' (*op. cit.,* p. 10). What exactly does this mean? Of the six points provided, it is only the last which is on the right track: 'there are strong and positive relationships between people from different backgrounds in the workplace, in schools and other institutions within neighbourhoods' (*loc. cit.*). This closely approximates to our 'points of contact' – and lack thereof – of those in segregated neighbourhoods. The problem is how to bring this about and, in this regard, the report is rather lacking: there is little concern for desegregating minorities, the problems of faith schools (see below) or of achieving the erosion of religious identities.

In a follow-up report by the Department of Communities and Local Government, published in 2008, entitled *Face to Face and Side* *by Side*, the subtitle makes explicit its understanding of British society: *A framework for partnership in our multi faith society* (DCLG, 2008). Investment of £7.5m over three years is set aside to bring together 'faith groups' in 'partnership' to deliver local services via the creation of a new local 'Faiths in Action fund' and 'Regional Faith Forums'. This is clearly a retreat from the COIC report and a mistaken and dangerous espousal of multifaithism.* Dangerous precisely because, as has been highlighted in previous chapters, the 'partners' in question are invariably the dominant forces within faith communities, that is male religious 'elders' and community leaders (who are, in the main, highly committed to the faith). These men tend to be profoundly reactionary, antithetical to gender equality, and help maintain, through coercive means, the oppression of women and children. Involving such people in delivering local services is a folly and must be rejected: provision of public services must remain on a secular basis.

The 7/7 London bombings, as well as other actual and planned attacks emanating from the radicalisation of young Muslims, has naturally concentrated the mind of the government as to how to tackle this problem. A key plank has been the creation of, in April 2007, 'The Preventing Violent Extremism: Winning Hearts and Minds' fund, totalling £76 million over three years towards various local projects.† Then Communities Secretary Hazel Blears rationalised this endeavour as follows:

> What I want to do is strengthen the mainstream moderate Muslims in this country, who are the overwhelming majority, but also those vulnerable youngsters so they have the ability to say 'You are ex-

---

* Indeed, the Department's website's entry on 'Faith communities' retains the emphasis on 'different faiths': 'Multi-cultural communities are often multi-faith communities and this should be fully recognised in policies aimed at promoting diversity. Fostering understanding and respect between different faiths is vital in practically implementing community cohesion strategies', http://www.communities.gov.uk/communities/racecohesionfaith/faith/faithcommunities/

† See Improvement and Development Agency, 'Background to PVE', http://www.idea.gov.uk/idk/core/page.do?pageId=7946870

treme. Your version of my faith is not correct. I don't want to be part of that' (Beckford, 2008).

The problem is that there is no guarantee whatsoever that this initiative will root out Islamist radicalisation and 'extremism', for it does not tackle its root causes. What this version of pork-barrel politics is, however, likely to do is to cement the power of *soi disant* 'mainstream, moderate Muslims' – the community leaders and those controlling mosques – adding fuel to the reactionary fire of 'faith communities' and faith identities. Moreover, it shall inevitably alienate the majority society as well as giving cause to non-Islamic groups to demand funds for similar faith-based projects. All these are, surely, contrary to the goals of integration and social cohesion.

So this is a misguided and irresponsible waste of resources. As we argue below, the main cause of Islamist radicalisation and 'extremism' and appeal of terror tactics is an unjust foreign policy – as was made abundantly clear by Mohommed Siddique Khan, one of the London 7/7 bombers.* Replace this with a just policy, which necessarily means non-militarist, and you remove at one fell swoop much of the *raison d'être* of Islamist grievances and the material basis of extremism and terrorism.

In conjunction with this, what is of urgent necessity are measures to help religious-ethnic minority citizens to break free from their isolation and the segregation that is rife within faith communities. Minimising inter-communal stress and tension, and increasing integration and cohesion, requires a concerted inclusiveness into mainstream society, in both mental and material terms. The *sine qua non* of egalitarian universalism, which we have advocated as a superior

---

* In a videotape, made prior to the bombing, Siddique Khan explained his motives thus: 'Your democratically elected governments continuously perpetuate atrocities against my people all over the world. And your support of them makes you directly responsible, just as I am directly responsible for protecting and avenging my Muslim brothers and sisters. Until we feel security, you will be our targets. And until you stop the bombing, gassing, imprisonment and torture of my people we will not stop this fight. We are at war and I am a soldier. Now you too will taste the reality of this situation' (BBC News 1/9/2005).

alternative to multiculturalism and multifaithism, is the tackling of racial and gender discrimination in all its forms, notably in the fields of employment, housing, policing, other public services, and in the private sector. A 'colour and difference blind approach' is the best guarantee to root out discrimination, and would approximate to what John Rawls terms the 'veil of ignorance'. This is a conceptual device whose aim it is to:

> nullify the effects of specific contingencies which put men at odds and tempt them to exploit social and natural circumstances to their advantage ... As far as possible, then, the only particular facts which the parties know is that their society is subject to the circumstances of justice and whatever this implies. It is taken for granted, however, that they know the general facts about human society (Rawls, 1971, pp. 136–137).

The *raison d'être* for this approach, therefore, is to ensure justice. Granted that the conditions required to meet it are extremely severe, and apply to what Rawls describes as the 'original position', the purpose behind the veil of ignorance nonetheless retains its positive force in 'normal' conditions. For our purposes, the result from this is that religious-ethnic identities, in particular, must be hidden beneath a veil of ignorance.

Desegregating community schools and phasing out faith schools
At heart, the problem of desegregation of schools is of desegregating communities – which necessitates dismantling segregated neighbourhoods. If the latter can be achieved, the former will naturally follow. Yet the deep entrenchment of segregated neighbourhoods is such that it will take a prolonged and sustained effort of great political and financial will to bring this about. So far in Britain, however, there has been no sign of this level of genuine desire or commitment by any of the political parties to do so. Moreover, this is also certainly the case with 'community leaders'. Indeed, matters may actually worsen,

including bouts of riots and urban unrest, before any concerted action is embarked upon, by which time it may be a case of too little too late, as was the case with ghetto riots in the US during the 1960s (see, for example, Kerner, 1967). The danger is that the entrenchment of pure religious-ethnic neighbourhoods may come to be accepted as the 'normal' state of affairs, as is the case with Black ghettos in so many large US cities.

Given that race/ethnicity is potentially a powerful force for causing divisions, given that we are still in a society sharply divided by class, it behoves us to minimise further divisions of peoples – and very few other social identities divide as much, or in so pernicious a manner, as religion. Whereas one's race/ethnicity is purely an accident of birth that cannot be changed, one's religion, to an overwhelming extent, is also an accident of birth but with the crucial difference that it has the potential of being changed. This distinction suggests that divisions based on religion have an artificial quality, which is to say are 'man made', notwithstanding the enormous difficulties of effecting a change of religion, or abandoning it altogether.

Accordingly, we make the value judgement that a gradual withering away of 'faith identities' will enormously aid the cause of social justice, integration, and cohesion. Public policy, above all in regard to school education, can significantly rein in this artificial division, a task that is made inordinately easier as a consequence of the relentless decline in belief in the UK (excepting Northern Ireland and small parts of Scotland) so that religious identity has become largely irrelevant to the mass of the population. In the previous chapter, we saw unambiguous evidence and cogent reasons as to the inherently divisive nature of faith schools. Minority-faith schools are especially toxic given that they are an ideal conduit for the entrenchment of a mono-faith straitjacket on children. This unanswerable fact most obviously points to the solution of removing the tag of religious identity in schools. Of necessity, this requires the immediate cessation of more minority-faith schools and for the phasing out of all faith schools (notably Anglican, Catholic and Jewish) and their conversion into secular community schools. That way, the charge of discrimination against the newer, minority faiths does not hold. No one can deny that this will not be easily achieved, and will attract great hostility from advocates of faith schools and the various faith communities. But any serious attempt at achieving a socially cohesive integrated society requires such firm and principled actions.

One fear a government may have regarding abolishing faith schools is that of an electoral backlash. This is certainly a strong possibility in regard to the minority of the electorate which supports and utilises faith schools, and undoubtedly there will be some electoral impact in those constituency wards where they are located. Notwithstanding the opposition to faith schools, it is argued by proponents that they provide higher academic standards and this is the crucial reason why they are popular, often heavily over-subscribed, and helps explain why families sometimes move house and feign faith to ensure their children's attendance. The implication is that this outweighs any actual or perceived disadvantages. But research on faith schools challenges this view. For example, research by Steven Gibbons and Olmo Silva on primary faith schools in England found:

- Faith primary schools could offer a very small advantage over secular schools in terms of age-11 test scores in Maths and English. Attending the average Faith school rather than the average secular school could move a pupil around 1 percentile further up the test-based pupil rankings.
- Any benefit of attending a primary Faith school is linked to the more autonomous admission and governance arrangements that characterised 'Voluntary Aided' schools during the period covered by our data. Pupils in religiously affiliated schools where admissions were under the control of the Local Education Authority ('Voluntary Controlled' schools) do not progress faster than pupils in secular primary schools.
- All of the apparent advantage of Faith school education – particularly for Church of England schools – could be explained by

unobserved differences between pupils who apply and are admitted to Faith schools and those who do not: pupils who *do not* attend a Faith primary school up to age 11 but attend a Faith secondary school thereafter perform just as well at age 11 as students who attended a Faith primary school but then attend a secular secondary school (Gibbons and Silva, 2006, P. 4).

But findings such as these are blithely ignored. Be that as it may, given the fact that some two-thirds of the population oppose faith schools (as we saw in the previous chapter), the net electoral impact is likely to be favourable, all the more so if secular, community schools are provided with the same resources. Moreover, there is a precedent for such a programme – that of converting grammar schools to comprehensives in the 1970s. Indeed, this policy by the Labour government (and attendant phasing out of the highly divisive 'Eleven Plus' entrance test) had widespread support which the Conservative governments that followed, from 1979 onwards, did not undo.* There is no reason to believe that, once implemented, a similar acceptance will not follow by the populace at large and, indeed, by all the major political parties.

We noted above that the COIC report failed to deal with the issue of faith schools. Yet the report unequivocally acknowledges the importance of the issue (COIC, 2007, pp. 116–117):

> We noted in our Interim Statement that many people had told us that they see faith schools as a significant barrier to integration and cohesion. Others, especially from faith communities, had said that faith schools are vital to helping their young people develop as strong and confident British citizens. During the further period of consultation, we continued to find these very different perspectives and the online user forum received a number of inputs from those who are troubled by the existence of 'faith schools', which they saw as potentially divisive.

* The policy was not fully implemented as some grammar schools, albeit a small percentage, remained.

Inexplicably, the report's recommendations regarding faith schools simply ignore these powerful – and truthful – inputs. Instead, what is recommended is decidedly meek and evasive:

> And although state supported faith schools are not required to teach multi-faith Religious Education, we note that in February 2006, leaders from the main UK faiths signed a joint statement to promote a scheme to teach pupils about other religions as well as their own, and to follow the guidance in the national non-statutory framework for RE. Together with promoting opportunities for meeting students from other backgrounds through twinning schemes and beyond the school gates activities, it will be important for Government to monitor the effectiveness of this voluntary agreement on RE in faith schools. We also recommend consideration of whether Ofsted inspections should cover RE teaching in faith schools (which is currently exempt) (*op. cit.*, p. 117).

Another government report that avoids tackling the dangers of faith schools, and of faith identities, is the Ajegbo Report (2007). Entitled *Curriculum Review: Diversity Citizenship,* this was commissioned by the Department for Education and Skills (now Department of Children Schools and Families), and led by a former headteacher, Sir Keith Ajegbo. This report examines the important issue of education and diversity. Unlike the COIC report, however, it does not discuss faith schools, let alone provide an explanation as to why these schools are opposed by two-thirds of the population. Nor does it engage with the divisiveness of faith identities which will inevitably be accentuated by a rise in the numbers of minority-faith schools. These issues should surely have constituted the core of the report. Instead what is served up are apologetics such as this:

> Throughout the [Non-Statutory National Framework for Religious Education] framework the importance of diversity is stressed: 'Religious education encourages pupils to develop their sense of identity

and belonging ... It enables them to flourish individually within their communities and as citizens in a pluralistic society and global community' (Ajegbo Report, 2007, p. 55).

This illustrates a complete failure to comprehend that within 'faith communities' especially, the possibility of a more rounded view of the world, and of fellow citizens, must largely come from outside the confines of the family and community. The 'danger' of contacts with 'outsiders' is one crucial reason why 'leaders' of faith communities are so keen to establish faith schools. Indubitably, the potential for questioning religious doctrines is much higher in mixed schools – indeed, as was pointed out in the last chapter such questioning is not likely to be tolerated if all the children are from one faith. Also noted was the poll which showed that two-thirds of children of 12–19 years old do not have a religion – these will overwhelmingly be White. Hence we would expect White school children to be the most critical and challenging of religious beliefs, a fact surely not lost on such leaders, and why they incessantly worry about the secular mainstream society. But it is undeniably the case that White children will not wish to attend minority-faith schools and, will, in any case, be discouraged from doing from so by their parents.

The suggestion by the Labour government to bring in more 'faith-based' schools should, therefore, be fiercely resisted. Not only do they entrench ghettoisation, but they also largely deny children a proper understanding of others by cementing in them the belief that 'their faith' is superior to all others. As such, they can potentially act as a conduit for intolerance. Just as we require schools to be free of racism and of racial stereotyping and prohibit them from allying with political parties, so we should require them not to ally with a religion or grant exemptions to the curriculum on the grounds of religious belief. This acts as an important counterweight to the often intense indoctrination of one faith that children of devout parents receive at home. Indeed, this is analogous to the influence of racist thinking and language that some White children may receive from their parents. It is imperative that a child's accident of birth should not preclude a broad, critical, tolerant education.

Accordingly, a critical education is obviously best provided in mixed community schools which are *rigorously secular*. This is not to suggest that there should be a complete absence of religion from the curriculum; on the contrary, religion should be taught as an academic subject and not as dogmatic instruction in rituals of a particular faith. The privilege accorded to Christianity in the daily act of worship that is required by law must be ended. In practice, this would enable the school to become a religion-free space for children so that they would not be artificially divided by the accident of birth stemming from their parents' religions. They thus would leave behind religious accoutrements at home, and be able to learn in a free, equal, less divisive and more tolerant environment. Secular schooling is, therefore, a necessary – though not necessarily sufficient – condition for eroding these religious divisions and any attendant tensions and animosities.

A rigorous pursuit of this policy might then enable children, as they matured, to take up a critical view of customs foisted on them, as well as being more understanding and tolerant of differences between various peoples. This would go an enormous way towards immunising them from bigoted views – and negating what can be termed the *segregation of the mind* (which can later facilitate high levels of psychic detachment). Consequently, the wearing of religious items should be disallowed in all state schools. It follows, therefore, that there is an urgent need for a law equivalent to that passed in France on religious symbols in schools (as discussed in Chapter 5). This is an absolutely essential element in enabling desegregation to occur and to assist in integration and social cohesion. Religious critics will no doubt argue (as they did in France) that this represents a type of 'secular fundamentalism' to which the response is obvious: only by an inclusive, secular and equal schooling can children obtain a rounded education. Recall from the previous chapter the stark danger of faith schools highlighted by Sen: 'young children are powerfully placed in the domain of singular affiliations well before they have the ability to reason about different systems of identification that may compete for their attention'. Consequently, it is of paramount importance that young children must be protected from the domain of 'singular affiliations'.

Changing the habitus through 'creolisation'
The process of desegregation will certainly be fraught with difficulties and it may take at least a generation to effect real, lasting, change – assuming that the necessary policies have been put in place. The entrenched, segregated neighbourhoods of religious-ethnic minorities, with high levels of psychic detachment, will necessitate the altering of what Pierre Bourdieu has termed their *habitus*, which he elaborates upon as follows:

> The structures constitutive of a particular kind of environment (e.g. the material conditions of existence characteristic of a class condition) produce *habitus,* systems of durable, transposable *dispositions* … it also designates a *way of being*, a *habitual state* … and, in particular, a *predisposition, tendency, propensity or inclination* (Bourdieu, 1977, p, 72; fn 1, p. 214).

Although Bourdieu uses this concept to refer to social class, it can also fruitfully be applied to segregated religious-ethnic communities. But altering their *habitus*, their 'way of being', will not at all be easy given that it requires the loosening and ultimate dissolution of closed cultural and religious mores. A corollary to this is transforming what Baumann and Gingrich (2004) have termed the 'grammars of identity' (that is, the construction of identity formation, and exclusion of the 'other') and, ultimately, identity itself. A *sine qua non* for this is physical and mental de-segregation. That said, we have acknowledged that self-segregation is quite explicable given that the familiarity and trust it engenders provides a powerful impulse for remaining within the confines of close-knit communities. Nonetheless, those 'trapped' within tend to be the poorest, most vulnerable, section of society, cajoled and coerced into identifying with the frequently reactionary ideas and customs of their culture and religion.

There is, therefore, a double struggle necessary in order to alter the oppressive features of the *habitus*: one against economic deprivation and racism in all its manifestations but, in tandem, one against oppressive customs. In both struggles, it is women who benefit the most. A sense of this can be gleaned by the existence of a multitude of organisations and refuges in Britain who have, for decades, brought into the public domain inside knowledge of abusive practices in regard to women. Importantly, they have conducted this important social task without any significant support from the state or, indeed, from mainstream feminist and 'left' organisations that ordinarily campaign for women's rights. The key proposition here is that the struggle against racial and gender discrimination and for equal rights is weakened, even demeaned, by the pervasive, oppressive practices that are oft-committed, but silently tolerated, within religious-ethnic minority communities.

Indubitably, attempts at changing the *habitus* of segregated communities are likely to be resisted on the grounds of the fear of 'dilution of culture' (or, more accurately, its transformation through absorbing aspects of other cultures, and the creation of new cultural traits). Such thinking is prevalent in all communities but is, undoubtedly, greatest in Asian ones. Perhaps it is least prevalent among Afro-Caribbeans. Socio-economic advancement, alongside a diminution of racism, is a necessary, but not a sufficient, condition for the reduction of this fear of change. Nonetheless, the argument needs forcefully to be made that, rather than this transformation being something to be alarmed about, it can be enormously enriching in an increasingly closer and integrated world. And for good reasons that have already been given: it increases understanding and awareness of others, reduces ethnic tensions, and provides a bulwark against bigotry. Yet, it is clear that, out of fealty to the 'home' country, religion, traditions and customs, there remains a very great reluctance and even hostility to change.

But the world changes, and is changing rapidly. A key contributory factor of this is the mass migrations of people, in the main from the developing to the developed world. The coming together of different peoples has, in many ways, brought about the altering of lifestyles of significant numbers of both host and settler populations. Indeed, in countries where the ruling regimes fear external influences, and the possibility of social and cultural transformation, the prevention of this is achieved only by the severest state-sanctioned repressive measures. In stark contrast, in societies with a more liberal outlook, where groups and individuals do not feel bound by 'essentialist' group identities, change has flourished. Indeed, we can describe the change in identity and lifestyle that has occurred in many parts of the world, including in developed heartlands, as a form of 'creolisation', a term which Robin Cohen argues has 'universal applicability':

> It describes a position interposed between two or more cultures, selectively appropriating some elements, rejecting others, and creating new possibilities that transgress and supersede parent cultures, which themselves are increasingly recognized as fluid. If this is indeed happening on a significant scale, we need to recast much traditional social theory concerning race and ethnic relations, multiculturalism, nation-state formation, and the like, for we can no longer assume the stability and continuing force of the ethnic segments that supposedly make up nation-states. Likewise, we cannot assume that the nation in international relations has a continuously uniform character. To accept the force of hybridity and creolization is also to accept that humankind is refashioning the basic building blocks of organized cultures and societies in a fundamental and wide-ranging way ... Behind the strident assertions of nationalism, 'old ethnicities,' and religious certainties is an increasing volume of cultural interactions, interconnections, and interdependencies and a challenge to the solidity of ethnic and racial categories (Cohen, 2007, pp. 99, 100).

Creolisation is, therefore, the process of a thoroughgoing integration through *meaningful contacts* between different people of cultural and racial groups, which stimulates the creation of *new* cultural patterns and altered identities by the absorption of parts of more than one culture.* It is conducive to miscegenation and so breaks down 'the solidity of ethnic and racial categories', bringing in its wake the existence of 'new people', that is, those of 'mixed heritage'. Indeed a 'Creole' is precisely someone of more than one ethnic/racial category.

It is this dynamic and outcome that multiculturalism and multifaithism, with fixed identities and mindsets, seek to resist and prevent, and have done so with considerable effect and with minimal resistance. The challenge to those seeking a truly integrated and cohesive society is to resist and reverse such fixed identities and mindsets in a most concerted manner whilst being cognisant of the fact that the loosening of ethnic, religious, and racial categories is a force for social good. We make the explicit value judgement that, in the hierarchy of a desired outcome (to include, say, assimilation, creolisation, multiculturalism/multifaithism), where people from different ethnicities and backgrounds live in close proximity and with equality under the law, creolisation is certainly the most desirable, with the caveat that oppressive beliefs and practices from whatever source are intolerable. Though it is rarely acknowledged, to a significant extent there has been a process of creolisation in Britain since the 1950s – accelerating through the decades, which is most evident in London. The most marked aspect of this has indeed been the increase in inter-racial marriages and partnerships – but mixing of peoples in all aspects of society, be it work, leisure, or civic activities, has given impetus to creolisation. It is *mixing* that is the key and offers the potential for social cohesion and lessening of stress caused by ethnic, religious, or cultural divisions. To stress, once more, the reason why

---

* The term 'fusion' also has a similar meaning as in 'fusion music' and 'fusion food' etc. Along the same lines though somewhat different is the term 'hybridity', which signifies an entity of two fairly distinct components. 'Hybrid' persons are those with parents of different ethnic/racial groups but are more commonly referred to as 'mixed race' or 'mixed ethnicity' (for a helpful discussion, see Verkuyten, 2006, pp. 151–156). Bhaba (1994) has an interesting discussion of hybridity in the context of the post-colonial era.

multiculturalism is the least favourable outcome is that it *discourages* and even *prevents* the mixing of peoples, a corollary of which is a high degree of isolation and separation.

In the previous chapter, we noted the possibility that even if neighbourhoods are mixed – meaning that people from different ethnic and religious backgrounds live in the same geographical space – there is no guarantee that the residents will intermingle in a meaningful manner. Our assumption is that intermixing is a societal good and its obverse, segregation, is harmful – especially for children. But we now wish to stress the possibility/danger that, even in geographically mixed neighbourhoods, forcible separation of children can start soon after birth. How? One avenue is through what is known as 'faith-based' nursery care. For those with a strong sense of religious identity, nursery facilities run by appropriate religious organisations are an appealing means of ensuring that their offspring, soon after birth, only intermingle with those of 'their' religious identity; moreover, the process of indoctrination into the faith occurs from a very young age. Though such a development has thankfully not as yet taken off in Britain, it is a common phenomenon in the US and Canada.*

Given the costs involved, such faith-based nursery care is likely to be the preserve of the middle classes. For religious-ethnic minority middle class people such faith-based care becomes a powerful mechanism in denying children the opportunity of mixing with those from different backgrounds. Moreover, the logical follow up for those parents who send their children to these types of nurseries is to try and ensure that they subsequently enrol in faith-based schools. The consequence is clear: such children will lead parallel lives, soon after their birth, through absolutely no choice of their own. Naturally, the implications of this are enormous so the problem has to be nipped in the bud by the prevention of faith-based nurseries. Hence, unless multiculturalist policies, including the focus on 'faith communities', are reversed, this troubling phenomenon is entirely possible in the UK.

---

* See for example the website canadianchristianity.com. Adherents think it preferable to have daycare in a church basement than in a non-profit secular state-run nursery.

Challenging oppressive cultural and religious mores

Andrew Kernohan has persuasively argued that there are analogies to be drawn between cultural oppression and environmental pollution:

> People can dispute about what the thresholds are, but at some level of pollution they will agree on the existence of a problem. Cultural oppression is not like that, [it] is covert: it functions to make inequality of moral worth seem natural to both dominant and subordinate groups. Those afflicted by cultural pollution frequently will truly believe inequality to be appropriate. Unlike the people of Mexico City [who notice traffic pollution], they will not notice their affliction. However, we can draw a parallel to another type of environmental pollution where the harm is hidden, and we must appeal to theory to discover it. For instance, it often takes chemical analysis to reveal the pesticides in the drinking water, and it may take further scientific research to decide what the threshold of harm is. Cultural oppression is more like the pesticide case. As in the pesticide case, we have to appeal to theory – here, the agreed-upon liberal principle of the equal moral worth of persons* – to see that people's beliefs in inequality are false. Then, to justify state action, we have to seek further arguments to show that leading people to have false ethical beliefs is a harm (Kernohan, 1998, p. 10).

It should be clear from this book that a primary reason for our opposition to multiculturalism and multifaithism is that they not only tolerate but provide intellectual cover for oppressive beliefs and practices of religious-ethnic minorities, which can be considered as polluting of the cultural environment. There is a double standard at play here given that such toleration is most certainly not afforded to 'cultural pollutants' (such as racism and sexism) emanating from the majority White society. The phenomenon of White liberal post-colonial guilt (discussed in the previous chapter) that so often tolerates this double standard must be set aside.

---

* 'Agreed upon' as Kernohan is engaging with avowed liberals.

Hence, strong support must be provided to those struggling to shake off the oppressive shackles within religious-ethnic communities, particularly to girls and women. True, women's oppression exists in all societies but this offers no defence for inaction given that the differences in degree are massive. In the West, economic development and the concomitant rise of a high degree of economic dependence for women has led to incessant campaigns for equality in all spheres of life; and laws enacted that, in intent at least, outlaw systematic discrimination. Though full equality has yet to be achieved, the gains have been real and tangible. Yet, there is often a profound clash of these gains with those of values of religious-cultural minorities that accord primacy to the woman's role as wife, mother and homemaker, all of which place her in a generally subservient position to the assumed breadwinner, the husband. Women have, of course, the right to be homemakers and to be subservient to their husbands. But this should not be based on a denial, as is so often the case, of their right to higher education, to work and to build careers. Hence, 'unequal moral worth' of persons must not be tolerated in the name of cultural relativism, or religious or cultural sensitivities.

There is evidence to show that unwarranted religious and cultural sensitivities can have a deleterious impact on the health and well being of those to whom the sensitivities are directed. Take, for example, breastfeeding. When women MPs for the Green Party in Germany were first elected to the Bundestag in the 1980s and 1990s, there was initial unease when those with infant children started breastfeeding in the debating chamber. But the Greens were right to point out that this was an entirely natural act, which set an important social example, for which no shame should be attached when conducted in public. Moreover, it was an important assertion of gender equality. This sent a powerful signal to the rest of German society (and beyond) that not only was breastfeeding important, it was an acceptable practice in public spaces. Furthermore, mothering of babies was not a barrier to women fulfilling important roles. True, this was novel and exceptional but what it highlights is that religious or cultural morals were not invoked to prevent breastfeeding in the German parliament: what took precedence for its advocates was the well-being of the infant and, on this, critics were wrong-footed or silenced. The Venezuelan government has taken the most principled stance by passing a law that grants all working mothers the right to breastfeed, requiring employers to set aside an allotted time for this.* One would find such a phenomenon and eventuality well-nigh impossible in those societies and cultures that were infused with powerful religious mores and lobbies.

The issue of breastfeeding has arisen in public life also in the UK. The Department of Health advocates it as the best method of feeding a baby. One way it has done this is by producing an information document freely available in GP surgeries and hospitals (Department of Health, 2004). The document offers guidance on how to breastfeed (importance of good sitting posture, how to hold the baby, the need to be patient) through the use of clear photographs of two representative mothers undertaking the different stages of breastfeeding. The document is socially progressive, not in only its advocacy of breastfeeding and how it is done most effectively, but also by its use of examples: one being a Black and one a White mother.

Curiously, however, no photo of an Asian mother is shown – even though the percentage of Asian women in the UK is much higher than that of Black women. One can conjecture that the reason for this is because of cultural and religious sensibilities: it is not deemed appropriate to show partially naked images of Asian women, even when performing a most natural act which the health service advocates as best practice for *all* women with babies. But might not images of an Asian woman breastfeeding further encourage Asian women to take up breastfeeding? The NHS could not assume that this was unnecessary on the grounds that Asian women, in the main, breastfeed in any case. Whether this is true or not, it does not override the argument for not allowing such sensibilities to interfere with good health practices. In regard to health and well-being, cultural and religious

---

* In article 393 of the Organic Law of Labour.

sensibilities must be set aside.*

Legislation is an important tool for change and laws exist which prohibit egregious cultural practices such as female genital mutilation, forced marriages, Shia-style self-flagellation and polygamy. In regard to the outlawing of forced marriages, there is also an implicit criticism of the system of arranged marriages – which rely, to varying degrees, on at least an element of coercion even when 'voluntarily' entered into.† Whilst the outlawing of such practices is positive and necessary, it is not always a sufficient preventative measure. True, by making these illegal, a powerful signal is sent out, not just to those perpetrating such acts but to those who are the victims, and ought to give some confidence to those resisting such abuse. Nonetheless, these oppressive practices still occur probably in significant numbers (accurate data are notoriously difficult to obtain) as with the cases of young women being taken to Pakistan and entered into forced marriages with local men, or of Sudanese women being taken back to their home country (sometimes voluntarily) for vaginal mutilation. Accordingly, the challenge to such beliefs and practices must begin at a young age through the creation of a social *milieu* in which such

---

* A notorious instance of religion acting directly against the interest of human health is that of Jehovah's Witnesses' refusal to allow blood transfusions: such an inhuman injunction represents the most blatant breach of the Hippocratic Oath and must be discarded.

† A seemingly cogent argument in defence of arranged marriages is that they seem to work, whereby the divorce rate that results is much lower than that emanating from 'love marriages'. In fact, the argument is bogus. The divorce rate is a product of the changing nature of society and the refusal of women in particular to put up with intolerable husbands, in an era when there has been a major advance in women's economic independence. The divorce rate in previous generations was, as in arranged marriages, minimal. In Britain, Asian women are much less economically independent so have less real choice in leaving unhappy marriages. This is compounded by pressures from 'honour and shame' to keep the marriage intact. But, with a rise in educational levels and economic independence, we can expect the divorce rate also to rise and, at the same time, to see a decline not just in arranged marriages but marriage in general, slowly to be replaced by co-habitation, as is happening in mainstream society (see, for example, Berthoud, 2000; McSmith, 2009).

activities as these are considered taboo – as is of course the case with the vast majority of the population. Secular schools, again, are of supreme importance in this regard.

As in all aspects, living in segregated communities makes it almost impossible to create a climate where a challenge to oppressive prevailing customs can be made. This is why a mixed education, a mixed living environment, a mixed working environment are a *sine qua non* for the achievement of unity across racial, ethnic, and religious barriers. Revealingly, the lack of integration as particularly manifested in mono-religious-ethnic neighbourhoods, which has become embedded as a result of multiculturalism, plays into the hands of racist organisations who resent and oppose precisely such mixing. For example, the far right BNP has campaigned for barriers to divide Asian from White areas in Northern towns – a policy clearly modelled on the divisions between Catholics and Protestants estates in towns in Northern Ireland. Plainly, their ability to effectively make such a demand would be limited were such neighbourhoods mixed.[*]

In America's Deep South, in the 1950s and 1960s, the civil rights movement aimed to destroy the *de facto* apartheid that existed there; in the northern states, urban rebellions were directed against the brutal poverty and racism of the segregated Black areas (Marable, 1985, ch. 2). In stark contrast, religious-ethnic minorities in Britain have not shown much interest in breaking down cultural barriers and segregation. We can hypothesise that strong adherence to cultural traits and religious identities militate against the desire for integration. Thus, myriad cultural and religious constraints mean that Asians, in particular, relatively infrequently attend pubs, clubs, leisure centres and swimming pools, sports events, theatre, evening classes, non-Asian concerts, non-Asian (Bollywood) cinema, and non-Asian restaurants. Given that colour bars have disappeared, it appears that much of Asian *social* segregation is not so much because of racism, but rather

---

[*] In Padua, in Italy, a brutal racism by the authorities led to the construction of a steel wall to keep apart Italians and migrants (Fraser, 2006). The moral of this is surely that segregation is a social ill and all policies (racist or multicultural) that bring it about must be resisted.

is voluntary, a corollary of residential self-segregation. True, there is a gender divide, with men partaking in the above activities rather more than women, but the proportional involvement for both sexes is much less than for Whites and Black Caribbeans.[*]

Thus, social mixing needs to be encouraged – particularly amongst young people. Schools, community centres, and civic groups need to be at the forefront of this. Sadly, in making what are rather obvious, even banal, suggestions, the stark reality is that this will not be easy, and will take considerable time. Innovative, challenging, ideas and actions are needed, especially from the young of all ethnicities. If such a dynamic can be created, then so too will struggles against cultural and racial oppression be intensified – and the tide can slowly turn towards inclusiveness, mixing, and de-segregation.

It is right and proper that the law outlaws practices that are truly egregious such as those listed above, but this must also be followed up by both the abandonment of the laissez-faire approach and the firm refusal to grant privileges in the form of exemptions and exclusions to beliefs and practices based on culture and religion. Now it is certainly the case that such legal privileges constitute 'recognition' for the relevant religious-ethnic minority communities. But such recognition has, as we have seen, increasingly given rise to demands for separate legal provisions and exemptions so that pressure for a pluralistic approach to the law is mounting and providing further impetus to separation, divisiveness, and psychic detachment of faith communities. In other words, the embedding of multifaithism has generated demands for *legal pluralism* and the codification in law of the reality of parallel lives. But such demands must be resisted as they represent a severe breach of universal and egalitarian principles and, as we have repeatedly stressed in this book, it is the most vulnerable members of these

---

[*] Participation in sporting leisure activities tends to be less for both Asian men and women in comparison with Blacks and Whites. However, Pakistani and Bangladeshi women partake in much less such activity than Indians. The same applies to young people and various leisure activities. See ONS, 1996, tables 5.17 and 5.18. Unfortunately, an update of this report has not been conducted – but there is no reason to believe that reality has changed significantly.

communities who invariably suffer, and so are denied justice.

We need, however, to be cognisant of the fact that 'indirect discrimination' is a clear and present reality, which can particularly impact on ethnic minorities. Hence it is prohibited under the 1976 Race Relations Act. But it can be – and sometimes is – abused by those of a religious persuasion, who may seek legal privileges. A recent example of this is the case of a *hijab*-wearing woman who took the owner of a hair salon in London to an employment tribunal on the grounds of 'religious discrimination' after being rejected for a job as a hair stylist. Astonishingly, though the tribunal panel dismissed the claim for religious discrimination, it upheld her complaint of 'indirect discrimination' and awarded £4,000 damages for 'injury to feelings'. The salon owner argued that she expected her staff to reflect the 'funky, urban' image of her salon and that she 'never in a million years dreamt that somebody would be completely against the display of hair and be in this industry'. (BBC News, 2008).

This sets a dangerous precedent: devout believers of other faiths would also feel justified in making claims for indirect discrimination and 'hurt feelings', if they are turned down for jobs which are in breach of their religions' injunctions. Countless examples could be provided: Muslims in the banking and gambling industry, vegetarians (including Hindus) as restaurant critics (Muslims and Jews also for non-halal or non-kosher restaurants) and so on.

A number of policy prescriptions flow from this avowedly secular perspective. Most obviously, religious courts and tribunals, which *de facto* operate on the basis of a parallel legal system, must be prohibited. There has of late, for example, been the demand made by Muslim organisations that elements of Islamic Sharia law be introduced into the body of UK civil law (similar to the Jewish Beth Din). Indeed Rowan Williams, the Archbishop of Canterbury averred, in February 2008, that this was 'unavoidable'. The controversy that ensued was entirely justified for there should be no doubt that Sharia law breaches fundamental human rights, especially of women and children.[*] This

---

[*] This is because, in Islam – and therefore, in Sharia law, which is based on the Koran and Hadith – there is systematic discrimination against women, children, apos-

has been recognised by Britain's highest court concerning a case in which the government attempted to remove a woman and child to Lebanon. In a 5–0 ruling the Law Lords argued 'that there was no place in sharia for the equal treatment of the sexes. It would be a "flagrant breach" of the European Convention on Human Rights for the Government to remove a woman to Lebanon, where she would lose custody of her son because of sharia-inspired family law' (Verkaik, 2008).

To argue that Muslims will retain 'choice' in regard to the courts and laws is to forget the reality of so many Muslims trapped in close-knit isolated communities. In other words, there is simply no *real* choice – especially for women and children. Importantly, the establishment of even a minimal Sharia jurisdiction will enormously increase the power of the mullahs and imams, who will then inevitably push for more exemptions to the law, and more Sharia laws and courts. Moreover, it will give the green light for religious leaders of other 'faith communities' to push for their own separate legal jurisdictions, a vista that cannot at all be appealing to anyone seeking a more just, unified, cohesive society.

In Canada, the Ontario state government deliberated upon introducing Sharia civil law that had been demanded by Islamic organisations. However, after a vigorous campaign against this proposal, the government abandoned it in September 2005. The reasons were succinctly given by Ontario Premier Dalton McGuinty:

> 'There will be no Shariah law in Ontario. There will be no religious arbitration in Ontario. There will be one law for all Ontarians'. Moreover, he asserted that religious family courts 'threaten our common ground ... Ontarians will always have the right to seek advice from anyone in matters of family law, including religious advice ... but no longer will religious arbitration be deciding matters of family law (CTV, 2005).

---

tates, blasphemers, non-believers (infidels), adulterers, and homosexuals. Sanctions can be barbaric, including amputations of limbs, lashes, and stoning to death.

Precisely the same approach should be universally applied. Thus, not only should religious arbitration be precluded from family law, it should be precluded from all laws.

We now turn to another example, one in which religious sensibilities have triumphed – that of religious slaughter of animals. Concern for the welfare of animals has taken root in recent years, one important consequence of which has been the banning of fox hunting. The government ultimately rejected the argument (as made by, for example, The Countryside Alliance) that this was a cultural practice of great import to the people of the countryside, going back many generations. The ethics of prevention of cruelty to animals trumped those of cultural tradition and its recognition. Precisely the same ethics and legal principle must also be applied to religious slaughter, which evidence shows causes unnecessary suffering to animals. Accordingly, in regard to this, the Farm Animal Welfare Council has long advocated the cessation of religious slaughter without stunning. Hence, in 1985, in a report to the then Conservative government, Recommendation 92 was as follows:

> We have been convinced during the course of our enquiries that the slaughter of animals is most humane if they are effectively stunned before bleeding ... However, we have to acknowledge that over centuries the acts associated with religious slaughter have assumed a cultural significance in their own right and have become symbols that are important in the traditions of those who adhere to those religions ... (FAWC, 1985, pp. 24–25).

Following these findings, Recommendations 93 and 94 offer clear guidance:

> 93. We therefore recommend that Ministers should require the Jewish and Muslim communities to review their methods of slaughter so as to develop alternatives which permit effective stunning. Their findings should be presented to Ministers so that the legislative pro-

visions which permit slaughter without stunning of animals (including poultry) by Jews and Muslims can be repealed within the next three years.

94. [Regarding] ... Sikh slaughter (*Jhatka*) we noted that instantaneous slaughter of the unstunned animal by decapitation is currently permitted ... We recommend that within three years the legislation permitting slaughter by decapitation without stunning of all animals (including poultry) should be repealed (*ibid.*, p. 25).*

Worried by the religious lobbies, the government did not enact these recommendations. But the Farm Animal Welfare Council reiterated its stance in 2003: 'Council considers that slaughter without pre-stunning is unacceptable and that the Government should repeal the current exemption' (FAWC, 2003, Recommendation 201, p. 60). But like its Conservative predecessor, the Labour government has also shied away from repealing the exemption. The response by DEFRA (Department for Environment, Food, and Rural Affairs) was as craven as it was unequivocal:

> Response: Do not accept. The Government does not intend to ban the slaughter of animals without prior stunning by religious groups.
>
> We agree with FAWC that the scientific evidence indicates that animals that receive an effective pre-cut stun do not experience pain at the time of slaughter. The balance of current scientific evidence also suggests that those cattle which receive an immediate post-cut stun are likely to suffer less than those that do not. However we recognise that this latter conclusion is disputed.
>
> The Government is committed to respect for the rights of religious groups and accepts that an insistence on a pre-cut or immediate post-cut stun would not be compatible with the requirements

---

* Note that this was not an unusual recommendation: the report shows that Norway, Sweden, and Switzerland provided no exemption for religious slaughter (FAWC, 1985, p. 39).

of religious slaughter by Jewish and Muslim groups (DEFRA, p. 17).

This is a clear case of religious privilege, in direct contradiction to scientific advice and the needs of animal welfare. Moves are afoot to bring in EU legislation which outlaws religious slaughter and, should this be passed, one fervently hopes that the UK government will not seek an exemption.

Another egregious, indeed quite inhumane, example of religiously-dictated behaviour that has come to light in recent years (albeit still of a relatively rare occurrence), is that of Muslim taxi drivers refusing to transport blind people with guide dogs because of religious objections (NSS, 2006). Such refusal arises because, in Islam, dogs are regarded as being 'unclean' in the same way that pigs are. This is another instance of the alienating (and irrational) religious behaviour that we have discussed in previous chapters. The practice is in breach of the Disability Discrimination Act 1995. It needs to be buttressed by the implementation of clear guidelines for taxi drivers (bearing in mind that, in several parts of the country, a significant proportion are Muslim), indicating that this is simply unacceptable behaviour.

What this discussion points to is unambiguous: the foundational principle of an integrated, cohesive society that is based on justice and egalitarianism must be *one law for all*. This sends out a powerful signal that the government is sincere and determined in attempting to build society on the basis of common citizenship and social justice, thereby casting aside the emphasis on 'difference' which has had such a corrosive, divisive, effect. Indeed, we can make the case that integration and social cohesion are improved the more religion is confined to the private sphere.

An identity based on commonality not difference
We can think of multiculturalism as enabling the fusion of the trinity of culture, religion, and community into a distinct identity, the

apotheosis of which is 'faith identity'. Respect and recognition of an individual is predicated on the respect and recognition of the person's culture and faith and, by extension, community. By this transmutation, the individual ceases to be a person in his/her own right as his/her autonomous identity is subsumed within this trinity; indeed it is best thought of as a coercively imposed identity, devoid of any real choice. It naturally follows that 'culture' and religion' are reified and, in the process, individuality is lost so that a person in a faith community has identified his/her own being with that of the faith and community. A profound consequence of this reification and loss of individual autonomy is that oppressive beliefs and practices become internalised within and tolerated (even respected) without. Our value judgement is that this is intolerable and without justification because it is not only harmful to the individuals concerned but to society in general, and so must be opposed. In this final section, we discuss how we can move away from oppressive identities based on difference – which are necessarily divisive and sectarian – to ones based on commonalities.

A striking feature of British public life over the past three decades, and one which points to an emphasis on commonality rather than difference is that the number and frequency of ethnic minority (especially Black) faces in television has increased significantly. The appearance of two Black newsreaders – Trevor McDonald on ITV and Moira Stuart on the BBC – was of great symbolic and social importance. The fact that millions of viewers would view Black faces on most nights during peak hours naturally increased the familiarity and, more importantly, acceptance of Blacks in British society. Hardened racists would doubtless have been appalled by their homes being 'invaded' by Black faces in such public, authoritative roles and accordingly switched channel or switched off. But this is likely to have been only a small percentage of the population – for audience ratings did not appreciably diminish; in fact, in McDonald's case, the ratings proved over time to be high as he became one of the most popular and respected news broadcasters and, in due course, TV personalities.

In their footsteps followed many other ethnic minority newsreaders, reporters, and programme presenters. Was this a triumph of multiculturalism? Not at all – it was rather an affirmation and assertion of multi-racialism: the increasing prevalence of non-White faces on TV screens starkly emphasised the increasingly multi-racial/ethnic character of Britain. This was emphatically not about 'culture' for there was nothing distinctive about the cultural or religious attributes of the presenters. Indeed the form of attire and appearance was standard and formal – which, in modern Britain, we could think of as being 'neutral'.* The unambiguous message then was that ethnic minorities are a legitimate part of society but there was no 'multiculturalist' element to this legitimacy. That is to say, there was no stress on cultural differences of non-White presenters vis-à-vis their White counterparts. For this to have been a 'triumph' of multiculturalism, there would have to have been a focus on overt differences, such as women adorned in saris, shulwaar-kameez, *hijabs*, burkas, or with red dots on forehead; or men in dhotis, turbans, dreadlocks, religious beards, caps and hats. But this was not the case – the only difference was (and remains) physiognomic and not cultural; and to this day no news presenter or reporter on any of the main TV channels has been allowed to veer away from this neutrality.†

So, multiculturalism on news-related programmes and channels was checked, with the principles of formality and neutrality taking strong roots. Provided the presenters and reporters articulately speak with one of the 'national' accents (though 'BBC English' with its received pronunciation and not the excessively pompous 'Queen's English' remains the 'standard') then skin complexion is deemed not to be of relevance and, in this regard, the major terrestrial TV stations have become far more inclusive over the past three decades. In contrast, by allowing the free expression of cultural and religious

---

* The only time this neutrality is breached is the almost universal, in reality coercive, adorning of the 'poppy' for about two weeks prior to, and including, Remembrance Sunday in November.
† Though Hardeep Singh Kohli who, on occasion, presents BBC2's cultural programme 'Newsnight Review', wears a turban.

identity on TV, the multicultural emphasis on 'difference' would, in this context, have been deeply alienating to the public at large and inevitably drawn strong complaints in very significant numbers. It would doubtless have generated an unwarranted animus towards ethnic minorities and intensified the feeling of their being 'the Other'. By consciously avoiding this approach, there has been an important, albeit somewhat hidden, recognition of unity and commonality in which race or ethnicity is downgraded and, of necessity, cultural and religious differences purposely disregarded. The salutary lesson that should be drawn from this example is surely that such unity and commonality need to be nurtured and extended.

Diminution of religious identity
We saw in Chapter 1 that the mayor of Amsterdam has advocated religion as an 'anchor' for the integration of Muslim settlers. It should be plain from our analysis that there is now a vital and urgent need to abandon the religious anchor so as to weaken religious identity. As already noted, among the indigenous population, only in Northern Ireland (and, to a minimal extent, in some parts of Scotland) is religion a significant mark of identity – and indubitably an extraordinarily divisive one. It is clearly the case that most British people have become increasingly estranged from religion and, as a corollary, find the notion of a strong religious identity of migrants alienating and a barrier to interaction and integration. Consequently, it is the height of political irresponsibility, as we argued above, to advocate this as a means of integration – and buttress it with funds for 'faith' groups, communities, and schools. This is an enormous disservice especially to the young and women given that it hinders them from breaking loose from the 'anchor' that holds them back in so many aspects of their lives. Responsible politics rooted in the vision of breaking down barriers and ghettos should be about ensuring the *de-anchoring* of religion as the basis of identity of ethnic minorities. However, breaking free from long-held beliefs and identities can be extraordinarily difficult given the years of systematic indoctrination that are firmly

etched in the mind and well-nigh impossible to remove. This is precisely why the education of the young, in a rounded manner, is so absolutely vital. Alongside this, there must be a relentless struggle against discrimination and racism in all their forms, thereby removing a key rationale for strong religious or ethnic identities. There has indubitably been considerable progress in this regard (in employment, housing, the media, at sports (especially football) matches, the intolerance of racist jokes etc.) which has been an enormous gain not only to non-White minorities, but to society as a whole. This must be built upon and there can certainly be no room for complacency.

The unifying force of secularism
Given that so much of the oppressive thinking and practices within religious-ethnic minorities stem from religious edicts and attendant interpretations, the key principle for *unifying* cultural traits must, of necessity, be *secularism*. Crucially, there is a trade-off between secularism and communalism/sectarianism so that when the former is weakened the latter is invariably strengthened, which is why communalism/sectarianism and social cohesion cannot easily be reconciled. Therefore, to keep communalism at bay requires a strong, unrelenting emphasis on secularism.

We provided evidence, in the previous chapter, of how religion was rapidly fading in importance to the mass of the British population yet the state, in stark contrast, is resolutely not secular. The compelling and just solution is for a realignment of the constitution so that it becomes consonant with reality. This necessitates the disestablishment of the Church of England and rescinding of the right afforded to 26 of its bishops to sit in the House of Lords. Such a privilege is a gross violation of democracy and equal rights and, if it is not removed, there will doubtless be a clamour (just as there is for state-funded faith schools) from other religious groups for a similar right to seats in the House of Lords alongside the CoE bishops. Moreover, the fairest and just solution is for members to the House of Lords to be elected democratically: any bishop or religious figure wishing to serve can stand for election. Again, as with the phasing out of faith schools, such a constitutional change is likely to have significant majority support, so there is no reason for any government implementing this reform to fear an electoral backlash.

Secularisation of public life, in combination with a stress on justice and equality, can be the progenitor for an inclusive 'secular identity' that takes away the roots of racial, communal, and sectarian divisions. What can enormously assist in this is the pursuance of a genuinely 'ethical foreign policy' – the termed coined by the former Foreign Secretary, Robin Cook, when Labour came to power in 1997. But this proved, almost from the start, to be a dead letter. Instead there has been a profoundly unethical and unjust foreign policy, steeped in mendacity and hypocrisy. This is attested by Britain's partaking in the invasions and occupations of Afghanistan and Iraq, and by its unstinting support for Israel, despite that country's appalling oppression of Palestinians and attendant breaches of myriad human rights conventions and UN resolutions.

We noted in Chapter 5 that one consequence of this misguided foreign policy has been to accentuate an Islamic identity among large numbers of Muslims, an identity that appears to have heightened self-segregation and psychic detachment, and the leading of parallel lives. Governments genuinely concerned about the creation of an integrated and cohesive society must learn the lessons from these gross foreign policy failures. One of monumental importance must be that unjust wars of aggression, inevitably leading to the slaughter of innocents in foreign lands, are felt with an extraordinary personal passion by those who feel a close bond with those at the receiving end of such aggression. In the cases of Afghanistan, Iraq, and Palestine, the bond is of course achieved by religion, specifically by the notion of the *umma* in Islam.

The days of empire may be long gone, but the imperial impulse and arrogance of the UK establishment remains – given succour by the 'special relationship' with the world's only superpower, in which Britain is especially loyal to US military forays. Like a recovering alcoholic, Britain, drunk on the militarism of empire, no matter which party is in power, finds it extremely difficult to become militarily abstemious. But achieving such abstemiousness remains a challenge of supreme importance. The defence budget must be for this stated purpose and not for wars of aggression, invasion, and occupation (the War Office was terminated in 1963). If this can somehow be achieved, a *sine qua non* for a foreign policy with ethical pretensions, then the task of a more socially cohesive society becomes that much easier.

A further, related lesson therefore is that not only will people of those countries which are attacked resist, but the resistance will 'come home' – as has precisely happened with respect to the wars in Afghanistan and Iraq, and to the Israeli assaults on Lebanon in the summer of 2006 and on Gaza in January 2009 (in both cases, the British government did not oppose these). However, opposition and resistance have been truly widespread, far beyond the ranks of Muslim communities incensed by 'Muslim' lands being attacked, invaded, and occupied. This hugely important phenomenon of modern British life has not been reflected in parliament. This gives hope – and reason – to believe that there is the possibility of the creation of not only a secular identity, but also a 'post-imperial identity', based on international solidarity and justice; one that is defined on the basis of Britain's dealings with the outside world in a just and ethical manner. In fact, such an identity is already a *de facto* reality for a significant percentage of the population who, it should be noted are, in the main, devoid of any religious allegiance or identity, being profoundly secular.

Amartya Sen makes the important and valid point to which the British government, with its great concern for potential terror attacks and violence emanating from Islamic extremism, should pay special heed:

> The vulnerability to influences of sectarian extremism is much greater if one is reared and schooled in the sectarian (but not necessarily violent) mode. The British government is seeking to stop

> the preaching of hatred by religious leaders, which must be right, but the problem is surely far more extensive than that. It concerns whether citizens of immigrant backgrounds should see themselves as members of particular communities and specific ethnicities first, and only *through* that membership see themselves as British, in a supposed federation of communities. It is not hard to understand that this uniquely factional view of any nation would make it more open to the preaching and cultivation of sectarian violence (Sen, 2006, p. 164).

A further danger is that the straitjacketing of people into pre-determined religious-ethnic identities is tantamount to the suppression of individuality, a point we stressed above. This suppression powerfully stultifies both the mind and personality – producing a mindset that is at once both hostile to external influences and fearful of challenges to religious doctrines and cultural hegemony. Critical, let alone original, thinking is crushed, leaving insipid conformity to reign supreme. To emphasise the point, we can take the example (admittedly extreme) of the Islamic 'madrassas'. These Koranic schools for boys are seminaries of the most oppressive form of thought control, infused with relentless, double-distilled indoctrination, whereby not a spark of critical quizzical thought is permitted to enter the minds of the boys within their grip. The young males that emerge from their clutches are no more than automatons, quite impervious to life's varied riches, knowledge and pleasures. Indeed, this is precisely why Jihadist groups make great use of madrassas, fully aware that their 'graduates' exercise a discipline which even the most ruthless army would have reason to envy. In a milder, yet unmistakeable form, the same process and diminution of humanity occurs to those in 'faith communities'. Lest one imagine that this is only a danger to Muslims, here is an account which makes any such assumption impossible, the reality facing those brought up as Orthodox Jews:

Simon Rocker, in his article on Haredim (strictly Orthodox) Jews, may be correct to say that they 'suffer little defection from their ranks'. But in stating merely that 'Haredim are far warier of secular culture', Rocker glosses over the level of ideological control to which young Orthodox Jews are subjected via a total exclusion from civil society, including an education entirely composed of faith schools from synagogue-administered nursery school to yeshiva or seminary (Maher, 2009).*

The dissolution of strong religious identities, therefore, enables the loosening of the 'ideological control' that is rife in faith communities under the grip of community and religious elders and leaders. Concomitantly, this can ensure the flourishing of *personal* identities, that is to say, where individuals can discover, determine and transform their own identities. Peer pressure and fashion will certainly still exist, but that is not necessarily an unalloyed ill – and far less harmful than cultural and religious taboos, diktats, and sanctions. The insular, sectarian, identities of segregated faith communities engender a 'grammar' which is conducive to Kipling's 'The ballad of East and West', or its modern equivalent, the 'clash of civilisations'. A just foreign policy can provide a powerful buffer to this reactionary outcome and contribute to the dissolution of the myriad tensions among communities divided by ethnicity, culture, and religion – and assist in the creation of an alternate, inclusive, and unifying grammar of identity.

What is neglected is that the focus on one all-embracing faith identity is not necessarily what many individuals designated as being of faith communities would want, and it is certainly not without profound costs to their well-being, notwithstanding the benefits of security which accrue within an enclosed community. We can posit that the most important costs are those of diminution of equality,

---

* The author's name, Tzipporah Maher, is a pseudonym. This may be because in the article she makes the powerful allegation: 'Orthodox youth's lack of access to adults outside the community can lead to child sexual abuse by family members and religious leaders' (Maher, 2009).

opportunity, freedom of conscience, and social justice. Furthermore, by accentuating faith identities, we return to the motif of heightened social divisions and tensions, including alienation and racism from the majority society. The long history of privileges accorded to the established Church of England, and to religion in general in Britain, has left an indelible imprint on society, including the seemingly unshakeable belief that the mark of religion on any societal phenomenon is inherently a good thing so that religious institutions, beliefs, practices, ethics, and morality are bestowed great respect by default. It is precisely this reasoning that has spilled over into a generalised positive attitude towards minority faiths adopted by the government and opposition parties. But we have attempted to demonstrate that this is a mistaken view and one fraught with dangers: social progress necessitates its abatement, and the pursuance of policies in a vigorous and principled manner, in which cultural and religious considerations are no longer accorded their current privileged status.

If the solutions put forward in this chapter are implemented, then the centrifugal dynamic of multiculturalism and multifaithism can be checked and reversed, allowing for deepening of integration, opportunity, commonality, and community cohesion. For the sake of future generations, the sooner this is done, the better.

Chapter 8

Concluding remarks

Much of this book has been written during what evidence suggests is the greatest global recession since the 1930s. The theoretical underpinning of the modern global economy was, for a long period, based on neoliberal laissez-faire economics, and labelled 'The Washington Consensus', named after the Bretton Woods institutions based in the US capital city, which had been the prime mover behind this economic model. Precipitated by the financial crisis, this 'consensus' is, however, encountering a sustained and robust challenge, with alternatives being actively sought. Though no new consensus has obtained, what is clear is that there will be no returning to laissez-faire capitalism any time soon.

It is the contention of this book that, in a similar manner, the laissez-faire approach to culture and religion, underpinned by theories of multiculturalism and cultural relativism, must also cease and better alternatives be found and adopted. Freedom of cultural and religious expression has too often transgressed into freedom of cultural and religious *oppression* and so has become, in reality, a *carte blanche* for all manner of abuses, obscurantist practices, and domination by predominantly male community and religious 'leaders', with only the most egregious beliefs, practices, and traditions being deemed out of bounds. In the preceding chapters, we have attempted to provide arguments and evidence against this approach, to assert that it is a denial of equality and basic human rights for many, and to offer policy prescriptions which can help undo the harm that has ensued and so offer a better way forward for societies with significant ethnic minority populations.

The economic crisis is having a terrible impact on the lives of countless millions around the globe and vigorous actions must be taken to counter it. In the UK, there is a clear and present danger that, in the context of recession, financial hardship, and mass unemployment, the divisive politics engendered in the discourse of multiculturalism and attendant dangers of pork-barrel politics already highlighted in previous chapters can, albeit unintentionally, help unleash a backlash against ethnic minorities, who can easily become scapegoats – a familiar tactic that the far right will anyhow doubtless adopt relentlessly. Indeed, this was precisely the case in the elections to the European Parliament in June 2009 when, for the first time, two BNP members were elected. Such a menacing scenario must not be allowed to spread – and provides an added and urgent reason as to why such misguided policies must be abandoned.

The paradoxical feature, and inconvenient truth, of multiculturalism and multifaithism is that whilst they advocate an autonomous, laissez-faire approach to culture and faith, the reality is that no such autonomy is proffered to members *within* the ghettoised religious-ethnic minority communities. On the contrary, from birth and in virtually all aspects, their lives are dictated by incessant levels of intervention, so that the outcome for them is distinctly devoid of laissez-faire, that is to say, of individual liberty. The paradoxical and often highly oppressive consequence of this for these citizens is *mono*-culturalism and *mono*-faithism, with concomitant rising levels of self-segregation, isolation, and psychic detachment.

This is surely not the outcome that was envisaged by advocates of multiculturalism. We do not deny that their motives were sincere and that, at a theoretical and philosophical level, the doctrine does possess a degree of elegance and deceptive appeal; particularly for those afflicted by White post-colonial liberal guilt. But we do contend that reality has put paid to the high hopes and we can argue that this is perhaps an example of the 'law of unintended consequences'. Even though a reasonable case can be made that the ensuing *negative* consequences may have indeed been unintended, nevertheless, a reasonable case can also be made that they should not have been unforeseen. Be that as it may, what is now desperately needed, above all for the ethnic minority citizens in whose interests multiculturalism was espoused, is, to utilise a term powerfully invoked by Thomas Kuhn (1996 [1962], ch. 5), a new 'paradigm', an epistemological break from the past. Powerful interest groups will naturally and inevitably provide tough resistance but, as we have stressed in previous chapters, there is now an urgent need for firm actions and policies.

In order to cope with the reality of the modern world – specifically of Western dominance – many in the West from religious-ethnic minorities, hailing from developing countries, hark back to a glorious past where important advances (in science, mathematics, medicine, warfare etc.) were made outside Europe.* This is particularly true for Muslims of a fundamentalist persuasion who, depressed at the generally appalling state and profound impotence of the Islamic world, yearn for the return of the glory days of Islam's expansion, genuine power and advances a thousand or so years ago. Whilst this is an important truth that should be asserted, and needs to be acknowledged by the host society – being, for example, a necessary part of the educational curriculum – nonetheless, this line of reasoning retains severe limitations: past achievements and splendour do not and cannot compensate for present inadequacies and failures. Moreover, this is merely a temporary palliative to salve the torn conscience and emphatically does not help in addressing the myriad problems of the present. So true, a degree of pride can be restored by recourse to past achievements of an 'imagined community' – especially when confronted with abrasive 'Orientalists' – but this is not a good basis for taking an holistic, truthful account of present reality.

Indeed it is precisely such thinking, such a *weltanschauung*, that has afflicted so many Muslims in the West and contributed to their psychic detachment. For them, adherence to a sectarian faith identity is so strong that living in a modern Western secular society appears to be intolerable and is deemed to offend against many of

---

* As Amartya Sen (2006, p. 56) points out: 'A large group of contributors from different non-Western societies – Chinese, Arab, Iranian, Indian, and others – influenced the science, mathematics, and philosophy that played a major part in the European Renaissance and, later, the Enlightenment.

their core beliefs – any critical self-examination seems well nigh impossible. Accordingly, self-segregation and isolation have increasingly become their 'solution'. But there is an element of hypocrisy here: a principled, consistent, stance would see a much greater desire on their part to return to their countries of origin or to countries that are based on their cultural and religious mores. Although such a principled view is rarely offered in public, neither is it so novel or unreasonable. Indeed, this is precisely what the former imam of Finsbury Park mosque in North London, Abu Hamza, has advocated: he rejects the identity and category of 'British Muslim' and has called for a 'hijrah' to Muslim lands so as 'not to melt away in this society' (cited in McRoy, 2006, p. 195).[*] From an opposing, progressive, perspective the Mayor of Rotterdam, Ahmed Abu Talib (who is of Moroccan origin), calls on Muslims who have made the voluntary choice to live in the Netherlands to 'integrate or go home'.[†] This certainly appears unduly harsh but Talib is, in essence, exposing their hypocritical attitude; moreover, there is an ethical seriousness to his position for he makes clear that his concern is for the children of such settlers, whose future will be in the new country, which is also their country of birth. What is clear is that the likes of Talib have laid down the gauntlet to those espousing and implementing the policies of multiculturalism, including the regressive segregationists; in the name of future generations, the status quo cannot continue.

Undoubtedly the most egregious and nefarious act emanating from a breach of a cultural and religious code is that of 'honour killing', a phenomenon that is rife in many religious-based

---

[*] Another example is that of a woman Islamist tutor at London's Regents Park Mosque who urges her female tutees to leave Britain for Muslim lands. This was revealed by a hidden camera on Channel 4's *Despatches* documentary 'Undercover Mosque: The Return', broadcast on 1 September 2008.

[†] Interview given for BBC World Service's *Outlook* programme; aired on 5 February 2009. Talib describes how he came from a small village in the Riff Mountains in Morocco and, 'from nothing', became Mayor of one of the Netherlands' largest cities. However, for his straight talking, he has received death threats and been afforded police protection.

communities and societies. Now 'honour' is an important precept in various cultures and nations across the world but, in some, its breach is sanctioned by death. In the lexicon of multiculturalism, such a breach is tantamount to disrespect or 'misrecognition'. We use this extreme example to make the point that a discourse of recognition, respect, and honour for culture and religion can have potentially devastating consequences. Take the following example.

In her interviews with Turkish men who have committed honour killings, the Turkish journalist Ayse Onal (2008, pp. 254–255) cites a research study which found that 67 per cent of the Turkish population views crime and sin as synonymous. She then makes some insightful remarks about honour killings:

> they lived not according to the law but according to their religion … Religion could help stop honour killings but religious authorities have not used their influence to this end … This silence has been interpreted as an endorsement of the murder of 'immoral' women … Religion, in fact, contributed to the murders that were not condemned.

Onal then draws the following powerful conclusion about this shocking phenomenon:

> the culture assigned traits such as dignity and virtue to women and gave men the job of supervising women and safeguarding these qualities … Men killed these women to be treated as men by their neighbours, their friends, their families. Therefore to classify honour killings as domestic violence is misleading. It is an internal societal violence that goes beyond families.

In the introduction to Onal's book (*ibid.*, p. 12), Joan Smith quotes Crown Prosecution lawyer Nazir Afzal regarding the honour killing of a 20-year-old Kurdish woman, Banaz Mahmoud, in South London. The sentiment expressed is similar to that of Onal's:

> ... members of the community did not assist and support prosecutors; instead they supported the family members who were responsible for the killing. They really didn't care and it showed... we don't see this as domestic violence – it's beyond that. The murder of Banaz was so brutal that it was a clear warning to others; it was a way of saying 'don't step out of line or this could be you'.

Smith (*ibid.*, p. 17) concludes her introduction by pointing out that:

> men who live in honour-based cultures are perpetually fearful, suspicious and angry, fuelling the violence with which they react when they believe their anxieties have been confirmed ... In Turkey and the UK, there is a striking correlation between honour-based codes and a reluctance to educate girls and young women, which results in girls failing to finish their education and being married at an early age.

In the UK and indeed Western context, what is incontrovertible is that 'honour-based' codes and cultures are overwhelmingly centred on a strong religious-ethnic identity. Though this is mainly a phenomenon among Asian communities, it is also evidenced in some of the newer settler communities such as Kurdish, Somali, and West African. The stark conclusion is that multiculturalism and multifaithism have unwittingly given the green light to notions of 'honour' as being an integral part of culture, religion, identity, and community. That is not to suggest that multicultural and multifaith policies condone honour killings, but to assert that such policies are unable to challenge the context of honour-based cultures precisely because they view society through the prism of cultural relativism.

Max Weber provided an insightful distinction which is apposite here: that of 'ethic of ultimate ends' (often referred to as 'ethic of conviction', which expresses the idea rather better) and 'ethic of responsibility':

We must be clear about the fact that all ethically oriented conduct may be guided by one of two fundamentally differing and irreconcilably opposed maxims: conduct can be oriented to an 'ethic of ultimate ends' or to an 'ethic of responsibility'. This is not to say that an ethic of ultimate ends is identical with irresponsibility, or that an ethic of responsibility is identical with unprincipled opportunism. Naturally nobody says that. However, there is an abysmal contrast between conduct that follows the maxim of an ethic of ultimate ends – that is, in religious terms, 'The Christian does rightly and leaves the results with the Lord' – and conduct that follows the maxim ethic of responsibility, in which case one has to give an account of the foreseeable results of one's action (Weber, 1967 [1919], p. 120).

With respect to adherents of multiculturalism, we can conjecture that an ethic of ultimate ends is dominant – that is to say, it is underpinned by a theoretical and philosophical framework that stems from a strong ethical conviction: 'this is the right way'. This is not to suggest that there is an absence of responsibility, but rather that little regard is paid to 'foreseeable results'. However, this should not be mistaken as an advocacy of crude utilitarianism: long-term consequences are notoriously difficult to foresee with accuracy. Rather, it is to assert that what is now required is a decisive reversal of this ethical stance and to advocate a move towards an ethic of responsibility, which is necessarily rational in approach and explicitly seeks to take account of consequences. This can facilitate a break from the past and the shift to egalitarian universalism and attendant policies which, we have argued, provides a better – and necessary – alternative.

Bibliography

Ahmed L. (1992) *Women and Gender in Islam*, London and Newhaven: Yale University Press.
Ajegbo Report (2007) *Curriculum Review: Diversity Citizenship*, Nottingham: DfES, www.teachernet.gov.uk/publications
Al-Hibri A. (1999) 'Is Western patriarchal feminism good for third world/minority women?', in Okin, *Is Multiculturalism Bad for Women?* Princeton: Princeton University Press pp. 41–46.
Allen C. and Nielsen J. (2002) *Summary Report on Islamophobia in the EU after 11 September 2001*, Vienna: The European Monitoring Centre on Racism and Xenophobia.
Amnesty International (2000) 'Saudi Arabia: Asian workers continue to suffer behind closed doors', *Amnesty International Index*: MDE 23/33/00, 1 May.
Anwar M., 1998, *Ethnic Minorities and the British Electoral System*, University of Warwick: Centre for Research in Ethnic Relations.
Bahceci M. (*et al.*) (2006) 'Evaluation of bone mineral density in terms of veiling, socio-economic status and educational level in Turkish women over 40 years: veiling may be a risk factor for osteoporosis', *Turkish Journal of Endocrinology and Metabolism*, vol. 3, pp. 63–68.
Barker (1981) *The New Racism: Conservatives and the Ideology of the Tribe*, London: Junction Books.
Barry B. (2001a) *Culture and Equality: An Egalitarian Critique of Multiculturalism*, Cambridge: Polity Press.
Barry B. (2001b) 'The muddles of multiculturalism', *New Left Review*, vol. 8, pp. 49–79.
Barry B. (2002) 'Second thoughts – and some first thoughts revived' in Kelly P (ed.) (2002), *Multiculturalism Reconsidered*, pp. 204–238, Cambridge: Polity Press.
Baumann G. and Gingrich A. (eds.) (2004) *Grammars of Identity/Alterity: A Structural Approach*, New York and Oxford: Berghahn Books.
BBC News (2001) 'Social worker "made cultural judgement"', 23 November, http://news.bbc.co.uk/1/hi/england/1672265.stm
BBC (2005) *Nation on film Part 6*, 'Make yourself at home' (video-recording), BBC for Open University.
BBC News (2004) 'Aborigines' fury over topless ban', 27 February, http://news.bbc.co.uk/1/hi/world/asia-pacific/3493408.stm
BBC News (2007) 'UK Muslims "more loyal than most"', 15th April, http://news.bbc.co.uk/1/hi/uk/6557003.stm
BBC News (2007) 'Racial 'time bomb' in UK schools', 26th April, http://news.bbc.co.uk/1/hi/education/6594911.stm

BBC News (2008) 'Man sentenced over Shia flogging', 24 September, http://news.bbc.co.uk/1/hi/england/manchester/7634275.stm

BBC News (2008) 'Muslim stylist wins £4,000 payout', 16 June, http://newsvote.bbc.co.uk/mpapps/pagetools/print/news.bbc.co.uk/1/hi/england/london/7457794.stm

BBC News (2009) 'Dutch MP refused entry to Britain', 12 February, http://news.bbc.co.uk/1/hi/uk_politics/7885918.stm

Beckett C. and Macey M. (2001), 'Race, gender and sexuality: the oppression of multiculturalism', *Women's Studies International Forum*, vol. 24, no. 3/4, pp. 309–319.

Beckford M. (2008) '£86 million scheme to prevent Muslim radicalisation is 'gravy train' for local groups', *Telegraph*, 25 October, http://www.telegraph.co.uk/news/newstopics/politics/labour/3255325/86million-scheme-to-prevent-Muslim-radicalisation-is-gravy-train-for-local-groups.html

Bentham M. (2007) 'Britons oppose Muslim veils in schools', *Evening Standard*, 13 November, http://www.thisislondon.co.uk/standard/article-23420747-details/Britons+oppose+Muslim+veils+in+schools/article.do

Berthoud R. (2000), 'Family formation in multi-cultural Britain: three patterns of diversity', ISER Working Paper: University of Essex, http://www.iser.essex.ac.uk/pubs/workpaps/2000-34.php

Bhaba H. (2007 [1994]) *The Location of Culture*, Routledge: London and New York.

Bhugra D. (2007) 'Deliberate self-harm among South Asians in London', Downloads, http://www.dineshbhugra.net/

Bittles A. H., Mason W., Greene J., and Rao N. (1991) 'Reproductive behavior and health in consanguineous marriages', *Science*, vol. 252. no. 5007, pp. 789 – 794.

Blanc M. (1998) 'Social integration and exclusion in France: some introductory remarks from a social transaction perspective', *Housing Studies*, vol. 13, no. 6, pp. 781–792.

Bogardus E. (1932) 'Social distance between Catholics, Jews, and Protestants', *Sociology and Social Research*, Nov-Dec, pp. 167–173.

Bogardus E. (1933) 'A social distance scale', *Sociology and Social Research*, Jan-Feb, pp. 265–271.

Bolognani M. (2007) 'The myth of return: dismissal, survival or revival? A Bradford example of transnationalism as a political instrument', *Journal of Ethnic and Migration Studies*, vol. 33, no. 1, pp. 59–76.

Boseley S. (1989) 'Injudicious record of male judges on sexual attacks',*Guardian*, 13 March.

Bourdieu P. (1977 [1972]) *Outline of a Theory of Practice*, Cambridge: Cambridge University Press.

Bourdieu P. (1993) *The Field of Cultural Production*, Cambridge: Polity Press.

Bowen J. (2007) *Why the French Don't Like Headscarves: Islam, the State, and Public Space*, Princeton and Woodstock: Princeton University Press.

Bradford Race Review, 2001, *Community Pride not Prejudice*, Bradford Vision, http://www.bradford2020.com/pride (*The Ouseley Report*)
Brown R., Rutland A, and Watters C (2008) ESRC Research Project, 'Identities in transition: A longitudinal study of immigrant children', http://www.secularism.org.uk/uploads/ecrcdiversity.pdf
Brubaker R. (1996) *Nationalism Reframed: Nationhood and the National Question in the New Europe*, Cambridge: Cambridge University Press.
Bruegel I. (2006) 'Social capital, diversity and education policy', Families & Social Capital ESRC Research Group, London South Bank University, http://www.lsbu.ac.uk/families/publications/SCDiversityEdu28.8.06.pdf
Bungawala I. and Wahid A. (2005) 'Is Islamophobia a Myth?' *Prospect Magazine*, Issue 108, March
Bunting M. (2007) 'Saturday interview: we were the brothers', *Guardian*, 12 May.
Burgess S., Wilson D (2004) 'Ethnic segregation in England's schools', LSE: Centre for Analysis of Social Exclusion, http://sticerd.lse.ac.uk/dps/case/cp/CASEpaper79.pdf
Burgess S., Wilson D. and Lupton R. (2005), 'Parallel lives? Ethnic segregation in schools and neighbourhoods', LSE: Centre for Analysis of Social Exclusion, http://sticerd.lse.ac.uk/dps/case/cp/CASEpaper101.pdf
Burkett E. (1997) 'God created me to be a slave', *New York Times Magazine*, 12 October, pp. 59–60, cited in Okin, p. 142, fn 1.
Buruma I. (2007) *Murder in Amsterdam: The Death of Theo Van Gogh and the Limits of Tolerance*, London: Atlantic Books.
CAMSIS (Cambridge Social Interaction and Stratification Scale) 'Introduction', http://www.camsis.stir.ac.uk/
Canadian Charter of Rights and freedoms (1982), Schedule B, Constitution Act 1982, http://laws.justice.gc.ca/en/charter/#titre
Cantle T (Chair) (2001) *Community Cohesion: A Report of the Independent Review Team*, Home Office, http://www.communities.gov.uk/documents/communities/pdf/independentreviewteam.pdf
Cantle Report (Report of Institute of Community Cohesion) (2006) *Challenging Local Communities to Change Oldham*, http://www.oldham.gov.uk/cantle-review-final-report.pdf
Casciani D (2007) 'The fallout from Forest Gate', *BBC News*, 13 February, http://news.bbc.co.uk/1/hi/uk/6358041.stm
Catholic News Agency (CAN) (2008) 'Spanish cardinal criticizes 'Christophobic' ruling removing crucifixes from schools', 24 November, www.catholicnewsagency.com
Channel 4 (2007) *Undercover Mosque*, broadcast on 18 January.
Charrad M. (2001) *States and Women's Rights: The Making of Postcolonial Tunisia, Algeria, and Morocco*, Berkley: University of California Press.

Chrysafis A. (2008) 'Sarkozy declares war on elitism and offers return to liberty, equality and fraternity', *Guardian*, http://www.guardian.co.uk/world/2008/dec/18/sarkozy-diversity-policy-france-obama

Cohen R. (2007) 'Creolization and diaspora: the cultural politics of divergence and (some) convergence' in Totoricagüena G (ed.) *Opportunity Structures in Diaspora Relations: Comparisons in Contemporary Multi-level Politics of Diaspora and Transnational Identity*, Reno, Nevada, Center for Basque Studies: University of Nevada Press.

Coleman D. A. (1994) 'Trends in fertility and intermarriage among immigrant populations in Western Europe as measures of integration', *Journal of Biosocial Science*, vol. 26, no.1, pp. 107–136.

Commission for Racial Equality (2001), *Top Ten TV: Ethnic Minority Group Representation on Popular TV*, http://www.cre.gov.uk/media/nr_arch/nr010402b.htm

Commission on Integration and Cohesion (2007) *Our Shared Future*, http://collections.europarchive.org/tna/20080726153624/http://www.integrationandcohesion.org.uk/Our_final_report.aspx

Conway C. (Chair) (1997) *Islamophobia: a Challenge for Us All*, London: Runnymede Trust.

Cooley J. (2000) *Unholy Wars: Afghanistan, America and International Terrorism*, London: Pluto Press.

Cote S. and Healey T. (2001) *The Well Being of Nations: The Role of Human and Social Capital*, Paris: OECD.

CTV (2005) 'McGuinty rules out use of sharia law in Ontario', 12 September, http://www.ctv.ca/servlet/ArticleNews/story/CTVNews/1126472943217_26/?hub=TopStories

Darity W.A (Jnr) and Myers S.L (1998) *Persistent Inequality: Race and Inequality in the United States since 1945*, Cheltenham: Edward Elgar.

Dawkins R. (2006) *The God Delusion*, London: Bantam Press.

Department of Children Schools and Families (DCSF) (2007) *Faith in the System: The Role of Schools with a Religious Character in English Education and Society*, http://publications.teachernet.gov.uk/eOrderingDownload/FaithInTheSystem.pdf

DEFRA (nd) *FAWC Report on the Welfare of Farmed Animals at Slaughter or Killing – Part 1: Red Meat Animals: DEFRA Response to Recommendations*, http://www.defra.gov.uk/animalh/welfare/farmed/final_response.pdf

Dejevsky M. (2008) 'Women's rights cannot be forced on Arab societies' *Independent*, April 22, http://www.independent.co.uk/opinion/commentators/mary-dejevsky/mary-dejevsky-womens-rights-cannot-be-forced-on-arab-societies-813349.html

Department of Communities and Local Government (2008) *Face to Face and Side by Side*: *A framework for partnership in our multi faith society*. London: DCLG, http://www.communities.gov.uk/documents/communities/pdf/898668.pdf

Department of Health (2004) Leaflet on 'Breastfeeding', http://www.dh.gov.uk/en/Publicationsandstatistics/Publications/PublicationsPolicyAndGuidance/DH_4084370

Dhaliwal S. (2003) 'Orange is not the only colour: young women, religious identity and the Southall community', in Gupta R (ed.) *From Homebreakers to Jailbreakers: the Work of Southall Black Sisters,* London: Zed Press, pp. 188–211.

Dixon J, Durrheim K, and Tredoux C (2005) 'Beyond the optimal contact strategy', *American Psychologist,* vol. 60. no. 7, pp. 697–711.

Dobson R. (2007) 'Many young south Asian women in UK lack vitamin D, study finds', *British Medical Journal,* vol. 334, p. 389, 24 February.

Dombey D. and Ward A. (2007) 'Bush under attack over Iran', *Financial Times,* 4 December, http://www.ft.com/cms/s/0/e9e67502-a430-11dc-a28d-0000779fd2ac.html?nclick_check=1

Doward J. (2008) 'Church attendance "to fall by 90%"', *Observer,* 21 December.

Durkheim E. (1996) [1897] *Suicide: A Study in Sociology,* London: Routledge and Kegan Paul.

Dwyer C. (2008) 'The geographies of veiling: Muslim women in Britain', *Geography,* vol. 93, part 3, Autumn, pp. 140–147.

Eagleton T. (2007) 'Rebuking obnoxious views is not just a personality kink', *Guardian,* 10 October, http://www.guardian.co.uk/commentisfree/2007/oct/10/comment.religion

El Fadl K. A. (2005) 'Dogs in the Islamic Tradition and Nature', in *Encyclopedia of Religion and Nature,* London: Continuum International Publishing Group, pp. 497–498.

The European Monitoring Centre on Racism and Xenophobia (EUMC) (2005) *Impact of 7 July 2005 London Bomb Attacks on Muslim Communities in the EU,* November, http://www.tirol.gv.at/fileadmin/www.tirol.gv.at/themen/gesellschaft-und-soziales/integration/downloads/Leitbild-neu-Stand_Jaenner_2009/AK7aReligion/London-Bomb-attacks-Muslim_Comm_05-11-07.pdf

Farm Animal Welfare Council (FAWC) (1985) Report on the Welfare of Livestock when Slaughtered by Religious Methods, London: HMSO.

Farm Animal Welfare Council (FAWC) (2003) *Report on the Welfare of Farmed Animals at Slaughter or Killing Part 1: Red Meat Animals,* http://www.fawc.org.uk/reports/pb8347.pdf

Fenton S. (2004) 'The sociology of multiculturalism: is culture the name of the game?' pp. 19–55, in Rex and Singh, *Governance in Multicultural Societies,* Aldershot and Burlington: Ashgate.

Foot P. (1965) *Immigration and Race in British Politics,* Harmondsworth: Penguin.

Forced Marriage Unit (2005) *Dealing with Cases of Forced Marriage: Guidance for Education Professionals,* http://www.fco.gov.uk/resources/en/pdf/FMarriageGuidance-Education

Forced Marriage Unit (2008) 'Escaping Forced Marriage', http://www.fco.gov.uk/en/fco-in-action/casestudies/forced-marriage#

Forster E. M. (1951) *Two Cheers for Democracy*, London: Edward Arnold.
Forum against Islamophobia and Racism (FAIR) (2001) *Promoting a Multi-Faith and Multi-Ethnic Britain*, London: FAIR.
Fraser C. (2006) 'Ring of steel divides Padua', BBC News, http://news.bbc.co.uk/1/hi/world/europe/5385752.stm
Freud S. (2008 [1927]) *The Future of an Illusion*, London: Penguin Books.
Fryer P. (1984) *Staying Power: The History of Black People in Britain*, London: Pluto Press.
Gallagher T. (2005) 'Faith schools and Northern Ireland: review of research', in Gardner R, Cairns J, and Lawton D., *Faith Schools: Consensus or Conflict?* Abingdon: Routledge Falmer, pp. 156–165.
Gates B. (2005) 'Faith schools and colleges of education since 1800' in Gardner R, Cairns J, and Lawton D., *Faith Schools: Consensus or Conflict?* Abingdon: Routledge Falmer, pp. 14–35.
George R. (2003) 'Revolt against the rapists', *Guardian,* April 5, http://www.guardian.co.uk/world/2003/apr/05/france.gender
Gibbons S. and Silva O. (2006) 'Faith primary schools: better schools or better pupils? CEE DP 72, Centre for the Economics of Education, London School of Economics,
http://cee.lse.ac.uk/cee%20dps/ceedp72.pdf]
Giddens A. (2001) *Sociology*, Cambridge: Polity Press.
Glanville J. (2008) 'Respect for religion now makes censorship the norm', *Guardian*, 30 September.
Glover J. and Topping A. (2006) 'Religion does more harm than good – poll', *Guardian*, 23 December.
Grayling A. C. (2007) 'A force of evil?', *Guardian*, 9 July, http://commentisfree.guardian.co.uk/ac_grayling/2007/07/a_force_for_evil.html
Guardian Opinion Poll (2005), 23 August, table 19, http://image.guardian.co.uk/sys-files/Politics/documents/2005/08/23/Guardian-aug05.pdf
Hari J. (2009) 'Despite these riots, I stand by what I wrote', *Independent*, 13 February.
Harris N. (1986) *The End of the Third World*, Harmondsworth: Penguin Books.
Hasan R. (2003) 'Critical remarks on cultural aspects of Asian ghettos in modern Britain', *Capital and Class*, vol. 81, pp. 103–134.
Heath A., Martin J., and Elgenius G. (2007) 'Who do we think we are? The decline of traditional identities', in *British Social Attitudes Report 2007: the 23rd Report*, London: Sage.
Herbert I. (2007) 'Tough lessons in ending racial tension', *Independent: Education Section*, 15 February.
Herbert I. (2007) 'Veils block integration in UK, warns Lord Ahmed', *Independent*, Wednesday 21 February.
Hewitt R. (2005) *White Backlash and the Politics of Multiculturalism*, Cambridge: Cambridge University Press.

Hickman M. and Walter B. (1997) *Discrimination and the Irish community in Britain*, London: Commission for Racial Equality.
Hicks M. and Bhugra D. (2003) 'Perceived causes of suicide attempts by UK South Asian women', *American Journal of Orthopsychiatry*, vol. 73, no. 4, pp. 455–462.
Hiro D., 1992 [1973], *Black British, White British: A History of Race Relations in Britain*, London: Paladin.
Hirsi Ali A. (2007) *The Caged Virgin*, London: Pocket Books.
Howe D. (2004) 'Who you callin' a nigger', Documentary shown on *Channel 4*, 9 August.
Howlitt W. (1838) *Colonisation and Christianity: A Popular History of the Treatment of the Natives by the Europeans in all their Colonies,* London: Longman, available at http://books.google.co.uk/books
Human Rights Watch (2002) 'India: Gujarat Officials Took Part in Anti-Muslim Violence', http://hrw.org/english/docs/2002/04/30/india3885.htm
Hummel J. R. (1986) 'Not just Japanese Americans: the untold story of U.S. repression during "The Good War"', *Journal for Historical Review*, vol. 7, no. 3, http://www.ihr.org/jhr/v07/v07p285_Hummel.html
Independent Police Complaints Commission (PCC) (various years), *Deaths during or following contact with the police for England and Wales by Ethnic Origin* http://www.ipcc.gov.uk/
Independent (2009) 'California's Chinese ask US to apologise', 19 June, http://www.independent.co.uk/news/world/americas/californias-chinese-ask-us-to-apologise-1708997.html
Ingrams R. (2009) 'Richard Ingrams's Week: Not everyone was taken in by the master of the pause', *Independent,* 3 January, http://www.independent.co.uk/opinion/columnists/richard-ingrams/richard-ingramss-week-not-everyone-was-taken-in-by-the-master-of-the-pause-1222878.html
James W. (1988 [1907]) *Pragmatism: A New Name for some Old Ways of Thinking,* Hackett: Indianapolis.
Johnston R., Burgess S., Harris R. and Wilson D. (2006) '"Sleep-walking towards segregation?" The changing ethnic composition of English schools, 1997–2003: an entry cohort analysis', Centre for Market and Public Organisation at the University of
Bristol, Working Paper No. 06/155, September.
Jureidini R. (2005) 'Migrant Workers and Xenophobia in the Middle East', in Y. Bangura and R. Stavenhagen (eds) *Racism and Public Policy*, London: Palgrave Macmillan, pp. 48–71
Kanigal R. (1991) *The Man who knew Infinity: a Life of the Genius Ramanujan*, London: Scribners.
Kassir S. (2006) *Being Arab,* London and New York: Verso.
Kaufmann E. (2006) 'Breeding for God', *Prospect Magazine,* Issue 128, November, http://www.prospect-magazine.co.uk/pdfarticle.php?id=7913

Keith M. (1993), *Race, Riots and Policing: Lore and Disorder in a Multi-racist Society*, London: UCL Press
Kelly P. (ed.) (2002), *Multiculturalism Reconsidered*, Cambridge: Polity Press.
Kenber B. (2008) 'Ban headscarves, say teachers', *Telegraph*, 3 October.
Kerner O. (1968) *Report of the National Advisory Commission on Civil Disorders (Kerner Commission Report)*, New York: Bantam Books.
Kernohan A. (1998) *Liberalism, Equality, and Cultural Oppression*, Cambridge: Cambridge University Press.
Kinross P. (1993 [1964]), *Atatürk: The Rebirth of a Nation*, London: Weidenfeld.
Kipling R. (1940 [1889]) 'The Ballad of East and West', *Rudyard Kipling's Verse*, London: Hodder.
Koran (1988) Translated with an Introduction by A. J. Arberry, Oxford: Oxford University Press.
Kuhn T. (1996 [1962]) *The Structure of Scientific Revolutions*, Chicago: University of Chicago Press.
Kymicka W. (1998) *Finding Our Way: Rethinking Ethnocultural Relations in Canada*, Toronto: Oxford University Press.
Kymlicka W. (2003)[1995] *Multicultural Citizenship: A Liberal Theory of Minority Rights*, Oxford: Oxford University Press.
Kymlicka W., 1999, 'Liberal complacencies', in Okin, pp. 31–34.
Lakey J., 1997, 'Neighbourhood and Housing', in Modood T. and Berthoud R. (and others), pp. 184–223, *Ethnic Minorities in Britain*, London: PSI
Lash S. and Featherstone M. (2001) 'Recognition and difference: politics, identity, multiculture', *Theory, Culture, and Society*, vol. 18, nos. 2–3, pp. 1–19.
Levinson M. (2007) 'Gypsy children and education', *Thinking Allowed*, BBC Radio 4, 25 July, http://www.education.ex.ac.uk/staff_details.php?user=mpl202
Levitas R. (1996) 'The concept of social exclusion and the new Durkheimian hegemony', *Critical Social Policy*, vol. 16, no. 46, pp. 5–20.
Maher T. (2009) 'Orthodox Jews like me are facing indoctrination and abuse', *Guardian*, 20 March, http://www.guardian.co.uk/commentisfree/2009/mar/20/faith-schools-judaism-religion-ideology
Malik K. (1996) *The Meaning of Race: Race, History and Culture in Western Society*, Basingstoke: Macmillan Press.
Malik K. (2005) 'The Islamophobia Myth' *Prospect Magazine*, Issue 107, February.
Marable M. (1985) *Black American Politics: From the Washington Marches to Jesse Jackson*, London: Verso.
Marable M. (1991) *Race, Reform, and Rebellion*, Jackson and London: University Press of Mississippi.
Marx K., 1977 [1843/4], *A Contribution to the Critique of Hegel's Philosophy of Right. Introduction*. In *Marx's Early Writings*, Harmondsworth: Penguin and New Left Review

Mayor of London Press Release (2006) 'Same methods used to attack Muslims today as used against Jews, 8 October, http://www.london.gov.uk/view_press_release.jsp?releaseid=9467

McGoldrick D. (2006) *Human Rights and Religion: The Islamic Headscarf Debate in Europe*, Oxford and Portland: Hart Publishing.

McRoy A. (2006) *From Rushdie to 7/7: the Radicalisation of Islam in Britain*, London: Social Affairs Unit.

McSmith A. (2009) 'Why does the marriage rate continue to decline, and does it matter?, *Independent*, 13 February.

Meer N. and Noorani T. (2008) 'A sociological comparison of anti-Semitism and anti-Muslim sentiment in Britain', Sociological Review, vol. 56, no. 2, pp. 195–219.

Meikle J. (2006) 'MP supports suspension of school assistant for wearing veil', *Guardian*, 14 October.

Mernissi F. (1985) *Beyond the Veil: Male-Female Dynamics in Modern Muslim Society*, London: Al Saqi Books.

Mill J. S. (2008) [1859] *On Liberty and Other Essays*, Oxford: Oxford University Press

Millett K (1971) *Sexual Politics*, London: Rupert Hart-Davis.

Ministry of Justice (2007) Statistics on Race and the Criminal Justice System – 2006:

Ministry of Justice Publication under Section 95 of the Criminal Justice Act 1991, October 2007, http://www.justice.gov.uk/docs/stats-race-criminal-justice.pdf

Modood T. (1992) *Not Easy Being British: Colour, Culture, and Citizenship*, London: Runnymede Trust.

Modood T. (2005) *Multicultural Politics: Racism, Ethnicity, and Muslims in Britain*, Minneapolis: University of Minnesota Press.

Modood T. (2007) *Multiculturalism: A Civic Idea*, Cambridge: Polity Press.

Modood T. and Berthoud R (and others), 1997, *Ethnic Minorities in Britain*, London: PSI.

Modood T., Beishon, S, and Virdee S, 1994, *Changing Ethnic Identities*, London: PSI.

Modood T., Triandafyllidou A and Zapata-Barrero R (eds.) (2006) *Multiculturalism, Muslims, and Citizenship: A European Approach*, London and New York: Routledge.

Mundy P., Kasari C., Sigman M.(1995) 'Nonverbal communication and early language acquisition in children with Down Syndrome and in normally developing children', *Journal of Speech and Hearing Research*, vol.38, pp. 157–167, February.

Murray D and Verwey J-P (2008) *Victims of Intimidation: Freedom of Speech within Europe's Muslim Communities*, London: Centre for Social Cohesion.

Namazie N. (2007) 'The veil and violence against women in Islamist Societies', *The International Humanist and Ethical Union*, 7 August, http://www.iheu.org/node/2776

National Centre for Social Research (2007), *British Social Attitudes Report 2006*, http://www.natcen.ac.uk/natcen/pages/news_and_media_docs/BSA_%20press_release_jan07.pdf

National Secular Society [NSS] (2006) 'Objection to blind woman's "dirty dog" lands Muslim minicab driver in court' http://www.secularism.org.uk/objection-toblindwomansdirtydogla.html

Newham Inner City Multfund and Newham Asian Women's Project (1998) *Young Asian Women and Self-Harm: A Mental Health Needs Assessment of Young Asian Women in Newham, East London*, Wembley: Adept Press.

NOMIS (Official Labour Market Statistics) (2008) *Annual Population Survey*, Jan 2007-Dec 2007, https://www.nomisweb.co.uk/Default.asp

Office for National Statistics (ONS) (2005) *Focus on Ethnicity and Identity* http://www.statistics.gov.uk/focuson/ethnicity/default.asp

Office for National Statistics (ONS) (2006) *Focus on Ethnicity and Religion 2006*, http://www.statistics.gov.uk/StatBase/Product.asp?vlnk=14629

Okin S. M. (1999) *Is Multiculturalism Bad for Women?* Princeton: Princeton University Press.

Onal A. (2008) *Honour Killing: Stories of Men who Killed*, London: Saqi Books.

Parekh B. (2000) *Rethinking Multiculturalism: Cultural Diversity and Political Theory*, Basingstoke and New York: Palgrave.

Parekh B. (2002) 'Barry and the dangers of liberalism', in Kelly (ed.), *Multiculturalism Reconsidered*, Cambridge: Polity Press, pp. 133–150.

Parekh B. (2005) 'Multiculturalism is a civilised dialogue', *Guardian*, 21 January

Parekh B. (Chair) (2000) *The Future of Multi-Ethnic Britain (The Parekh Report)*, Report of the Commission on the Future of Multi-Ethnic Britain, The Runnymede Trust, London: Profile Books.

Park A., Phillips M. and Johnson M. (2004), 'Young people in Britain: the attitudes and experiences of 12 to 19 Year Olds', National Centre for Social Research, Research Report 564, http://www.dcsf.gov.uk/research/data/uploadfiles/RR564.pdf

Parker-Jenkins M., Hartas D., and Irving B. (2005) *In Good Faith: Schools, Religion and Public Funding*, Aldershot: Ashgate.

Phillips T. (2005) 'After 7/7: sleepwalking to segregation', 22 September, http://83.137.212.42/sitearchive/cre/Default.aspx.LocID-0hgnew07s.RefLocID-0hg00900c002.Lang-EN.htm#top

Pickles J. (1993) *Judge for Yourself*, Coronet Books: Sevenoaks.

Popham P. and Porthilo-Shrimpton T. (2008) "I despise Islamism': Ian McEwan faces backlash over press interview', *Independent*, http://www.independent.co.uk/news/world/europe/i-despise-islamism-ian-mcewan-faces-backlash-over-press-interview-852030.html

Porteous-Wood K (2007) 'NUT Faith Schools Working Party: Synopsis of evidence given by National Secular Society', http://www.secularism.org.uk/uploads/nutfaithschoolsworkingpartysubmi.pdf

Radtke F-O. (2004) 'Multiculturalism in Germany: the local management of immigrants' social inclusion', pp. 81–101, in Rex J and Singh G, *Governance in Multicultural Societies*, Aldershot and Burlington: Ashgate.
Ramadan T. (2005) *Western Muslims and the Future of Islam*, New York and Oxford: Oxford University Press.
Rashid A. (2000) *Taliban: Islam, Oil and the New Great Game in Central Asia*, London: I. B. Tauris.
Rawls J. (1971) *A Theory of Justice*, London and Cambridge MA: Belknap Press.
Rawls J. (1997) 'The idea of public reason' in Bohman J and Rehg W, *Deliberative Democracies: Essays on Reason and Politics*, Cambridge, Mass.: MIT Press, 1997, pp. 93–139.
Rawls J. (2005 [1993]) *Political Liberalism*, New York: Columbia University Press.
Rex J. and Singh G. (eds.) (2004) *Governance in Multicultural Societies*, Aldershot and Burlington: Ashgate.
Rojas J-P. (2006) 'Hate Bill protesters rally at Commons', *Independent*, 31 January, http://www.independent.co.uk/news/uk/politics/hate-bill-protesters-rally-at-commons-525311.html
Rose S., Kamin L., and Lewontin R. (1984) *Not in our Genes: Biology, Ideology and Human Nature*, Harmondsworth : Penguin.
Rowbotham S. (1973) *Hidden from History: 300 Years of Women's Oppression and the Fight Against It*, London: Pluto Press.
Roy D., Berry J., Pye S., Adams J., Swarbrick C., King Y., Silman A., O'Neill T. (2007) 'Vitamin D status and bone mass in UK South Asian women', *Bone*, vol. 40, pp. 200–204.
Russell B., 1987 [1957], *Why I am not a Christian*, London: Unwin.
Ruthven M. (2007) 'How Saudis used oil money to export a hardline ideology that fuels Islamist terror', *Independent*, 30 October.
Sahgal G. (1992) 'Secular spaces: the experience of Asian women organizing', in Sahgal G and Yuval-Davis N., *Refusing Holy Disorders: Women and Fundamentalism in Britain*, London: Virago Press, pp. 163–197.
Said E. (2003 [1978]) *Orientalism*, London: Penguin.
Sardar Z. (2006) Presentation at conference 'Fundamentalisms: Culture and Difference', University of Brighton, May 20.
Schofield Clark L. (2007) 'Fashion bibles and Muslim pop: the emergence of religious lifestyle branding in the west', paper presented at the *BSA Sociology of Religion Group* Annual Conference: *Religion, Media, and Culture*, April.
Scott J. W. (2007) *The Politics of the Veil*, Princeton and Oxford: Princeton University Press.
Sen A. (2006) *Identity and Violence: The Illusion of Destiny*, London: Penguin Books.
Seymour R. (2008) *The Liberal Defence of Murder*, London and New York: Verso.
Shachar A. (2001) *Multicultural Jurisdictions: Cultural Differences and Women's Rights*, Cambridge: Cambridge University Press.

Simpson, L. (2004) 'Statistics of racial segregation: measures, evidence and policy',
Urban Studies, vol. 41, no. 3, pp. 661–681.
Smith J. (2008) 'Introduction', in Onal A, *Honour Killing: Stories of Men who Killed*, London: Saqi Books.
Sniderman P and Hagendoorn L. (2007) *When Ways of Life Collide*, Princeton and Oxford: Princeton University Press.
Social Trends 38 (2008), available at http://www.statistics.gov.uk/downloads/theme_social/Social_Trends38/ST38_Ch13.pdf
Southall Black Sisters (SBS) (1994) *Domestic Violence and Asian Women*, London: SBS.
Southall Black Sisters (SBS) (2001) *Forced Marriage: Interim Report*, London: SBS.
Sturcke K. (and agencies) (2006) 'Straw: I'd rather no one wore veils', *Guardian*, 6 October.
Sword K. (1996) *Identity in Flux: The Polish Community in Britain*, Occasional Papers No. 36, London: School of Slavonic and East European Studies.
Tawney R. H. (1964 [1931]) *Equality*, London: Unwin Books.
Taylor C (1994) 'The politics of recognition' in Gutman A (ed.) *Multiculturalism: Examining the Politics of Recognition*, Princeton: Princeton University Press.
Taylor M. (2005) 'Two thirds oppose state aided faith schools', *Guardian*, 23 August, http://www.guardian.co.uk/uk/2005/aug/23/schools.faithschools
Tempest M (2007) 'Cameron returns to Birmingham to address Muslims, *Guardian*, 5 February, http://www.guardian.co.uk/politics/2007/feb/05/conservatives.religion
The Swann Report (1985) *Education for all: Report of the Committee of Enquiry into the Education of Children from Ethnic Minority Groups*, Chairman: Lord Swann, Cmnd. 9453, London: Her Majesty's Stationery Office, available at http://www.dg.dial.pipex.com/documents/docs3/swann18.shtml
Tiryakian E. (2004) 'Assessing multiculturalism theoretically: *E pluribus unum sic et non*', pp. 1–18, in Rex and Singh, *Governance in Multicultural Societies*, Aldershot and Burlington: Ashgate.
Townsend M. (2005) 'The new colour of British racism: Behind the riots lies vicious hostility between the Asian and African-Caribbean communities in Birmingham', *Observer*, 30 October.
Toynbee P. (2005) 'My right to offend a fool', *Guardian*, 10 June.
Tran M. (2006) 'Australian Muslim leader compares uncovered women to exposed meat', *Guardian*, 26 October.
Triandafyllidou A., Modood T., and Zapata-Barrero R. (2006) 'European challenges to multicultural citizenship: Muslims, secularism, and beyond' in Modood T., Triandafyllidou A. and Zapata-Barrero R. (eds.) (2006) *Multiculturalism, Muslims, and Citizenship: A European Approach*, pp. 1–22, London and New York: Routledge.
Tully J. (1995) *Strange Multiplicity*, Cambridge: Cambridge University Press.

Tyler C. (2004) 'Strangers and compatriots: the political theory of cultural diversity', in Rex and Singh, *Governance in Multicultural Societies*, Aldershot and Burlington: Ashgate pp. 19–35
Unger C. (2007) *House of Bush House of Saud: The Secret Relationship Between the World's Two Most Powerful Dynasties*, (3rd edn) London: Gibson Square Books.
Vasta E. (2007) 'From ethnic minorities to ethnic majority policy: Multiculturalism and the shift to assimilationism in the Netherlands, *Ethnic and Racial Studies*, vol. 30, no. 5, pp. 713–740.
Verkaik R. (2008) 'Court rules Islamic law discriminatory', *Independent*, 23 October, http://www.independent.co.uk/news/uk/home-news/court-rules-islamic-law-discriminatory-969777.html
Verkuyten M. (2006) *The Social Psychology of Ethnic Identity*, Hove and New York: Psychology Press.
Verkuyten M .and Yildiz A. (2007) 'National (dis)identification, and ethnic and religious identity: A study among Turkish-Dutch Muslims', *Personality and Social Psychology Bulletin*, 33,10, pp. 1448–1462
Voas D. and Bruce S. (2004) 'The 2001 Census and Christian identification in Britain', *Journal of Contemporary Religion'*, vol. 19, no. 1, pp. 23–28.
Voas D. and Crockett A. (2005) 'Religion in Britain: neither believing nor belonging', *Sociology*, vol. 39, no. 1, pp. 11–28.
Wallis R. (1984) *The Elementary Forms of New Religious Life*, London: Routledge and Kegal Paul.
Wallis R. and Bruce S. (1992) 'Secularization: The orthodox model', in Bruce S (ed.) *Religion and Modernization: Sociologists and Historians Debate the Secularization Thesis*, Oxford: Clarendon Press.
Warrier M. (2007) 'Hinduism: a historical overview' in Partridge C (ed.) *The New Lion Handbook: The World's Religions*, Oxford: Lion Hudson.
Watson C. W. (2000) *Multiculturalism*, Buckingham and Philadelphia: Open University Press.
Watt N. (2007) 'Revealed: UK schools dividing along race lines', *Observer*, 27 May, http://www.guardian.co.uk/uk/2007/may/27/education.race
Weber M. (1967 [1919]) *Politics as a Vacation*, in Gerth H and Wright Mills C (eds.), *From Max Weber: Essays in Sociology*, London: Routledge and Kegan Paul, pp. 77–128.
West P. (2005) *Poverty of Multiculturalism* London: Civitas.
Williams J. (2007) 'Questions of murder', *BBC News*, 1 December, http://news.bbc.co.uk/newswatch/ukfs/hi/newsid_4480000/newsid_4489300/4489328.stm
Wolfe A. (2006) 'Realism on religion', *Prospect Magazine*, Issue 128, November, http://www.prospect-magazine.co.uk/pdfarticle.php?id=7928
Wollstonecraft M. (1995) [1790], *A Vindication of the Rights of Men, In A Letter to the Right Honourable Edmund Burke; Occasioned by his Reflections on the Revolution in France*, in *A Vindication of the Rights of Men* and *A Vindication of the Rights of Woman*, Cambridge: Cambridge University Press, pp. 3–64.

Wollstonecraft M. (1995) [1792] *A Vindication of the Rights of Woman: with Strictures on Political and Moral Subjects* in *A Vindication of the Rights of Men* and *A Vindication of the Rights of Woman*, Cambridge: Cambridge University Press, pp. 64–294.

Young I. M. (1990) *Justice and the Politics of Difference*, Princeton: Princeton University Press.

Zielenziger M. (2006) *Shutting Out the Sun: How Japan Created Its Own Lost Generation,* New York: Nan A. Talese.

Index

n against a page number denotes a footnote e.g. 183*n*

7 July bombings 124–6, 132, 234
9/11 terrorist attacks 123–4, 130

Aaronovitch, David 146
Aborigines 162
Abu Hamza 270
Abu Talib, Ahmed 270
adoption agencies 47*n*
Afghanistan 133–4
Afzal, Nazir 271–2
Ahmed, Leila 73
Ahmed, Lord 156–7
Ajegbo Report (2007) 239–40
alcohol 111, 112, 113
Algeria 181
Allen, Christopher 123
Amara, Fadara 178
Amis, Martin 221
Amish society 115
animal welfare 255–7
anti-racism 13–14, 59, 117
anti-Semitism 56–7, 121–2, 127, 147, 213–14
arranged marriages 17, 90–91, 250
arrests 136

Asians
 and criminal justice system 136–8
 cultural practices 86–7
 educational attainment 71
 extended family 69–70
 gender segregation 74, 111, 177
 importance of family 68–70, 90–92
 intra-Asian tensions 73
 middle-class 12–13
 police-related fatalities 137–8
 religious identity 9–10, 92–4, 109, 210
 settlement expectations in Britain 68
 socio-economic standing 24–5
 and sport 84, 252*n*
 and television 83–4, 86
 victims of crime 139–41
 women 75–9, 76–7, 249
 see also Bangladeshis; Pakistanis; segregation; veiling
asylum seekers 230
Australia 66–7

Bangladeshis 25, 71–2, 196–7
Barry, Brian 20, 21, 23–4, 33*n*, 34–6, 37
Beckett, Claire 87
Bellil, Samira 178

Bhugra, Dinesh 76–7
Black British, in the media 7–8, 83
Black Caribbeans 55, 65–6, 71, 82–3, 88
Black communities 82–3, 128, 136–8, 139–40
Blackburn 155, 198–9
Blair, Tony 47*n*, 124
blasphemy laws 47*n*, 141, 225
blood transfusions 250*n*
BNP (British National Party) 48–9, 251, 268
Bourdieu, Pierre 242
Bowen, John 173–4, 178–9, 181, 183*n*, 187
Bradford 9, 73*n*, 195–6, 199
Bradford Race Review (Ouseley Report) 9, 194, 195, 229
Brahminism 109–110
breastfeeding 248–50
British identity 21, 177
broadcasting
  religion in 225
  see also television
Brown, Rupert *et al* 209–210
Bruegel, Irene 200
Bunting, Madeleine 148–9
Burgess, S. *et al* 197
Bush, President George W. 133
Byers, Stephen 199

Canada 17–19, 254
Cantle Reports (2001, 2006) 194, 195
Carey, Archbishop George 124
Chakrabarti, Shami 166
Charles, Prince of Wales 124
Charrad, Mounira 159–60
Cherifi, Hanifa 177
children
  benefits of school diversity 209–210
  boys and young men 73–4
  faith-based nurseries 246
  indoctrination of religious belief 206–7, 240–42

rights of 27
and self-flagellation 50*n*
social detachment of Muslim girls 111–12
veiling of 180–81
Christianity 55, 205–6
  daily worship in schools 224, 241
Church of England 224, 241, 261
Climbié, Victoria 27*n*
Cohen, Job 53–4
Cohen, Nick 146
Cohen, Robin 244
cohesion
  Commission on Integration and Cohesion (COIC) 231–2, 238–9
  community 10
  and faith schools 201–2
  social cohesion 35
colonialism
  post-colonial rule 38
  white liberal post-colonial guilt 212–15, 218, 223–4
Commission on Integration and Cohesion (COIC) 231–2, 238–9
Commission for Racial Equality 83, 130, 194
Cook, Robin 262
corporal punishment 26–7
creationism 208, 226
creolisation 22–3, 244–5
crime, victims of 126, 139–42
criminal justice process 135–8
Cruddas, John 122
cultural pluralism 144
cultural practices, egregious 24, 44, 50, 250
cultural racism 57–9, 222
cultural relativism 30–32, 46–7, 144
cultural rights 39–42
cultural transformation 80
culture 23, 27–8, 86–7
Culture and Equality: An Egalitarian Critique of Multiculturalism (Barry) 20, 21, 34

Darfur 135
Dawkins, Richard 187–8, 226
deaths, police-related 137–8
Débray, Régis 177
Dejevsky, Mary 218–19
Deligöz, Ekin 182–3
Department of Communities and Local Government
  Commission on Integration and Cohesion (COIC) 231–2, 238–9
  Face to Face and Side by Side 232–3
Disability Discrimination Act (1995) 257
discrimination, indirect discrimination 253
dogs 112–13, 257
Dwyer, Claire 168

Eagleton, Terry 221
economic crisis 267–8
education 71
  see also faith schools; schools
employment
  Asians 71–2
  corporate culture 46–7
  and segregated schooling 115
  women 25, 71, 109
ethnic minorities
  and criminal justice process 135–8
  cultural rights 39–42
  duress within 42
  and economic crisis 267–8
  integration 51–4
  inter-ethnic conflict 81–2
  marrying out 43–4, 65–6, 88–9
  population statistics 70
  victims of crime 126, 139–42
ethnicity 55–7
European Monitoring Centre on Racism and Xenophobia (EUMC) 123–7
evolution, teaching of 208

Face to Face and Side by Side 232–3
FAIR (Forum against Islamophobia and Racism) 9
faith communities 233–4
  see also ethnic minorities; religious identity
faith organisations 49, 232–3
faith schools
  academic standards 237–8
  and community cohesion 201–2
  divisive nature of 211
  indoctrination of children 206, 240–41
  many in existence already 202
  minority faith schools 207–9, 236
  phasing out 236–7
  quotas from other faiths 209
  statistics 202–4
  teaching of religious education 239–40, 241
  see also segregated schools
Farm Animal Welfare Council 255–7
Fawcett Society 172
flagellation, self-flagellation 50*n*
Fong, Paul 129–30
forced marriages 74–5, 250
foreign policy 121, 132–5, 144–5, 169–70, 234, 262–3
fox hunting 47*n*
France 173–9, 181–2, 186, 187
freedom of choice 34
  see also turbans; veiling
freedom of expression 23–4, 29–30, 142, 145, 178
freedom of speech, India 226–7
Freud, Sigmund, on religion 107
Fryer, Peter 127–8
Future of Multi-Ethnic Britain, The (Parekh Report) 1, 24, 231

Galloway, George 217*n*
gender segregation 74, 111, 177
genital mutilation 44, 50, 250
Germany 60, 182, 214, 248–9

ghettoisation *see* segregation
Gibbons, Steve 237–8
Glanville, Jo 122
God Delusion, The (Dawkins) 187–8
grammar schools 238
Grayling, A.C. 216
Greek Orthodox Church 162–3
guide dogs 112–13, 257
guilt 214
  white liberal post-colonial 212–15, 218, 223–4
Gujarat 127
Gulf War (1991) 134
gypsies 46

Hagendoorn, Louk, *When Ways of Life Collide* 150
hairdressing salons 253
Hari, Johann 226–7
hate crimes 126–8, 139–42
headscarves *see* veiling
health, ill-effects of veiling 184–5
health service 225
al Hilali, Sheikh Aldin 160
Hinduism 108–110, 149
Hindus 82
honour (*izzat*) 91–2
honour killings 270–72
House of Lords
  composition of 224, 261–2
  Mandla v. Dowell Lee 36
house prices 114
housing segregation 193–4, 195–7
Howe, Darcus 81
Howitt, William 212–13
Hummel, Jeffrey 128–9
Husain, Ed 148

identity
  Black 82–3
  British 21, 177
  see also religious identity
immigration 7–9, 64–6, 67–9, 95

independent schools 204
India 127, 226–7
IRA bombings 130–32
Iran 217
Iraq war (2003) 156, 215–17
Irish, anti-Irish hostility 130–32
Islam 108–9, 149–53, 264, 269
  see also Muslims
Islamist, The (Husain) 148
Islamophobia: a Challenge for Us All (Runnymede Trust) 143–4
Islamophobia
  and anti-Semitism 121–2, 127, 146–7
  definition 121, 143
  doctrine of 121–32
  evidence against 132–42
  and freedom of expression 142
  offspring of multiculturalism 142–54
  perceived victimhood 153–4
  and Western foreign policy 121, 132–5
Israel 145–6, 214*n*, 263
Italy 251*n*

Jacobson, Howard 146
Japan 169
Jehovah's Witnesses 250*n*
Jews 56–7, 264–5
  see also anti-Semitism
Johnson, Alan 199–200
Johnson, Nick 194
Johnston, R. *et al* 195, 196
Justice and the Politics of Difference (Young) 15

Kanigal, Robert 109–110
Kassir, Samir 218*n*
Kernohan, Andrew 247
Koran 157–9, 165
Kosovo 134
Kuwait 134
Kymlicka, Will 13, 14, 19, 32–3

Index

language 115
legal privileges 21–2, 45–8, 252–3
Leicester 196
literacy 46
Livingstone, Ken 121–2
local services 233–4, 235
loyalty 27–8

McCabe, Steve 141*n*, 202
McDonald, Trevor 258
McEwan, Ian 221
Macey, Marie 87
madrassas 264
Mahmoud, Banaz 271–2
Malik, Kenan 64–5, 132*n*
Mandla v. Dowell Lee 36
marriage
 arranged 17, 90–91, 250
 conversion to Islam upon 220
 forced 74–5, 250
 mixed (marrying out) 43–4, 65–6, 88–9
 see also honour killings
Marx, Karl, on religion 107
Mernissi, Fatima 159
migrants
 from UK 66–7, 97–8
 Imperial identity 63–4, 66
 motive for settlement 98–9
Mill, John Stuart, *On Liberty* 29
Millett, Kate 79
Milosevic, Slobodan 134
Modood, Tariq 13–14, 32–3, 39, 58, 147–8
Mugabe, Robert 213*n*
Multiculturalism: a Civic Idea (Modood) 32–3
multiculturalism
 definition 10–11
 key concepts 13–17, 20–23, 27–32
multifaithism
 and contestation of religious beliefs 117
 dangers of 232–4

 definition 2
 and Islamophobia 153–4
 and segregation 49
 successor to multiculturalism 9–10, 21
murders 140
music 84–5
Muslims
 in Arab countries 134–5
 asylum seekers 127
 cultural factors 111–14
 domestic issues 145
 and foreign policy 121, 132–5, 144–5, 234, 262–3
 Hindus/Sikhs and 82
 opinion poll (2007) 140–41

Naseem, Mohammed 122
National Secular Society 207, 208*n*
Netherlands, Muslims in 53–4, 150, 270
New Zealand 66–7
Newham Asian Women's Project 172–3
Nielsen, Jorgen 123
9/11 terrorist attacks 123–4, 130
Northern Ireland, schools 202, 210–211
nurseries 246

Oldham 94, 195, 199
Onal, Ayse 271–2
Orientalism (Said) 39*n*
Ouseley Report (Bradford Race Report) 9, 194, 195, 229

Pakistanis 25, 71–2, 196
Palestinians 146, 214*n*
Parekh, Bhikhu 13–14, 23–4, 27–32, 34–5, 38–9, 174*n*
Parekh Report 1, 24, 231
Phillips, Melanie 146
Phillips, Trevor 1–2, 11, 199
Pickles, Judge James 160

police 136–8
Polish migrants 55
population statistics 70
Porteous-Wood, Keith 207–8, 209
Powell, Enoch 222
prison population 136
privileges, religious/cultural 21–2, 45–8, 252–3
psychic detachment
  components 100–103
  and religious identity 103–5, 108–111
  and segregation 95–100
  and veiling 183
public schools 211
public services 233–4, 235

Qatar 219
qualifications 71

Race Relations Act (1976) 36, 57
Racial and Religious Hatred Act (2006) 141–2, 225
racism
  anti-racism 13–14, 59, 117
  borderline racism 220
  cultural racism 57–9, 222
  declining levels of 229–30
  in France 181–2
  racist attacks on non-Muslims 127–32
  and skin colour 57
Raffarin, Jean-Pierre 187
Ramadan, Tariq 163–4
Ramanujan, A.K. 109–110
Rawls, John 223, 235
Raz, Joseph 15, 24, 78
religion
  declining significance 224–5
  and integration of migrants 53–5
  justification for war 216
  religious symbols in schools 175–6, 181–2, 241
  types of 106–9

  see also Christianity; Hinduism; Islam; Sikhism
religious education 239–40, 241
religious hatred 141–2
  see also hate crimes
religious identity
  Asians 9–10, 92–4, 109, 210
  decline of 11–12, 204–5, 260–61
  linked to segregation 103–4
  need for dissolution of 265–6
  see also veiling
religious slaughter 255–7
residential segregation 11–13, 193–4, 195–7, 242–3
Respect party 217*n*
Rethinking Multiculturalism (Parekh) 24
Richards, Judge Bertrand 160
rights
  children's 27
  cultural 39–42
  women's 222–4, 243, 248
riots
  1980s 7
  2001 8–9, 94
  Birmingham (2005) 81–2
  and segregation 194
Runnymede Trust 143–4
  see also Parekh Report
Rushdie, Salman 28, 142, 145

Sabuni, Nyamko 183
Said, E. 39*n*
Sardar, Ziauddin 163–4, 165
Sarkozy, Nicholas 176, 181
Satanic Verses, The (Rushdie) 28, 142, 145
Saudi Arabia 96–7, 133, 218–19
scarves *see* veiling
schools
  benefits of diversity 209–210
  daily act of worship 224, 241
  grammar schools 238
  religious education 239–40, 241

religious symbols in 175–6, 181–2, 241
uniforms 45–6
see also faith schools; segregated schools; turbans; veiling
Scotland, Baroness 74
Sebag, Yazid 181
secularism 33, 224–8, 261–2
segregated schools
  disadvantages of 114–15, 198, 199
  ethnic groups within 196–9
  government policies 199–201
  impact on integration 194–5
  and school twinning 200
  see also faith schools
segregation
  desegregation/creolisation 242–6
  gender segregation 74, 111, 177
  and ghetto mentality 72
  increasing through choice 230
  neighbourhoods 11–13, 193–4, 195–7, 235–6
  self-segregation 53–4, 242–3
  social detachment 102–3, 111–12, 251–2
Sen, Amartya 93, 201–2, 263–4, 269*n*
Serbia 134
7 July bombings 124–6, 132, 234
sex education 208
Shachar, Ayelet 39–40, 41–2
shame (*sharam*) 91–2
Shapiro, Ian 33*n*
Sharia law 253–5
Sheerman, Barry 211
Siddique Khan, Mohommed 234
Sikhism 108–9
Sikhs 34–7, 57*n*, 82
Silman, Alan 184
Silva, Olmo 237–8
Simpson, Ludi 195
Singh, Darra 231
Smith, Joan 271–2
smoking 111
Sniderman, Paul, *When Ways of Life Collide* 150
social capital 103–4
social cohesion 35
social detachment 102–3, 111–12, 251–2
social distance 100–101
Southall Black Sisters 75, 172–3, 222
Spain 182
sport 37, 84, 252*n*
state schools 203
stratification theory 101
Straw, Jack 155–6
Sudan 135
suicide 76–7
superstitions 105–6
Swann Report 194
Sweden 183

Talib, Abu Ahmed 270
Tasleem, Begum 75
Tawney, R.H. 211
taxi drivers 257
Taylor, Charles 13, 14–15
television 83–4, 86, 258–60
terrorism
  7 July bombings 124–6, 132, 234
  9/11 attacks 123–4, 130
  attacks by Muslims 128
  police arrests 138
Terrorism Act (2000) 137
Thatcher, Margaret 57–8
Third Worldism 38
Tiryakian, E. 59
tobacco 111
Touraine, Alain 177
Toynbee, Polly 141, 146*n*
Tully, James 13
turbans 34–7, 46
Turkey 134, 182, 185, 226
Turkish men, honour killings 271–2

unemployment 71
United Kingdom

foreign policy 144–5, 169–70, 234, 262–3
and Saudi Arabia 133
United States
and Afghanistan 133–4
Chinese-Americans 129–30
civil rights movement 170, 251
foreign policy 133–5, 169–70
and Islamic countries 133–5
Japanese-Americans 128–9

veiling
Abrahamic faiths 157
children 180–81
coercion 171, 178, 186
France 173–9, 181–2, 186, 187
freedom of choice 165–7, 185–7
Germany 182
health effects 184–5
Koran 157–9
opposition to 34, 187
oppressive nature of 179–80, 187–8
prevention of non-verbal communication 183–4
and public institutions 171–3
reasons for 158–63, 177–8, 186
and religious identity 168–9, 179–80
rise in 167–71
Sweden 183

Venezuela 249
Vigerie, Anne 178

Walker, Anthony 140
Wallis, Roy 106–8
Weber, Max 272–3
West Indians *see* Black Caribbeans
When Ways of Life Collide (Sniderman and Hagendoorn) 150
White flight 114, 198
Wilders, Geert 142*n*
Willets, David 201
Williams, Archbishop Rowan 253
Williams, Jon 140
Wollstonecraft, Mary 151–3, 188–9
women
conversion to Islam on marriage 220
egregious cultural practices 24, 44, 50, 250
employment 25, 71, 109
genital mutilation 44, 50, 250
oppression of 73, 218–19
subordinate beings 152–3
see also gender segregation; veiling
women's rights 222–4, 243, 248

Young, Iris 13, 15

Zelensky, Anne 178
Zimbabwe 213*n*